#BRING BACK OUR GIRLS: The Chibok Debacle

BOKO HARAM TERRORISM IN NIGERIA

VOL. 1

OKENWA ENYERIBE--B. PHARM.

By the Same Author:

Books:

Win the war…. Inside Biafra
The Expedient Nigerian Revolution Has Emerged; Log In
The Sorry State of Nigerian Prisons--My Kuje Experience
Centenary: Nigeria at 100 is a Bummer
Nigeria: 48 Years after Biafra
Nelson Mandela Joins the Saints; GDP: Equating Nigeria
With South Africa
An Anthology of the Nigerian State (Poems), ISBN—
10:1973244209; ISBN 13: 9781973244202,
Amazon.com/books/2017
Nigeria: House on Sand

Presentations:

Why I Climbed to the Roof-Top of the 9-Storey Head of
Service Abuja Block on 16 July, 2012
The Eagle Square Document, 2012
The Wuse Market Abuja Declaration, 2013
Our Stand on the State of Affairs in Nigeria Today, 2013
The Shame at National Human Rights Commission Abuja
September 10, 2012
Memo to President Good Luck Jonathan, 2012
Revolutionary Nigerianism, 2014
Letter to Chief Judge Federal High Court FCT, Abuja,
2013
How   Citizens   Can   Contribute   and   Participate
Productively In an Emerging Democracy Like Nigeria

Copyright © Okenwa Enyeribe 2018

All rights reserved

All rights reserved

No part of this publication should be reproduced, stored in a retrieval system, or transmitted in any form or by any means, electronic, mechanical, photocopying, recording, online or otherwise without the prior permission of the copyright owner.

Enquiries:
CORRUPTION-FREE GOVERNMENT IN NIGERIA
THE REVOLUTIONARY COUNCIL OF THE NIGERIAN PEOPLE
Website: www.revolutionarycouncil.org.ng.
E-mail: corruptionfreegovernmentng@yahoo.com;
enyeribeokenwa@gmail.com
Face Book: Anticorruption Nigeria
Tel: +2348059853212

CONTENTS

Dedication

To you phlegmatic and noble Nigerian People who groan under the weight of outrageous wretchedness, poverty, squalor, misery, hopelessness and insecurity precipitated by Mephistophelian and devious politicians and elite, do not despair; the Respectable Revolution to restore sanity to the Federal Republic of Nigeria has finally emerged. Let us join hands to take back our country from the hands of marauders. Our victory is a surefire. It is also a consolation to The Masses that are daily traumatized by unconscionable insecurity which has culminated in the abduction of over 300 school girls from Chibok in North Eastern Nigeria.

And to you intrepid emancipator, Dr. Nelson Rolihlahla Mandela - the Madiba, for taking the pains and indignation, deserting hearth, company and luxury, to liberate a segment of this earth from Boer bestiality and oppression.

Okenwa Enyeribe - B. Pharm.

January 2018

Acknowledgements

I thank you for the copy of your book: 'Win the War…Inside Biafra' sent to me and indeed appreciate your courageous anticorruption struggle. Please accept the assurance of my best wishes. *Senator Uche Chukwumerije, Chairman Nigerian Senate Committee on Education, 2nd November 2012*

Thank you /The White House. Thank you for contacting the White House. Thank you again for your message. *The Office of Presidential Correspondence, The White House Washington D.C., United States of America, October 2, 2012*

Re: Presentation of New Book-WIN THE WAR…Inside Biafra

I wish to acknowledge with thanks your letter dated 12th June 2012 pertaining to the above subject. I wish to inform you that the book will be kept in the Embassy's Library for reference. *EMBASSY OF THE REPUBLIC OF LIBERIA, ABUJA, June 25, 2012*

Your current Sweeping Revolution is a GODSEND to the Nigerian State - **Head, Management of Federal High Court Abuja officially welcoming members of the Revolutionary Council of the Nigerian People on May 7, 2013**

Subject: "The President wants to see you"
From: The White House (info@mail.whitehouse.gov)

To: corruptionfreegovernmentng@yahoo.com
Date: Tuesday, July29, 2014 7:22 PM
THE WHITE HOUSE
Tuesday, July29, 2014
WASHINGTON

"The President wants to see you"
"Would you be willing to have dinner with the President Tuesday night?"

This email was sent to
corruptionfreegovernmentng@yahoo.com

Sign up for updates from the White House

The White House -1600 – Pennsylvania Ave NW – Washington D.C. 20500 – 202-456-1111

INDEPENDENT CORRUPT PRACTICES AND OTHER RELATED OFFENCES COMMISSION: ICPC/P/NC/172/2015
Okenwa Enyeribe—B. Pharm.,

Head, Revolutionary Council of the Nigerian People,
C/o Stan Dioka & Co, 46 Durban Str.,
Wuse 2, Abuja.
RE: A CITIZEN'S LETTER OF COMMENDATION AND REQUEST FOR FURTHER INVESTIGATION OF CORRUPTION CASES IN GOVERNMENT PURSUANT TO SECTIONS 14(2C), 24B AND 39 OF THE 1999 CONSTITUTION OF THE FEDERAL REPUBLIC OF NIGERIA AS AMENDED

I am directed to acknowledge the receipt of your petition dated 12th March, 2015on the above matter,
You will be notified of further development if necessary. Quote the reference number above in further correspondence with the commission on this issue.
Please accept the assurances of the Hon. Chairman's highest regards.
Abdullahi M.M.
For the Hon. Chairman
Special thanks to Mr. Okwuchukwu Emeka Alfred,

Project Director, Mankind Development and

Rehabilitation Organization (MANDERO), Abuja.

Veronica Bakam: indefatigable freedom fighter and

change agent, you will always be remembered for your

other-centred service to humanity.

Missiles and thoughts

"The current situation in the country where some children have taken arms against their own country is totally unacceptable. Parents must share in the blame. I have been an advocate for dialogue with the Boko Haram elements in this country. But things have gone absolutely beyond bound and no government will negotiate with Boko Haram as long as they keep our girls and our boys". —*Past Nigerian Senate President, David Mark at a funeral ceremony in Delta State early May 2014*

"Like millions of people across the globe, my husband and I are outraged and heartbroken over the kidnapping of more than 200 Nigerian girls from their school dormitory in the middle of the night. This unconscionable act was committed by a terrorist group determined to keep these girls from getting an education – grown men attempting to snuff out the aspirations of young girls" --*United States of America First Lady, Michelle Obama launching the #Bring Back Our Girls campaign, May 8, 2014*

"This abduction could have been prevented."-- Amnesty spokeswoman, Susanna Flood, Commenting on the abducted Chibok girls, May 9, 2014

"Terrorist attacks carried out by Boko Haram rebels since 2009 have caused large-scale and devastating loss of life and represent a threat to the stability and peace of west and central Africa." --*The UN Security Council on Friday May 9, 20014*

"Nigeria has made bad choices, not hard choices. They have squandered their oil wealth; they have allowed corruption to fester, and now they are losing control of parts of their (own) territory because they would not make hard choices...The seizure of these young women by this radical, extremist group, Boko Haram, is abominable, it's criminal, it's an act of terrorism, and it really merits the fullest response possible, first and foremost from the government of Nigeria. The government of Nigeria has been, in my view, somewhat derelict in its responsibility toward protecting boys and girls, men and women in northern Nigeria over the last years." -- *Former United States First Lady, Senator Hillary Clinton rebuked the monumental corruption and incompetence in President Good Luck Jonathan's Government at the International Crisis Group and a philanthropy parley in US (CNN), early May 2014*

"Boko Haram has become a franchise with which many people commit several crimes. Abu Kakar and Abu Shekau are dead. Those bearing these names are fake" ...Nigeria will not in any way negotiate with Boko Haram." --*Spokesperson of the SSS, Deputy Director Marilyn Ogar at a press briefing, May 12, 2014*

"Corruption prevents supplies as basic as bullets and transport vehicles from reaching the front lines of the struggle against Boko Haram...induced low morale and desertions on soldiers of the 7th Army Division fighting the rebels." --*United States Under Secretary of State for Civilian Security, Democracy and Human Rights, Sara Sewall addressing US House of*

Representatives Committee on Foreign Affairs,
Wednesday 21 May 2014

"**The government has stated its position on this issue. Men and women are out there combing everywhere, collaborating with international support. As far as we are concerned in this issue, all options are still open and we will apply international best practices all over the world.**" *--Coordinator of the National Information Centre on the Chibok Girls crisis, Mr. Mike Omeri at a press conference with journalists in Abuja, May 22, 2014*

"**Tell your CP (Commissioner of Police) that there is a message for him. Nigeria will not always be like this. People have to be careful what they do with the citizens of this country. We sent a letter today, acknowledged telling you that there was rising trend of aggression towards us. And yet you deployed police to guard the rented crowd. And the police stood. They witnessed, it happened. Let the FG and associates know that we the women, men, youths and children of Abuja family of #Bring Back Our Girls are resolute to keep standing.**" *--Convener of the notable #Bring Back Our Girls crusade party, Mrs. Oby Ezekwesili searing at a policeman after her group was attacked by thugs, May 28, 2014*

"**My family will be worried**".

"**I never expected to suffer like this in my life**".

"**They have taken us away by force**".

"**We are not getting enough food**" *--Four of the abducted Chibok Girls in distress pleaded for their*

*release in a purported video, The Mail on Sunday June 1,
2014*

"The vast majority of the Chibok girls are not being
held in Nigeria. They are in camps across the Nigerian
borders in Cameroun, Chad and Niger. I say the vast
majority as I know a small group was confirmed to me
to be in Nigeria last week when we sought to have
them released." *--Australian negotiator, Dr. Stephen
Davis on the arduous efforts to facilitate release of the
Chibok Girls held captive by Boko Haram, June 1, 2014*

"The trend is now posing a serious security threat to
those living around and as the FCT Police boss; I
cannot fold my hands and watch this lawlessness.
Information reaching us is that too soon dangerous
elements will join the groups under the guise of
protests and detonate explosives aimed at
embarrassing the Government. Accordingly, protests
on the Chibok Girls are hereby banned with
immediate effect." *--Commissioner of Police FCT Abuja,
Mr. Mbu Joseph Mbu arbitrarily banning further protests
in Abuja for the release of the abducted Chibok girls,
June 2, 2014*

"The Police High Command wishes to inform the
general public that the Force has not issued any order
banning peaceful assembly/protests anywhere in
Nigeria... Consequently, citizens are strongly advised
to reconsider their positions on the issues of rallies and
protests in FCT until the existing threats are
appropriately neutralized and removed from our
midst by relevant security agencies."--Nigerian
Inspector General of Police (IG), Mr. Mohammed

Abubakar refuted within 24 hours the earlier authoritarian order of his lieutenant CP of FCT June 3, 2014

"The Boko Haram itself has not helped matters since it has never come out by its actions to define what type of war it is fighting….in spite of professional advice to the Presidency including two Memos submitted by my humble self, it does not seem to know what it is facing and the type of war it should be fighting. Is it a war against terrorists, insurgents or as people are coming to believe, a nurtured war against the people in Northern Nigeria?" --*Murtala Nyako, Governor of beleaguered Adamawa State at the 3-Day Symposium on Current Economic, Social and Security Challenges Facing Northern Nigeria in Washington D.C., organized by the US Institute of Peace, March 17-19, 2014*

Corruption had been: "The grand open sesame to the chambers of power, the prime qualification for the most important appointments, the tie which bound the powerful and ruthless. Rather than serving as that high temple from which all goodness flows, our Presidential Villa became the bulwark of the beastly, the den of the desperado, and the last unfailing refuge of fugitives from justice". *Renowned scholar, Professor Niyi Osundare denouncing grotesque corruption in former President, Goodluck Jonathan's government at the 80th Anniversary Lecture of Christ School, Ado Ekiti, Ekiti State, in Lagos on May 17, 2015*

"You see this card? It is what we shall use to sweep out the government thieves. If the incoming government is not better, we shall use it to sweep them away too". *Two Yoruba women displaying their*

Permanent Voter's Card (PVC) before they voted at the 2015 Presidential elections

"He should be wary of wolves in sheep clothing, sycophants and all political jobbers who jumped ship to identify with the winning party". *Bishop Emeritus of Lagos Archdiocese, Cardinal Olubumi Okojie, in a statement urged the incoming President of Nigeria, Muhammadu Buhari, to avoid fraudulent and egocentric sycophants at the corridors of state power, May 20, 2015*

"In the first place Jonathan should not have been President of Nigeria because he lacks both the competence and experience to run the country successfully…I will advice Buhari to convince himself that he is morally and politically capable to undertake the responsibility of cleaning up Nigeria. I will ask him to constitute a government of national unity involving all the political parties in Nigeria in the task of rebuilding Nigeria."

Activist Second Republic Governor of Kaduna State, Alhaji Balarabe Musa, on August 21, 2015 stated that the anti-corruption tack of President Muhammadu Buhari was subjective and therefore flawed.

"The campaign was the most iconic fight of a freedom struggle. The fight will be won some day. No injustice will can last forever. But for the sake of these girls, it must be won soon". *Former British Prime Minster and now the UN special envoy speaking on the one year anniversary of abduction of the Chibok school girls* *celebrated by the Bring Back Our Girls group, Zpril 15, 2015*

"**Boko Haram came and told us they were moving out and said that we should run away with them. But we said no. Then, they started stoning us. I held my baby to my stomach, bending over to protect her.**" *May 2015: Lami Musa, 27, one of the first female hostages rescued from Boko Haram insurgents in the Sambisa Forest narrating gory stories of brutality*

"**Our Chibok girls have stayed away beyond an acceptable amount of time in the hands of savages. It is now time for their government to bring them back. There is no time left.**" *Mrs. Oby Ezekwesii addressing President Muhammadu Buhari on the need to rescue the 219 Chibok school girls still held by Boko Haram insurgents in the northeast, during the Presidential meeting with the Bring Back Our Girls*

"**Rescuing the Chibok girls is a top agenda for both US and Nigeria. We however call on Nigeria and all concerned persons globally to keep tweeting about the Chibok girls. Finding them will break Boko Haram, make them less powerful and bring an end to extremism in Nigeria**". *US Congresswoman, Wilson Frederica, speaking during the solidarity visit of a contingent of the United States of America Congress to the Bring Back Our Girls in Abuja, August 4, 2015*

"**Many say our world is at a tipping point. If we do not act together, if we do not act responsibly, if we do not act now, we risk slipping into a cycle of poverty,** degradation, and despair."--*Ban Ki Moon, United Nations Secretary General on the need for humans to safeguard the world*

"Nigeria really needs to think that relative its level of wealth, it is really far behind" -- *Bill Gates, Microsoft Founder and billionaire deplored extreme wretchedness and poverty in the midst of affluence in Nigeria, February 2013*

"Many things are going wrong and nothing seems to be working. Bad leadership is the cause of insecurity in Nigeria" --*Sultan of Sokoto and President–General Jama'atul Nasril Islam, Alhaji Muhammadu Sa'ad Abubakar 111 decrying preposterously egregious leadership in the Nigerian polity, June 2013*

"Nigeria needs strong institutions not strong men. In too many countries, the actions of thugs and warlords and human traffickers hold back the promise of Africa. History shows us that progress is only possible where governments exist to serve their people and not the other way round" --*US President, Barack Obama, at Cape Town University, South Africa, June 30, 2013*

"When a man is denied the right to live the life he believes in, he has no choice but to become an outlaw." --*Dr. Nelson Mandela, First Black South African*

President, on the dark days of apartheid oppression in his
fatherland

"...the most compelling reasons for revolution
throughout the ages were injustice, crushing poverty,
marginalization, rampant corruption, lawlessness,
joblessness and general dissatisfaction with the ruling
elite. That these conditions exist is well known to the
people in authority but the successive efforts have
failed to yield the radical change from the present
approach to a revolution one"--*Remorseful Speaker of*
the Nigerian House of Representatives calling for
Revolution in the Country, July 2, 2013

"Nigerian Government–A criminal Enterprise" --*Prof*
Pat Utomi, Former Head of Lagos Business School
decrying the gravity of corruption and deceit in the
Nigerian Polity THE NEWS: MAY 7, 2012

"Nigeria Needs Revolution" --*Alhaji Maitama Sule,*
Former Nigerian Permanent Representative to the United
Nations, addressing the Northern Peace Summit in
Kaduna, January 2013

"I entirely agree with the connotation Boko Haram if
it means one going to school to acquire Western
education that guarantees one to steal public funds" --
Governor Sule Lamido, welcoming members of Bauchi

*State House of Assembly to the Government House ,
Jigawa State on 28 February 2012*

**"Our sacred mandate, that is the protection and
preservation of our nation which is our collective
patrimony"**--*Mr. Ekpeyong Ita, Director-General State
Security Services, at a ceremony to honour his 10 security
operatives slain by Ombatse militia cult group in
Nassarawa State Nigeria, May 26, 2013*

**"The inability of the state to punish criminals as
criminals has created the illusion that there is a
conflict between Christians and Moslems. Nigeria is
changing because Nigerians are taking back their
country from the grip of marauders. Christians and
Moslems together in solidarity are protesting against
corruption beyond the false hood of religion"**--*Dr.
Hassan KUKAH, Bishop of Sokoto Diocese on the need
for Christians and Moslems to ferociously fight their
common enemy-Ruinous Corruption in the Nigerian
State, 15 January 2012*

CHAPTER 1

DAY OF CATASTROPHE

On April 14, 2014 more than 276 female students of Government Girls Secondary School Chibok were abducted by Boko Haram insurgents in Borno State of north-eastern Nigeria. The group, Boko Haram, (literally meaning: Congregation of Followers of the Prophet for the Religion of Islam and the Struggle) which started violent attacks in 2009 says it is fighting for an Islamic State of Northern Nigeria. Two deadly assaults were carried out by the sect at Nyanya--an Abuja outskirts on 14 and 29 April 2014 in which an estimated 100 people died. This bestial kidnapping of Nigerian school girls had elicited outrage and protests around the world.

Various groups: religious, civil society and trade unions staged demonstrations across the country for the release of the girls. The protests were spearheaded by the Bring Back Our Girls movement. The group held the first protest with massive turn-out on 29 April 2014; exactly 15 days after the girls were kidnapped.

On May 8, 2014 former Nigerian Minister for Education and Vice President of World Bank, Mrs. Oby Ezekwesili led a mammoth assembly of women including the wife of former Nigerian Vice President, Mrs. Titilayo Atiku Abubakar, along the streets of Abuja to the National Assembly demanding immediate freedom of the abducted girls (front cover). The crowd was bedecked with red t-shirts, badges, caps and banners bearing the hash tag: #Bring Back Our Girls (BBOG). They were assured by Senators and Congress members that the hostages will be released. Addressing Nigerians at the

Presidential Media Chat on Nigerian Television Authority on May 4, 2014, then President Goodluck Jonathan said security agencies were combing communities around Chibok to secure the release of those traumatized girls. He also mentioned that the Nigerian government had approached some foreign countries to assist in tracking the rebels. [1]

Speaking at a funeral ceremony in Delta State early May 2014, previous Nigerian Senate President--David Mark--voiced repugnance over the abduction over 250 female students of Government Girls Secondary School Chibok, Borno State on 14 April by insurgents. David Mark seared that:

"The current situation in the country where some children have taken arms against their own country is totally unacceptable. Parents must share in the blame. I have been an advocate for dialogue with the Boko Haram elements in this country. But things have gone absolutely beyond bound and no government will negotiate with Boko Haram as long as they keep our girls and our boys".

He audaciously declared that:

".... they must never test the will of the Nigerian people because we must stand united against evil." [2]

I want to ask: are we united against the most dreadful evil in Nigeria--corruption? Is monstrous institutional corruption not the root cause of present despicable insecurity? Can there ever be true democracy amid monumental corruption?

THE WORLD OUTRAGED BY TRAGEDY

The British Prime Minister, David Cameron, while addressing Parliament on May 7, 2014 described the abduction of more than 200 Nigerian school girls as an 'act of pure evil', promising to offer further assistance in the rescue efforts.

"Britain stands to provide any assistance as we can, working very closely with the US. We already have a British military training team in Nigeria the foreign office has counter terrorism experts and we should be proud of the role we play in that country, where British aid is helping to educate 800, 000 Nigerian children including 600,000 girls," Mr. Cameron said.

On Thursday May 8, 2014 the United States of America First Lady, Michelle Obama took the rare step of delivering her husband's weekly video address to express anger over the plight of more than 250 schoolgirls kidnapped by Islamist militants in Nigeria. Displaying a demonstration poster which read #Bring Back Our Girls, Mrs. Obama said:

"Like millions of people across the globe, my husband and I are outraged and heartbroken over the kidnapping of more than 200 Nigerian girls from their school dormitory in the middle of the night. This unconscionable act was committed by a terrorist group determined to keep these girls from getting an education – grown men attempting to snuff out the aspirations of young girls".

On the possibility of the US helping to rescue the girls Michelle Obama said,

"I want you to know that Barack has directed our government to do everything possible to support the

Nigerian government's efforts to find these girls and bring them home. In these girls, Barack and I see our own daughters. We see their hopes, their dreams, and we can only imagine the anguish their parents are feeling right now."[3]

The international attempt to rescue the 276 schoolgirls being held captive by Islamic insurgents in northeastern Nigeria was boosted Friday May 9 when British security experts joined the Nigerian and American forces trying to set free the missing students. Also Canada, France, Israel, China and Japan had enlisted with the salvaging operations. Meanwhile Amnesty International claimed Nigerian commanders were warned that armed men were beginning to arrive near Chibok where the girls were kidnapped from their school, but the military were unable to raise enough troops to respond.

"This abduction could have been prevented," said Amnesty spokeswoman, Susanna Flood.

The UN Security Council called on Friday May 9, 20014 for the Nigerian terrorist group Boko Haram, which is holding hostage 276 schoolgirls, to be held accountable for what might amount to crimes against humanity. The declaration approved by all 15 Council members was the strongest by the UN's most powerful body on terrorist attacks in Nigeria. The Council expressed "profound outrage" at Boko Haram's abduction of 276 schoolgirls on April 14 and eight girls on May 5, and demanded their immediate and unconditional release.

It also stoutly condemned a May 5 attack that caused hundreds of deaths and injuries. The Council said terrorist attacks carried out by Boko Haram rebels since 2009 "have caused large-scale and devastating loss of life and represent a threat to the stability and peace of west and central Africa."[4]

On May 9, 2014, the United Nations Secretary General, Ban Ki Moon divulged that the world body had concluded arrangements to send a special envoy on security to assist the country in the search for the abducted school girls. He said the UN will make sure over 10 million non-schooling girls are effectively sent back to classes soon. This was disclosed by the UN Special Envoy for Global Education and former British Prime Minister, Gordon Brown, at the end of the World Economic Forum on Africa held in Abuja. [5]

UNDER JONATHAN, NIGERIA SQUANDERED OIL WEALTH, BREEDS CORRUPTION-- HILLARY CLINTON May 9, 2014

The credibility and competence of the Nigerian Government under President Goodluck Jonathan was challenged by former United States First Lady, Senator Hillary Clinton. Mrs. Clinton accused the Jonathan administration of ineptitude, debauchery and monumental corruption which precipitated the country into rot and insecurity. Those searing reproofs were delivered early May, 2014 at a public function organized by the International Crisis Group and a philanthropy parley, as she was widely quoted by several American media outlets, including CNN. At the function organized by the International Crisis Group, Hillary Clinton scorched that: *"Nigeria has made bad choices, not hard choices. They have squandered their oil wealth; they have allowed corruption to fester, and now they are losing control of parts of their (own) territory because they would not make hard choices."*

On the present insurgency crisis in Northern Nigeria she emphasized that,

"The Nigerian government has failed to confront the threat, or to address the underlying challenges. Most of all, the government of Nigeria needs to get serious about protecting all of its citizens and ensuring that every child has the right and opportunity to go to school. Every asset and expertise should be brought to bear. Everyone needs to see this for what it is, it is a gross human rights abuse, but it is also part of a continuing struggle within Nigeria and within North Africa".

In a chat with ABC-TV's Robin Roberts on American national television, Hillary Clinton said:

"The seizure of these young women by this radical, extremist group, Boko Haram, is abominable, it's criminal, it's an act of terrorism, and it really merits the fullest response possible, first and foremost from the government of Nigeria. The government of Nigeria has been, in my view, somewhat derelict in its responsibility toward protecting boys and girls, men and women in northern Nigeria over the last years"

Senator Clinton avowed that:

"The Nigerian government must accept help – particularly intelligence, surveillance and reconnaissance help – their troops have to be the ones that (are) necessary, but they could do a better job if they accept the offers that are being made. Nigeria has made bad choices, not hard choices". [6]

BOKO HARAM DEMANDS PRISONER SWAP

On the 12th of May 2014, in a video believed to have been posted by Boko Haram, the leader of the group, Abu Shekau, said he would release the abducted girls if the Federal Government freed his members held in detention centres across the country. In the 17-minute speech with rapid fire Hausa and Arabic pyrotechnics, Shekau said:

"All I am saying is if you want me to release your girls that we kidnapped; you must release our brethren that are held in Borno, Yobe, Kano, Kaduna, Abuja, Lagos and Enugu. We know that you incarcerated our brethren all over the country."

The federal government of Nigeria said it was scrutinizing authenticity of the video. In a World Press Conference same day, the joint coordinator of the National Briefing Centre and Director of the National Orientation Agency, Mr. Mike Omeri, said government was studying the footage. On the question of negotiation with the insurgent group, Mr. Omeri said "all options are opened" to effect release of the girls.

Nevertheless, the State Security Services (SSS) insisted that Abu Shekau was dead. Spokesperson of the SSS, Deputy Director Marilyn Ogar, said after the press briefing:

"Boko Haram has become a franchise with which many people commit several crimes. Abu Kakar and Abu Shekau are dead. Those bearing these names are fake".

She foreclosed the prospect of a sovereign government negotiating with terrorists, emphasizing that "Nigeria will not in any way negotiate with Boko Haram". [7]

POROSITY AND CORRUPTION OF THE NIGERIAN ARMY

On May 14, 2014 rebellious soldiers shot at the General Officer Commanding (GOC) 7 Division Nigerian Army, Borno State, Major General Abubakar Mohammed. The mutineers were expressing distaste over an earlier failed operation in the Sambisa Forest war theatre in which four soldiers including a Lieutenant Colonel died. They accused the GOC of mishandling the operation resulting to their ambush and attack by Boko Haram members. Consequently, he was relieved of his post by the military authorities.

At the same time, the United States security agents in Nigeria said the Nigerian Government had complicated the efforts to rescue the abducted girls. The United States Defence Department stated on May 15, 2014 that Nigeria had initially been tardy in accepting the offer from the US to help rescue the girls from captivity. [8]

Wednesday 21 May 2014, while briefing the United States House of Representatives Committee on Foreign Affairs in a hearing tagged as: Boko Haram–The Growing Threat to School Girls, Nigeria and Beyond, the United States Under Secretary of State for Civilian Security, Democracy and Human Rights, Sara Sewall, revealed that corruption was hindering Nigeria's efforts at ending insurgency in the north-east. In her report, Sara Sewall said that the Nigerian Military must eliminate entrenched corruption and incompetence in its ranks for it to secure the release of over 200 school girls held hostage by Boko Haram.

Speaking alongside a top Pentagon African official, Amanda Dory, Sara Sewall was stunned that in spite of

Nigeria's $5.8 billion security budget for 2014, *"Corruption prevents supplies as basic as bullets and transport vehicles from reaching the front lines of the struggle against Boko Haram".*
The situation, according to Sewall reported in the New York Times, had induced 'low morale and desertions' on soldiers of the 7th Army Division fighting the rebels.

On the advancement in delivering the girls, Sewall said, "Given time I am hopeful that we will make progress".
At Abuja she told journalists that it was up to the Nigerian Government to accept or reject the prison exchange arrangement proposed by Abu Shekau. In her presentation, Amanda Dory said the Pentagon believes that the girls must have been dispersed into multiple smaller groups and that 'they may or may not all be in Nigeria'. President Good Luck Jonathan had in a meeting with President François Hollande of France in Paris on May 17, 2014 described Boko Haram as 'the al Qaeda of West Africa'.

Same day, Washington said 80 US troops were currently in Chad to support the advancing international struggle to rescue the abducted girls. In a statement formerly informing the US Congress of the deployment of the troops, the White House said the military personnel are not ground troops. They are mostly Air Force crew members, maintenance specialists and security officers for unarmed predator surveillance drones. The White House statement said that:

"Those personnel will support the operation of intelligence, surveillance and reconnaissance aircraft for

missions over Northern Nigeria and the surrounding area". [9]

#BRING BACK OUR GIRLS INTENSIFY OUTRAGE

On Thursday May 22, 2014 the BBOG campaign group was prevented from entering the Presidential Villa Abuja by State Security operatives. The assembly, led by former Nigerian Minister of Education, Mrs. Oby Ezekwesili, and past Congressman, now Senator Dino Melaye, was seeking the release of teenage girls abducted from Government Girls Secondary School, Chibok in Borno State. Armed with placards and chanting songs of outrage and despondency, the protesters who had planned to take their complaint to the President to address them on the fate of those girls were restricted by security agents to the Federal Secretariat within the Three Arms Zone, a few metres from the State House gate.

However, they were welcomed by Secretary to the Federal Government, Ayim Pius Ayim, Minister of Federal Capital Territory (FCT), Bala Mohammed, Minister for Information, Labaran Maku and other Government officials. President GoodLuck Ebele Jonathan, represented by the Minister of State, Federal Capital Territory, Olajumoke Akinjide, advised the protesters to 'direct their cries also to Boko Haram' insurgents and that the federal government was making concerted efforts to free the teen captives. [10]

In another development May 22, the coordinator of the National Information Centre on the ongoing crisis, Mr. Mike Omeri told journalists at a press conference in Abuja that:

"The Nigerian government welcomes growing support from the International Community for Nigeria's effort to locate and secure the release of the school girls abducted from Chibok."

Asked if the Nigerian government has opened deliberations with the insurgent group, Mr. Omeri said:

"The government has stated its position on this issue. Men and women are out there combing everywhere, collaborating with international support. As far as we are concerned in this issue, all options are still open and we will apply international best practices all over the world. The result of this international cooperation will be the rescue of the school girls and the restoration of peace and normalcy in our sub region."

The United Nations Security Council on May 22, 2014 affirmed Boko Haram an al Qaeda-linked terrorist organization. All 15 members of the world body unanimously concurred with this critical decision. To this effect it has imposed travel bans and arms embargo on Boko Haram. Assets of key Boko Haram members around the world would henceforth be frozen.

QUEST TO STIFLE #BRING BACK OUR GIRLS COMMENCES

May 28, 2014 a counter group known as Release Our Girls, allegedly hired by government agents, stormed the Unity Fountain Square, venue of the BBOG campaign assembly and attacked the protesters. Leaders of the original campaign organization were descended upon by the rival camp with bottles under the watchful eyes of the Nigerian policemen sent to the area. The women among them were also beaten up.

In the ensuing skirmish, sitting chairs, cameras, telephones and other campaign materials were vandalized by the opposition faction. Ironically, the bellicose sect said it was also fighting for the release of the school girls abducted on April 14 by Boko Haram. It was a display of incivility and ignominy! Convener of the notable BBOG crusade party, Mrs. Oby Ezekwesili, looking directly at a standing policeman, said in a fit of rage:

"Tell your CP (Commissioner of Police) that there is a message for him. Nigeria will not always be like this. People have to be careful what they do with the citizens of this country. We sent a letter today, acknowledged telling you that there was rising trend of aggression towards us. And yet you deployed police to guard the rented crowd. And the police stood. They witnessed, it happened".

Vowing to continue with demonstrations, Ezekwesili seared:

"Let the FG and associates know that we the women, men, youths and children of Abuja family of #Bring Back Our Girls are resolute to keep standing".

Astoundingly, members of the Release Our Girls wing were all over the Unity Fountain ground with mobile electronic billboards and balloons flashing campaigns for President Good Luck Jonathan and Vice President Namadi Sambo. Meanwhile four of the abducted girls from Government Girls Secondary School, Chibok had escaped from their captors. Some sources purported that Boko Haram released the quartet on grounds of ill health.

In an emotion-laden assembly at the THIS DAY DOME in Abuja on 29 May, 2014 the leader of the Bring Back Our Girls group, Mrs. Oby Ezekwesili, chronicled the tortuous and arduous odyssey pushing for the release of the girls. She narrated how the campaign was formed and has been widely progressive and welcome. She also gave account of the indignities and torture meted to the patriotic protesters by security agencies, particularly the Nigerian Police. In spite of this, she said the camp would continue to keep vigil and protest until the abducted girls are released back to their parents. [11]

BOKO HARAM SHOWS FOOTAGE OF GIRLS IN DISTRESS

June 1, 2014 London-root newspaper, The Mail on Sunday, relayed a video footage allegedly released by Boko Haram showing some of the abducted girls in misery, distress and shock. The newspaper divulged that the video was taken a month after the girls had been kidnapped, showing them pleading for help. They really needed salvation from their look.

In the video reported by The Mail, 8 of the girls dressed in school uniform were paraded in turns to make public statements for their release. Four of them spoke in Hausa that they were taken by force and were hungry. One, a tall maiden of about 18, said with tears, "my family will be worried".

Another of the female teens said:

"I never expected to suffer like this in my life".

The other: "They have taken us away by force".

And the fourth: "We are not getting enough food".

It was accounted that video captured by an intermediary on May 19 had been shown to President Goodluck Jonathan. The Mail on Sunday reported that two attempts to release some of the girls were aborted at the last minute as Boko Haram instead took fright.

STEPHEN DAVIS MEDIATES FOR RELEASE OF CHIBOK GIRLS

Hitherto, an Australian, Dr. Stephen Davis who had advised three Nigerian Presidents on how to dialogue with militant groups in Nigeria spent about one month struggling to help release the girls. According to him:

"The vast majority of the Chibok girls are not being held in Nigeria. They are in camps across the Nigerian borders in Cameroun, Chad and Niger. I say the vast majority as I know a small group was confirmed to me to

be in Nigeria last week when we sought to have them released."

He stated that the negotiation process has been hard and complicated. In his remarks:

"One of the small groups of girls is ill and we had hoped we might convince the commander of the group holding her that she should be released so we could give her medical treatment".

He revealed that:

"There are other girls who are not well and we have come close to having them released but their captors fear a trap in which they will be captured in the handover process. One girl has what I assume is a broken wrist as they demonstrate to me how she holds her hand. I have been told that others are sick and in need of medical attention." [12]

NIGERIAN POLICE BANS #BRING BACK OUR GIRLS CAMPAIGN

BBOG HEADS FOR COURT

On the 2nd of June 2014, the FCT Abuja CP, Mr. Joseph Mbu issued a statement banning further protests in Abuja for the release of the abducted Chibok girls. Declaring the ban on Monday Mr. Mbu said:

"The trend is now posing a serious security threat to those living around and as the FCT Police boss; I cannot fold my hands and watch this lawlessness. Information reaching us is that too soon dangerous elements will join the groups under the guise of protests and detonate explosives aimed at embarrassing the Government. Accordingly, protests on the Chibok Girls are hereby banned with immediate effect".

The proclamation elicited instantaneous furious condemnation across the country and around the world. Citizens viewed that order as inhuman and repressive. Such a tyrannical directive was not unexpected as armed policeman with arrest trucks and ice sprayer tanks had been trailing and watching every meeting of the BBOG group.

Consequent on this, the BBOG represented by former Minister of Education, Dr. Mrs. Obiageli Ezekwesili, wife of former Chief Justice of Nigeria, Mrs. Maryam Uwais and 15 others on 3rd June filed a suit at the Federal High Court Maitama Abuja challenging the powers of the Nigerian Police Force to ban any form of peaceful protest within the FCT. In the application seeking the enforcement of their fundamental human rights to non-violent assembly and association, the plaintiffs through their lawyer, Mr. Femi Falana, SAN, stated that the FCT CP, Mr. Joseph Mbu, did not have the constitutional powers to stop the #Bring Back Our Girls campaign. He had just been deployed from Rivers State over controversies surrounding public protests.

The crusaders viewed that action as a gross infringement on their rights as enshrined in sections 38, 39 and 40 of the 1999 Constitution of the Federal Republic of Nigeria as amended and Articles 8, 10 and 11 of the African Charter on Human Rights. The CP of FCT was listed as the only respondent to the suit.

DEMANDS

The BBOG critically requested the FCT High Court to grant the following prayers:

1. An order for the enforcement of the fundamental human rights of the applicants to freedom of conscience, freedom of expression and freedom of assembly and association guaranteed by Section 38, 39 and 40 of the Constitution of the Federal Republic of Nigeria, as amended, and Articles 8, 10, 11 of the African Charter on Human and Peoples Rights (Ratification and Enforcement) Act, LFN, 2004 in terms of the reliefs sought in the statement accompanying the affidavit in support of this application.
2. A declaration that the decision of the respondent to ban protests and rallies in the Federal Capital Territory with effect from Monday, June 2, 2014, is illegal, unconstitutional, null and void as it violates the fundamental rights of the applicant to freedom of conscience, freedom of expression

and freedom of assembly and association guaranteed by Section 38, 39 and 40 of the constitution of the Federal Republic of Nigeria, as amended, and Articles 8, 10, 11 of the African Charter on Human and Peoples Rights (Ratification and Enforcement) Act, LFN, 2004.

3. A declaration that the respondent is not competent to ban protests and rallies in the Federal Capital Territory in any manner whatsoever and however without an order issued by a court of competent jurisdiction.

4. An order of perpetual injunction restraining the respondent, his agents and privies from further preventing the applicants or aggrieved Nigerians from taking part in protests and rallies in exercise of their freedom of conscience, expression, assembly and association as guaranteed by Sections 38, 39 and 40 of the Constitution of the Federal Republic of Nigeria, as amended, and Articles 8, 10, 11 of the African Charter on Human and Peoples Rights (Ratification and Enforcement) Act, LFN, 2004.

5. An order directing the respondent to pay to the applicant the sum of N200m only as damages for the said act of violation of applicants' fundamental rights to freedom of conscience, freedom of expression and freedom of assembly and association as guaranteed by Sections 38, 39 and 40 of the Constitution of the Federal Republic of Nigeria, as amended, and Articles 8, 10, 11 of the African Charter on Human and Peoples Rights (Ratification and Enforcement) Act, LFN, 2004.

Buttressing their rights to freedom of association, the first plaintiff, Hadiza Bala Usman in a 25-paragraph affidavit on behalf of the protesters told the court that they have been carrying out demonstrations on the fate of over 200 girls abducted from Government Girls Secondary School Chibok in Borno State under the aegis of Women for Peace and Justice #Bring Back Our Girls.

POLICE REPUDIATES BAN ON BRING BACK OUR GIRLS CRUSADE

In what might be seen as an afterthought, the Nigerian IG, Mr. Mohammed Abubakar refuted the authoritarian order of the CP of FCT within 24 hours. Addressing pressmen through the Police Force Public Relations Officer, CSP Frank Mba on 3rd June; the IG said:

"The Police High Command wishes to inform the general public that the Force has not issued any order banning peaceful assembly/protests anywhere in Nigeria. Against the backdrop of current security challenges in the country coupled with a recent intelligence report of a likely infiltration and hijack of otherwise innocuous and peaceful protests by some criminal elements having links with insurgents, the Police only issued advisory notice enjoining citizens to apply caution in the said rallies particularly in the Federal Capital Territory and its environs".

He expounded that:

"The IG calls on the General public to see the present position of the Force as a necessary sacrifice for the peace our nation needs as security is a collective responsibility. Consequently, citizens are strongly advised to reconsider their positions on the issues of rallies and protests in FCT until the existing threats are

appropriately neutralized and removed from our midst by relevant security agencies."

Reacting to the IG's counter directive, Mrs. Oby Ezekwesili said to journalists:

"We have already gone to court; therefore, I have nothing else to add." [13]

OBASANJO ADMITS ACCESS TO BOKO HARAM

Speaking on the Hausa Service of the British Broadcasting Corporation (BBC) on June 12, 2014 former Nigerian President, Chief Olusegun Obasanjo, acknowledged that he has access to the Boko Haram insurgents. He blamed the Nigerian government for stalling the process of negotiation for the release of the Chibok Girls by refusing to give him clearance to initiate talks with the sect. Obasanjo hinted that the terrorist group might release some of the girls that could be pregnant while some of them would not be seen again for years. According to Chief Obasanjo:

"I believe that some of them will never return. We will still be hearing about them many years from now. Some will give birth, but if they cannot take care of them in the forest, they may be released."

In his reaction, the coordinator of the National Information Centre for the crisis, Mr. Mike Omeri expressed disbelief at Obasanjo's statements. He claimed that the former Nigerian government leader has unrestricted access to the President to discuss release of the girls. He restated that the government has not stopped any individuals who have access to the group not to come

forward and intervene in this matter. Mr. Omeri recalled
that:

*"In our briefing we reiterated that there are three
options opened to the government to find those abducted
girls and the first is any individual with access to the sect
should help the government in securing the release of the
girls. Second is for the Army, in collaboration with our
international allies, to secure their release and for the
insurgents to voluntarily release the girls."*

Rebuking Chief Obasanjo, the crisis coordinator said:

*"If he actually said so, that means he has superior
equipment to those of the Government and its allies.
Besides, as a respectable statesman and former
President, I think he has unfettered access to the
President to discuss this. I don't think the pages of
newspapers is the appropriate avenue to make claims that
he has access to the insurgents. I sincerely don't
understand this".*

Going down memory lane, the former Nigerian Head of
State had at the early stage of the kidnapping cataclysm
accused President Goodluck Jonathan of not believing
that the girls were really taken away. In an interview with
a foreign media he said the President did not believe in
the news until 16 days after the abduction. In Obasanjo's
observation:

*"I believe that the girls would have been rescued within
28 hours, maximum 48 hours. Don't forget they were
almost 300 girls. The logistics of moving them around is
something and if action had been taken immediately; but*

unfortunately, the President had doubts. Is this true or is it a ploy to those who don't want me to be President again?"

Obasanjo revealed that his mediation proposals three years ago at the early stages of the insurgency were ignored by the government and its agents. Reminiscing of the botched attempt he said:

"Three years ago I went to Maiduguri. Actually that was when Boko Haram attacked the UN building in Abuja; and they accepted the responsibility. Then I went to Abuja to find out from security leaders, the Inspector General of Police, the National Security Adviser; who are these people? What are their objectives, their grievances and if we can reach out to them?

"The feeling I got was: Oh, they are just a bunch of riff-raffs, forget about them. I then went to the President and said, look, should I take it upon myself to go on fact-finding visit? I want to find out. And the President said: 'I trust your judgement. You can do that'.

"Of course, I reported back to the two important principals – the State Governor and the President at that time. I believe that if action had been taken at that time as I recommended maybe we would not have got to this stage." [14]

HIGH COURT DECLARES BRING BACK OUR GIRLS PROTEST LEGITIMATE

A Federal Capital Territory Abuja High Court presided over by Justice Abubakar Talba on June 12, 2014 declared that the Nigerian Police Force (NPF) lacked the powers to prevent or nullify rallies or protests being conducted by Nigerians with respect to the over 300 students of Government Girls Secondary School Chibok abducted in Borno State on April 14, 2014. In an epoch-making judgement, justice Talba upheld that the Public Order Act Cap 382 Laws of Nigeria 1990 which the Police relied on for its action *"does not authorize men of the Nigerian Police to disrupt rallies or processions on the issue of the abducted Chibok Girls."*

This landmark judgement was consequent on the suit filed by former Congressman, Dino Melaye, for enforcement of his fundamental human rights, challenging the interruption on May 9, 2014 of the rally he championed in Abuja calling for the release kidnapped Chibok Girls. The Judge affirmed as unconstitutional the arrest and assault on Dino Melaye during the event by the Nigerian Police. The suit identified as CV/1521/14 has the IG of Police and CP FCT Command as respondents. They were evidently absent in court.

Supervising Judge Abubakar Talba held that arrest of Dino Melaye in respect of rallies is unlawful. The court also declared the disruption of peaceful processions and protests by agents of 1ˢᵗ and 2ⁿᵈ respondents as illegal and unconstitutional. The Judge stated that failure of the respondents to file any counter claims to the applications submitted by the plaintiff Dino Melaye was an admission of the allegations made against them by the applicant.

In his ruling Justice Talba granted the applicant the following reliefs:

1. An order of perpetual injunction restraining the respondents and their agents from further

43

harassing, molesting, intimidating, obstructing, arresting, detaining and prosecuting the applicant in respect of peaceful rallies or processions in Abuja or any part of Nigeria.

2. The sum of One Hundred Fifty Thousand Naira (₦150, 000) awarded as costs and damages against the respondents in favour of the applicant.

3. An order that the IGP, Mohammed Abubakar and CP FCT, Mr. Joseph Mbu "tender a written apology to the applicant as provided for under section 35(6) of the Constitution of the Federal Republic of Nigeria as amended." [15]

Meanwhile the suit instituted at the Federal High Court Maitama Abuja by the #Bring Back Our Girls group challenging the powers of the Nigerian Police Force to ban any form of peaceful protest within the FCT came up for hearing on June 12, 2014. The application seeking the enforcement of their fundamental human rights to non-violent assembly and association was argued by their lawyer, Femi Falana (SAN). The case was subsequently adjourned to 14th July 2014 for judgement.

GERMAN PARLIAMENT VISITS #BRING BACK OUR GIRLS GROUP IN ABUJA

An eleven-man contingent of the German Bundestag led by the Vice President, Mr. Johannes Singhammer on June 20 paid a solidarity visit to the BBOG Abuja camp at Unity Fountain. This meeting had been arranged earlier on by German representatives in the evening of June 6. Addressing the group at the Fountain adjacent to the Transcorp Hilton Hotel, Mr. Johannes said that sequel to the atrocious incident the German Parliament held special meeting to express solidarity with the campaign group. In his remarks the Vice President said:

"For the mothers and relatives of the girls that have been abducted in such a cruel way, a terrible thing has happened and that is why the German Parliament installed a special meeting to express our solidarity with you. On behalf of the German Parliament we express that you are not alone."

He called for immediate release of the kidnapped girls as requested by his parliament:

"This is an occasion for me to launch an appeal to those that perpetrated this terrible deed that on behalf of the German Parliament, they should stop it and give the girls back to their mother and families. This is an official expression of German Bundestag."

On the prospect of assisting the Federal Government to rescue the girls he said:

"I think the government should do what is possible. In Germany we have stamped out the rebel, so the government should do what is possible. All we can do will be revealed as soon as possible."

In her contribution, a woman member of the delegation, Mrs. Ernstberger Petra said:

"You are not only fighting to bring back our girls but at the same time, you are giving face to all children abducted, injured kidnapped or killed. You are representing all of them here. You will also give a voice and face to all mothers and women who are suffering

seeing their families destroyed and their husbands killed. You are here to fight for women's rights also. You should be proud about that because you are not alone and can no longer be condemned to silence."

Consolidating support for the Nigerian crusade group, she promised that the slogan #Bring Back Our Girls would be adopted by the German Parliament. She said:

"On behalf of the Parliament, I will like to support you in this endeavour and the slogan #Bring Back Our Girls is ours now."

Leader of the BBOG camp, Mrs. Oby Ezekwesili expressed appreciation to the German representatives. In gratitude, she said:

"It is because the issue of Chibok girls has taken a humanitarian dimension that few weeks ago we were visited by the Minister of Economic Cooperation, Germany. The Parliament in any democracy is the symbol of citizen's rights and we are very delighted to welcome the Vice President and his delegation. Though we have had visits by the UN Secretary Genera's Representative for Africa, US Parliament and other countries, Germany keep coming and I think it's because the Germans in many ways understand the citizens' demands for accountability and that is exactly what we are doing here."

Mrs. Ezekwesili thereafter decorated the visitors with mementoes of face caps, badges and t-shirts bearing #Bring Back Our Girls. Amazingly the delegates immediately wore their shirts and fastened the emblems to pose for photographs. As usual, on their departure they were hounded by journalists. A member of the Mobilization Committee of the #Bring Back Our Girls group, Okenwa Enyeribe, presented two copies of his book 'WIN THE WAR...Inside Biafra' to the Vice President German Bundestag through one of his female media aides called Vanessa during the occasion. [16]

The Nigerian Army announced a major breakthrough in its fight against Boko Haram insurgents on June 30, 2014. In a press briefing, the Director of Defence Information, Major General Chris Olukolade, revealed the arrest of one Babuji Ya'ari suspected to be a mastermind of the Chibok Girls abduction in April. Olukolade also stated that Babuji, shockingly a member of the Borno State Civilian JTF Vigilante Group, participated in the murder of the Emir of Gwazo a couple of weeks back.

A lady, Hafsat Bako, who coordinated the payments to Boko Haram members, was likewise arrested by the Military. Another woman suspect, Haj Kaka, was also apprehended for espionage and arms dealing for the terrorists. Babuji Ya'ari, a businessman in tricycles is reported to have organized series of terrorist attacks against the Nigerian army as well as bombings in Borno State. Hafsat Bako--the terrorist pay woman --confessed that insurgents are paid a minimum of N10, 000 depending on the type of task undertaken. [17]

MALALA YOUSAFZAI JOINS #BRING BACK OUR GIRLS IN NIGERIA

On July 13, Pakistani teen women education rights activist, Malala Yousafzai, lent her voice for the release of over 500 women abducted by Boko Haram insurgents since April 14, 2014. Malala who survived a shot on her head by the Taliban while campaigning for girls' education rights came to express compassion to the government and people of Nigeria over the kidnapped girls. On this Sunday, she met with parents of the more than 200 girls, who were taken hostage by the militant group from a school in the northeastern village of Chibok. Energetically vowing to stand by the BBOG Campaign Malala said:

"I can see those girls as my sisters ... and I'm going to speak up for them until they are released. I'm going to participate actively in the 'Bring Back Our Girls' campaign to make sure that they return safely and they continue their education."

On Monday July 14, Yousafzai marked her 17th birthday with some of the released Chibok Girls. She also paid a solidarity visit to President Goodluck Jonathan and urged Boko Haram to free the women in their custody. She revealed that President Good Luck Jonathan has promised to visit the parents of the abducted girls. Dedicating her 17th birthday to the cause Malala said:

"My birthday wish this year is 'Bring Back Our Girls' now and alive."

In her appeal to the rebels to free the girls she stated:

"Lay down your weapons. Release your sisters. Release my sisters. Release the daughters of this nation. Let them be free. They have committed no crime. You are misusing the name of Islam ... Islam is a religion of peace. Protect girls from cruelty."

She insisted that girls should not be forced to marry or to leave school to become brides 'when they should be girls,' or to give birth to children 'when they themselves are children.' In her meeting with parents of the girls held in captivity, Malala told pressmen that President Jonathan, in a 45-minute meeting, *'promised me that the girls will be returned as soon as possible.'* According to the President:

"The great challenge in rescuing the Chibok girls is the need to ensure that they are rescued alive."

He affirmed that his government was '*actively pursuing all feasible option'* to achieve their safe return. Speaking on the day designated Malala Day by the United Nations, the teenage activist said:

"I can feel ...the circumstances under which you are suffering. It's quite difficult for a parent to know that their daughter is in great danger. My birthday wish this year is...Bring back our girls now and alive."

Yousafsai Malala spoke of the agony of the parents of the young girls. She said:

"I could see tears in their eyes. They were hopeless. But they seem to have this hope in their hearts, and they were asking if they could meet the president."

Women education rights activist, Yousafsai Malala, has won the European Union's prestigious human rights award. She also was one of the favourites to win the Nobel Peace Prize last year, although the award ended up going to the Organization for the Prohibition of Chemical Weapons. She pledged the sum of $102, 500 to facilitate girl education in Nigeria.[18]

Meanwhile, in a new video released same Sunday, the leader of the Islamic insurgent group Boko Haram, Abubakar Shekau, renewed his demand that the federal government should release his captured members in exchange for the freedom of the girls. Shekau declared that:

"Nigerians are saying 'Bring Back Our Girls,' and we are telling Jonathan to bring back our arrested warriors, our army."

PRESIDENT GOODLUCK JONATHAN ASSURES RESCUE OF THE GIRLS

While inaugurating the Terrorism Victims Support Fund Committee on July 16, 2014, President Goodluck Jonathan assured Nigerians that the war against Boko Haram will soon be over. Addressing the 28 persons committee headed by former Defence Minister, General Theophilus Danjuma, in the State House, the President described members of the Boko Haram as 'individuals whose minds have been so twisted and tutored to believe that they are doing God a service.' He likewise rebuked the furtive promoters and sponsors of the current calamitous insurgency in Nigeria. Expressing repulsion with the group, President Jonathan said:

"They have killed and maimed and struck fear into law-abiding citizens. They have destroyed villages, attacked property and terminated people's livelihoods. They have engaged our security agencies in a meaningless warfare that has wasted unimaginable human and material resources".

On the counter-terrorism efforts, the Head of Government stated:

"Our war against terrorism is gathering momentum. When you read about bombing incident in the mass media, they may come across to those not directly affected as mere statistics."

Accepting the assignment on behalf of the Victims Support Committee, Theophilus Danjuma said:

"One thing we will not do is to go to Sambisa Forest. The Commander-in-Chief will lead and we will follow him. But seriously, this war must be brought to an end. We must win this war immediately. It is taking too long. I called it war when it began but people say it is insurgency. The insurgents appear to be having upper hand at this very moment. We must win this war Mr. President, we must do so immediately."

On his part, the National Security Adviser (NSA), Sambo Dasuki, stated that it was time a clear battle line is drawn with the rebels coupled with hard choices. Meanwhile, the meeting between parents of the Abucted Chibok Girls and President Good Luck Jonathan brokered by UN Envoy and women rights activist, Yousafzai Malala, on Tuesday - July 15 failed to hold. The conference foundered on ineffective logistics between government agents and the Bring Back Our Girls Group which has been pushing for the release of the seized teens since April. It was also reported that to date, 57 of the Chibok Girls have gained their freedom by escaping on their own.[19]

GOODLUCK JONATHAN MEETS WITH PARENTS OF ABDUCTED GIRLS

On July 22 being Day 99 of the abduction of the Chibok School Girls, President Good- luck Jonathan had a conference with their parents and local community leaders. In attendance were the Governors of Borno and Bauchi States. The occasion was also witnessed by top military chiefs and other high government officials. It was a solemn moment as both guests and the State House hosts burst into tears while recounting the events of the tragedy.

During the meeting, the President assured the parents that he was doing everything humanly possible to secure release of the girls. On the apparent delay, he stated that the government is being careful to set the teens free safe, avoiding fatalities. Two members of the #Bring Back Our Girls campaign group who attended the meeting later addressed their sit-out camp at the Unity Fountain. They said they received commendations from Mr. President for conducting themselves with decorum in pressurizing for the rescue of the girls in hostage. [20]

SECURITY AGENTS DETAIN OBY EZEKWESILI AT ABUJA AIRPORT

On her way to London, Mrs. Oby Ezekwesili announced via Twitter--@obyezeks-- on early morning July 22 that the **State Security Service** detained her at the Nnamdi Azikwe Airport in Abuja and seized her passport. Billed for an interview with the BBC 'Hard Talk'show, shortly she was handed back her passport to proceed to London. On Tuesday, July 23, Ezekwesili narrated her ordeal to members of the Christian Association of Nigerian-Americans.

Afterwards, the leader of the BBOG discredited the insinuation that their campaign for the release of the girls was politically motivated. In an interview with Stephen Sackur of the BBC Programme--Hard Talk--Ezekwesili maintained in the 20 minutes or so chat that it was out of humanitarian compassion for the traumatized teenage girls and their families, and belatedness by the government that the group was formed to press for a quick rescue operation. She maintained that Nigeria was not a failed state but replete with failed institutions; which was the cause of egregious governance.[21]

The money given to the parents of the abducted Chibok Girls by President Good Luck Jonathan when he had a meeting with them on July 22 ignited discord in the homeland. The Nigerian public was awash with the news that Goodluck Jonathan gave to the community a munificence of N100 million. The distressed relatives of the maidens in captivity accused the Chibok community in Abuja of shortchanging them in sharing the donation from the President.

One parent of the girls who spoke with BBC's Abdu Halidu on July 29 said she was given only N200, 000. Another said she was presented with N7000 on her farm. Some real parents reported that they were schemed out of the contingent that visited President Goodluck Jonathan.

However, the Chibok community leaders in Abuja later denied any treachery, insisting that the Presidential bounty had been exaggerated. Leader of the Chibok Community in Abuja, Mr. Dauda Iliya explained in a press conference at the Unity Fountain on July 30 that President Jonathan gave the money directly to the parents and girls and not through the community. However, that contradicted the earlier announcement by the Special Assistant on Media and Publicity to the President that the Presidency never gave money to the parents. He failed to expound how the poor relatives found their way back to far-flung Borno State. [22]

INTEL THREAT ON #BRING BACK OUR GIRLS

On the 1st of August 2014 which marked Day 94 Sit-out of the BBOG Group, Mrs. Oby Ezekwesili depressingly informed the members of a 'credible and grave' threat to attack them. Citing a sensitive Intel, she expounded that the assault on their lives, if carried out, would result to fatalities thereby disrupting their advocacy and mission to continue pressurizing for the rescue of the abducted Chibok Girls. She therefore read a statement prepared by the Strategic Planning Committee of the assembly to the effect that they should suspend sitting at the Unity Fountain and remap lines of action.

The members were strongly divided on this critical issue. There was clear fury and despondency on their faces. While some concurred with the leadership to avert violence and disaster to the group, others insisted on staying at the venue despite any imminent danger. However, wise counsel prevailed at last and the camp synchronized to adjourn campaign at the Fountain to an undisclosed location of safety. [23]

DAY 120 OF THE KIDNAPPING OF THE CHIBOK GIRLS

On the 12th of August, being Day 120 of the kidnapping of the Chibok Girls, the BBOG Abuja group staged another protest march from their base at the Unity Fountain to the Eagle Square chanting songs of solidarity and revolution. Astoundingly, they were escorted this time by teams of the Federal Road Safety Corps and policemen. All along, the crusade had been repulsed by security operatives of the government.

At the Federal Secretariat, the leader of the camp, Mrs. Oby Ezekwesili, directed the members to rearrange in twos to move round the Eagle Square and circulate the resource materials to the public, searing for the rescue of the Chibok Girls. While some Nigerians on the way were sympathetic to the plight of the incarcerated maidens and encouraged the protests to go on, others expressed disinterest. The later viewed both the abduction and campaign as political scheming.

Hence the BBOG advocates had a ponderous task convincing fellow Nigerians that it was out of humanity sharing that they were pressurizing for the release of the girls. From there the campaigners marched to Transcorp Hilton Hotel junction at Maitama to display their placards, banners and continue the advocacy for about forty-five minutes. They later re-convened at the Unity Fountain for stock-taking. The group expressed profound gratitude to the Nigerian Police and Road Safety for leading them through. In turnout was former congressman, now Senator Dino Melaye. [24]

DAY 140 OF THE ABDUCTION

Monday September 1, 2014, the BBOG took their protest to Berger Junction Abuja. At the roundabout, some members of the group wore sealed lips, hands tied and placards depicting the trauma, distress and anguish of the girls in captivity. The outing which marked Day 140 of the abduction was led by Mrs. Aisha Yesufu who walked about the junction calling on fellow Nigerians in cars and passing by to join the pressure for the rescue of the kidnapped female teens.

Officers of the Civil Defence Corps and Nigerian Police were present to provide security and order. Expectedly, some encountered Nigerians sympathized with the group for the release of the girls. Others expressed lackadaisical attitude, preferring to go about their businesses. In any case, the campaign reawakened the consciousness of Nigerians to continue to push for the delivery of the Chibok Girls – a part of the Nigerian population brutally held hostage by Boko Haram insurgents since April 14, 2014. [25]

WASHINGTON POST BLASTS JONATHAN FOR CAMPAIGN SLOGAN

The Washington Post on Tuesday September 9, 2014 rebuked President Goodluck Jonathan over a campaign slogan in support of his re-election bid come 2015. In an editorial report of the United States-based tabloid titled: *'This may be the most inappropriate political hostage of the year'* it questioned the slogan's resemblance with that of the pressure group, #Bring Back Our Girls, seeking the release of the over 200 schoolgirls kidnapped in April. The article relayed that:

"It was the social media campaign of the year. #BringBackOurGirls awoke the world to the ravages of Boko Haram, an al-Qaeda-linked terror group in Nigeria, and the plight of the millions of people who live amid their insurgency.

"At the heart of the message were hundreds of missing schoolgirls, abducted in April from the remote village of Chibok by Boko Haram fighters who vowed to turn them

into slaves. The #BringBackOurGirls hostage channeled sympathy from abroad and local outrage and concern in Nigeria, with many angry at the government of President Goodluck Jonathan for being unable to free the captured women."

The Washington Post stated that more than 200 girls remain missing in suspected Boko Haram captivity while others had *"perished from snakebite, illness and deprivation in the wild."* It said:

"Nigerian forces are now fighting Boko Haram in pitched battles around Maiduguri, the capital of Borno State, the main hotbed of Boko Haram's operations. The US reports that, at least, 1.5m people have been displaced by the conflict since Jonathan's government declared a state of emergency in May."

The editorial divulged that:

"While #BringBackOurGirls was just a brief cause célèbre in the West--a passing moment to get morally exercised and then move on; it had a deeper meaning in Nigeria. It echoed the larger frustrations of a society that has little faith in its political leadership. It is fed up with endemic corruption and wants genuine reform and better governance. Boko Haram is a fanatical, murderous outfit, but its insurgency gained sway in a region that has been historically marginalized and neglected by Nigeria's central government."

The paper deplored the insouciance of President Jonathan towards the maidens in captivity. It relayed the scorn thus:

"In this context, the new campaign slogan is particularly galling. Jonathan has not brought back the girls, yet his campaign expects Nigeria to bring him back to power. One wonders if it will spawn more rich satire among Nigerians on social media. After all, there's plenty of precedent."[26]

In a quick reaction to the global outrage, President Goodluck Ebele Jonathan directed that the #Bring Back Jonathan 2015 campaign posters and banners around Abuja, which he and many Nigerians found offensive, be brought down immediately. This was revealed in a press statement from the Presidency on Wednesday, September 10, 2014 signed by the special adviser to the President on media and publicity, Reuben Abati. He stated that:

"President Jonathan wholly shares the widely expressed view that the signs which were put up without his knowledge or approval are a highly insensitive parody of the #Bring Back Our Girls hash tag. While President Jonathan appreciates the enthusiastic show of support for his administration by a broad range of stakeholders, he condemns the #Bring Back Jonathan 2015 signs which appear to make light of the very serious national and global concern for the abducted Chibok girl."

On Thursday September 11, the #Bring Back Our Girls group celebrated 150 Days of abduction of the Chibok school girls around the Games Village Junction Abuja. Members marched to the roundabout displaying their banners and posters. Fliers and the Citizens' Solution to End Terrorism, the Voice of Nigerians were distributed to Nigerians at the venue. When the congregation reconvened at the end of public engagement, Mrs. Oby Ezekweili informed the advocates that the Nigerian government remained tardy and ineffectual in rescuing the girls. She thus called Nigerians to prepare for more forceful public outcry and mass dissent to press for the delivery of the female teens.

#BRINGBACKJONATHAN2015: THE WAGES OF IMPUNITY--BY WOLE SOYINKA

Nobel Laureate, Professor Wole Soyinka, in September deplored the mockery of the #Bring Back Our Girls Campaign in Nigeria by a group demanding #Bring Back Jonathan instead of the abducted Chibok Girls. This scorn, he said, had further degenerated the image of Nigeria before the International Community as a country administered by deceitful, callous and inhuman leaders. In an editorial to Sahara Reporters on Septmember13, 2014, Wole Soyinka said:

"The dancing obscenity of Shekau and his gang of psychopaths and child abductors, taunting the world, mocking the BRING BACK OUR GIRLS campaign on internet, finally met its match in Nigeria to inaugurate the week of September 11 – most appropriately. Shekau's dance macabre was surpassed by the unfurling of a political campaign banner that defiled an entry point into Nigeria's capital of Abuja. That banner read: BRING BACK JONATHAN 2015."

On the effect of the ridicule on Nigeria before the world Soyinka seared:

"President Jonathan has since disowned all knowledge or complicity in the outrage but, the damage has been done, the rot in a nation's collective soul bared to the world. The very possibility of such a desecration took the Nigerian nation several notches down in human regard. It confirmed the very worst of what external observers have concluded and despaired of - a culture of civic

callousness, a coarsening of sensibilities and, a general human disregard. It affirmed the acceptance, even domination of lurid practices where children are often victims of unconscionable abuses including ritual sacrifices, sexual enslavement, and worse. Spurred by electoral desperation, a bunch of self-seeking morons and sycophants chose to plumb the abyss of self-degradation and drag the nation down to their level. It took us to a hitherto unprecedented low in ethical degeneration."

Wole Soyinka was of the view that persons such as General Ihejirika and Bunu Sheriff, indicted over the Boko Haram crisis by Australian negotiator, Mr. Stphen Davis, should be thoroughly investigated and prosecuted. According to the erudite scholar:

"Regarding General Ihejirika, I have my own theories regarding how he may have come under Stephen Davis' searchlight in the first place, ending up on his list of the inculpated. All I shall propose at this stage is that an international panel be set up to examine all allegations, irrespective of status or office of any accused."

Then taking a caustic descent on Sheriff he said,

"As if to confirm all such surmises, an ex-governor, Sheriff, notorious throughout the nation – including within security circles as affirmed in their formal dossiers - as prime suspect in the sponsorship league of the scourge named Boko Haram, was presented to the world as a presidential traveling companion. And the speculation became: was the culture of impunity finally receiving endorsement as a governance yardstick? So impunity now transcends boundaries, no matter how heinous the alleged offence?"

He expressed repugnance over President Goodluck Jonathan's accommodation of Sheriff. This, he saw as bringing back criminals and highly corrupt people into government. In the view of the professor:

"The Nigerian president however appeared totally at ease. What the nation witnessed in the photo-op was an affirmation of a governance principle, the revelation of a decided frame of mind – with precedents galore. Goodluck Jonathan has brought back into limelight more political reprobates - thus attested in criminal courts of law and/or police investigations - than any other Head of State since the nation's independence."

He declared that Sheriff has been supporting Boko Haram activities. Calling for thorough reconnaissance on the former governor, Soyinka said:

"Of the complicity of ex-governor Sheriff in the parturition of Boko Haram, I have no doubt whatsoever, and I believe that the evidence is overwhelming. Femi Falana can safely assume that he has my full backing – and that of several civic organizations - if he is compelled to go ahead and invoke the legal recourses available to him to force Sheriff's prosecution. The evidence in possession of Security Agencies - plus several diplomats in Nigeria - is overwhelming, and all that is left is to let the man face criminal persecution. It is certain he will also take many others down with him."

Soyinka lampooned the #Bring Back Jonathan thus:

"Those who stuck up the obscene banner in Abuja had accurately read Jonathan right as a Bring-back president. They have deduced perhaps that he sees "bringing back" as a virtue, even an ideology, as the corner stone of governance, irrespective of what is being brought back.

No one quarrels about bringing back whatever the nation once had and now sorely needs – for instance, electricity and other elusive items like security, the rule of law etc. etc. The list is interminable. The nature of what is being brought back is thus what raises the disquieting questions. It is time to ask the question: if Ebola were to be eradicated tomorrow, would this government attempt to bring it back?"

Professor Soyinka called for invitation of Stephen Davis by the Nigerian people to unravel the ambiguities surrounding the Boko Haram insurgency. Still talking about 'bring back' he exhorted:

"Well, while awaiting the Chibok girls, and in that very connection, there is at least an individual whom the nation needs to bring back, and urgently. His name is Stephen Davis, the erstwhile negotiator in the oft aborted efforts to bring back the girls. Nigeria needs him back – no, not back to the physical nation space itself, but to a Nigerian induced forum, convoked anywhere that will guarantee his safety and can bring others to join him. I know Stephen Davis; I worked in the background with him during efforts to resolve the insurrection in the Delta region under President Shehu Yar'Adua. I am therefore compelled to warn that anything that Stephen Davis claims to have uncovered cannot be dismissed out of hand. It cannot be wished away by foul-mouthed abuse and cheap attempts to impugn his integrity – that is an absolute waste of time and effort."

Wole Soyinka confirmed the financing of Boko Haram activities using the Central Bank of Nigeria as conduit. In his revelation, he said:

"Finally, Stephen Davis also mentions a Boko Haram financier within the Nigerian Central Bank.

Independently we are able to give backing to that claim, even to the extent of naming the individual. In the process of our enquiries, we solicited the help of a foreign embassy whose government, we learnt, was actually on the same trail; thanks to its independent investigation into some money laundering that involved the Central Bank. That name, we confidently learnt, has also been passed on to President Jonathan. When he is ready to abandon his accommodating policy towards the implicated, even the criminalized, an attitude that owes so much to re-election desperation, when he moves from a passive "letting the law to take its course" to galvanizing the law to take its course, we shall gladly supply that name."

Soyinka therefore warned President Goodluck Jonathan to restore the fallen glory of the Nigerian nation. In his entreaty, he affirmed:

"In the meantime, however, as we twiddle our thumbs, wondering when and how this nightmare will end, and time rapidly runs out, I have only one admonition for the man to whom so much has been given, but who is now caught in the depressing spiral of diminishing returns: "Bring Back Our Honour." [27]

RED CROSS INVOLVED IN SECRET BOKO HARAM PRISONER SWAP TO BRING BACK KIDNAPPED GIRLS

The Red Cross role represented the first official confirmation that Nigerian government was in talks with terror group--Boko Haram, despite a vow that it would not negotiate. The International Committee of the Red Cross (ICRC) based in Geneva had become involved in a secret prisoner swap deal to secure the release of the Nigerian schoolgirls kidnapped by Boko Haram. Officials from the Red Cross mediated on talks between the

Nigerian government and a senior Boko Haram leader
currently held in one of the country's maximum-security
prisons. Colin Freeman of The Telegraph reported that
while visiting a few prisons in Nigeria, the ICRC
identified 16 key Boko Haram Commanders that the sect
wanted released in exchange for the abducted female
teenagers.

The ICRC, whose global humanitarian work includes
prisoners' wellbeing, had decided to act as an independent
party in ensuring that the two sides, neither of which
trusted each other, kept to any prisoner exchange
agreement. It had also offered to reconnoiter and
supervise any arranged swap of the schoolgirls for the
militants. In a chat with The Telegraph Fred Eno, an
experienced journalist, who has been participating in the
meetings, said:

*"We felt the negotiations would go better with the
backing of a major international humanitarian
organisation like the ICRC. There have been two or three
ICRC people at each meeting - international staff rather
than Nigerians - and they accompany the government
security agents to the various prisons and detention
centres to identify the people that Boko Haram want
released."*

The negotiations actually commenced about the month of
August, when representatives of the ICRC alongside
government officials and mediators from Nigerian civil
rights groups, met with a senior Boko Haram leader
currently serving a life sentence in Kuje prison, on the
outskirts of the Nigerian capital, Abuja. The Boko Haram
commander, simply identified as 'Omar', acted as
spokesman for all the group's prisoners. Referring to the
16 prisoners that Boko Haram wanted released, Eno said:

"They were senior enough that some other commanders who had taken their place are worried about what will happen to their own positions if they are released."

However, he said they were not notorious names among the Nigerian public, but were still senior figures in the group. [28]

ANOTHER CHIBOK GIRL ESCAPES FROM INSURGENTS

One of the abducted Chibok girls on 23 September emerged from the Boko Haram den. The female teen named Susan Ishaya about 20, was dumped in the bush of Kalaha by the terrorists and she wondered about for several days to a rustic village. Looking haggard and demented, country dwellers thought she was a mad woman. However, a few of them cultivated enough courage to accommodate her and took her to the nearest police station at Maraban Mubi in Hong Local Government Area of Adamawa State. Susan, later discovered to be with four months pregnancy, underwent medical examination and rehabilitation under the custody of the Directorate of Military Intelligence (DMI).[29]

FOUR MORE GIRLS ESCAPE THROUGH JUNGLE

The New York Post relayed in October 2014 that four more girls had escaped from the captivity of Boko Haram in the Nigeria-Cameroun border. The girls, aged between 16 and 18 escaped with the help of a teenage boy prisoner. According to Dr. Stephen Davis who had previously negotiated for the rescue of the school girls for four months to no avail; the escapees were guided by the setting of the sun. Thus, they walked west for three weeks. Finally, they arrived at a Nigerian rural community, starving and traumatized.

"They are amazing – the first escape and then walk for weeks," Davis told the Times of London.

He went further to state that:

'They are the only ones that have escaped from a Boko Haram camp." *The girls in hostage have been daunted by Boko Haram insurgents that if they escaped, their families would be killed.*[30]

FURY, TEARS AND JEERS MARK 6TH MONTH ABDUCTION PROTEST, OCTOBER 14

Members of the Bring Back Our Girls Abuja family were once again prevented by security agents from conducting their peaceful protest on the day marking six months since the Chibok school girls were abducted. The group had earlier on the 12th of October held a candlelight vigil at the Unity Fountain to keep the crusade for the release of the teen maidens alive. This was boosted with contact to international humanitarian organizations, embassies, individuals and the social media.

The campaigners had planned as usual to assemble at the Unity Fountain before marching to the State House for their prearranged meeting with President Goodluck Jonathan. Early morning of Tuesday 14th October, a mammoth crowd allegedly hired by the government occupied the venue. To avoid scrimmage with the rented claque, the #Bring Back Our Girls sought an alternative convergence at the Giwa Garden in Asokoro.

From there the protesters proceeded to the Presidential Villa with banners, wearing red t-shirts and chanting solidarity songs. Approaching the Junction close to Protea Hotel, the army of freedom fighters was accosted by a large detachment of police women who hooked their hands thus forming a woman-block across the expressway as if to say: *'You cannot pass through here, no road, no way'*.

The crusaders marched to meet the police chain face to face. Sensing that they could move no further, campaign leader, Mrs. Oby Ezekwesili, said:

"I am speaking to the female police women that are blocking us; what will you do if these girls were your daughters. You can take down your arms; we are an orderly group and we will not try to break through your rank until you allow us. To be honest, all these security is not needed because we are a peaceful group.

"You should be at the Unity Fountain where some people are employed there to attack us. You should be at the fountain to bring order. We know that you are doing your jobs, but I want you to remember that inhumanity to one is inhumanity to all."

Members of the Bring Back Our Girls continued to sing their watchwords:

What are we demanding? .... Bring back our girls now and alive.
What do you want? ... Result from the rescue operation.
When shall we stop? ... Not until our girls are back and alive.
And when shall we stop? ... Not without our daughters.
Where are we from? Chibok.
Who are we? ... Chibok family

What are our core values? ... HUMANITEEDS

The FCT Commissioner of Police then came from among the security barricade to inform Mrs. Ezekwesili that a delegation from the Presidency will arrive in 10-15 minutes to address them. Meanwhile the advocates continued with unity chants. After some 30 minutes, the government representatives arrived.

They were ministers Hajia Zainab Maina (Women Affairs), Sarah Ochepke (Water Resources), Lawrentia Mallam (Environment) and Ekon Eyakenyi (Lands, Housing and Urban Development). Ezekwesili welcomed them and introduced the mission of her group thus:

"We wrote and requested to meet with Mr. President so that we can listen to him and to inform him of the incredible urgency concerning the rescue of the Chibok girls and to hear from him what is exactly going on concerning the rescue of these girls. We are not sure why we are not being allowed to proceed to our meeting and so we will need to get answers to that.

"We are simply requesting to meet the president concerning our Chibok girls whose only crime was attempting to acquire education. Just imagine how the whole world that is standing with us will see pictures of how you are stopping us from seeing Mr. President. We are speaking for the voiceless girls that cannot speak at all."

Then Hajia Zainab Maina replied:

"Madam, you were once a minister. Even though you wrote a letter to the President; he is the President and he can ask us to come and address you. That is why we are here to address all of you. So, you are the one who will tell us why you are out here. You wanted to meet with Mr. President to find out why up till now the girls are not

rescued and we are here to assure you that, as a responsible government, there is no government in the world that will sit comfortably while girls who are the mothers of the nation are abducted.

"It is not as if the government is sitting by and watching; the government is doing all it can to make sure that the girls are brought back alive. So, please, let us treat each other with all sense of responsibility and respect. We are all mothers.

"As much as it hurts you, it also hurts us. We all know that the government is doing something. There are some technicalities that border on security; we all know that our military personnel are all out there in the bush, doing all they can. Nigeria is a very large country; we are not like Cameroon; some people are talking about Cameroon. I was expecting that you people will stand here and speak maturely and respect yourselves. I am respecting you."

Mrs. Ezekwesili rebuked her on the issue of maturity and respect by telling her bluntly:

"No, no, no, Minister we can't take this from you. Members of this group are mature people. They are men and women of integrity and respect."

When Mrs. Ezekwesili asked Mrs Maina to listen to the request of one of the escapee Chibok girls that would be addressing her in Hausa because she could not speak English due to the decadence of the Nigerian educational system, Mrs Maina replied:

"It was during your tenure, Madam Ezekwesili that the educational system collapsed."

Mrs. Ezekwesili yelled: *"Shame on you."*

The rest of the group joined in the booing and some eldersin the group had to be restrained from wrenching the minister. A parent from Chibok said to the ministers, tears flowing down her eyes:

"I want you to think, if your daughter is abducted over six months, how will you feel? We know that the President is doing his best, but we want him to negotiate. When his uncle was abducted, we all know how hard he worked until he brought his uncle back.

"I know that the military is doing their best, but I don't trust them because the military is divided into two. I just came in from Chibok yesterday and there is nothing happening, most of the military men have turned this war into business and they don't want our girls back. Are you trying to tell me that Cameroon is stronger than Nigeria? Some people are with the President because they are looking for their daily bread. I am praying for Mr. President. I am praying that he does his job."[31]

Same day the White House United States released a press statement stressing their commitment to recue the abducted girls. A declaration from the Office of the Press Secretary issued for immediate release read thus:

The White House
Office of the Press Secretary
For Immediate Release
October 14, 2014
Statement by National Security Advisor Susan E. Rice on the Chibok Girls

"Six months ago, today, approximately 270 girls were abducted in the middle of the night from their school in northeast Nigeria, where they were learning the skills they need to create a better future for themselves, their

families, and their communities. The United States has made clear our commitment to supporting Nigeria's efforts to bring the girls home safely. Since then, we have aided in the investigations, including by deploying personnel on the ground, facilitated strategic communications, and provided assistance to the families. These efforts are part of our broader support to Nigeria's pursuit of a holistic counterterrorism strategy, which includes the rule of law and strengthened security institutions.

"We will continue to work toward the release of all the girls who remain in captivity, even as we celebrate the freedom of the few who have managed to escape Boko Haram's clutches. And, we will stand with girls everywhere who seek to achieve their full potential through education and to claim the universal rights and fundamental freedoms that are their birthright."

ALICIA KEYS DEMONSTRATES IN NY FOR NIGERIAN GIRLS

On that day, too a heavily-pregnant US singer, Alicia Keys, joined a small group of protesters outside the Nigerian consulate in New York demanding the immediate release of more than 200 schoolgirls kidnapped by Boko Haram. The Alicia Keys crowd shouted:

"Bring back our girls now."

The Grammy-winning 33-year-old New York R&B singer-song-writer wore jeans and wrapped her hair in black scarf. Coinciding with six months of the abduction, Alicia said:

"Today is my son's birthday, so I stand in solidarity with the mothers of the Chibok girls."

The star, who has sold more than 30 million singles across the world and is expecting her second child in December, held up "#bring back our girls NOW" signs with the others.

"It is so atrocious and horrible, the fact they have been gone for six months and have not been found," Keys said, emphasizing that it was vital for people to keep up the pressure for their release.

"It is important now more than ever because it is that pivotal six months time. It is too long."

Keys, who recently set up a movement called "We Are Here" to fight for greater social justice, said the world must show solidarity. She said to AFP:

"Nigeria needs to find these girls. We as an international community should support them finding these girls. These girls represent so much. They represent girls who are kept from education, they represent girls who are treated as property, they represent girls who are raped and have to live in violence as a weapon of war."

Among her group of some 40 demonstrators was Eva, who refused to give her second name but stopped off during her lunch break. She said:

"I had not realized it was already six months. How is it possible? We can find terrorists but we cannot find 200 girls?" [32]

Back home in Nigeria, police on Tuesday, October 14 blocked supporters of the 219 school girls kidnapped by

Boko Haram militants from marching to the President's official residence.

NIGERIA, BOKO HARAM REACH CEASE-FIRE, TO FREE SCHOOLGIRLS

The Nigerian government on the 17th of October 2014 allegedly struck a deal with Boko Haram on ceasefire and release of over 200 secondary school girls abducted by the sect from Chibok, Borno State six months back. The truce was reported to have been reached in Saudi Arabia. As part of the deal, some key Boko Haram leaders might be freed thereafter simultaneously with the abducted Chibok girls. The listed commanders would be moved from their detention centres to agreed locations in Chad.

A statement issued by Chief of Defence Staff (CDS), Air Chief Marshal Alex Badeh on the ceasefire agreement during the coordinating conference on Nigeria-Cameroun Trans-Border Military Operations held at the Defence Intelligence Agency (DIA), Abuja yesterday read:

"Without any prejudice to the outcome of our three-day interactions and the conclusions of this forum, I wish to inform this audience that a ceasefire agreement has been reached between the Federal Government of Nigeria and the Jama'atul ahlul Sunnah Lidda'awati Wal Jihad. I have accordingly directed the Service Chiefs to ensure immediate compliance with the development in the field."

Same day the coordinator of the National Information Centre on the crisis, Mike Omeri, alongside the spokesperson of the Defence Information unit, Major General Chris Olukolade, at a security briefing in Abuja, said President Goodluck Jonathan's Principal Private Secretary, Hassan Tukur, met with the Boko Haram representative, Danladi Ahmadu and the President of

Chad, Idris Derby, in Saudi Arabia and have reached an armistice. In his press release Mr. Omeri said:

"We can confirm to you that there have been contacts between the Government and representatives of Boko Haram. The discussions are essentially in relation to the general insecurity in the North East and the need to rescue all captives of the terrorists, including the students of the Government Girls Secondary school, Chibok."

He further stated that:

"From the discussions, they indicated their desire for and willingness to discuss and resolve all associated issues. They also assured that the school girls and all other people in their captivity are all alive and well. Already, the terrorists have announced a ceasefire in furtherance of their desire for peace, in this regard; the government of Nigeria has in a similar vein declared a ceasefire. This is to assure Nigerians that the greater goal of this process is to ensure the return of normalcy in the land, especially in parts of the country troubled by the activities of terrorists."

According to reports by the Voice of America (VOA) and British Broadcasting Corporation (BBC), the negotiations involved the Chadian President, Idris Derby, and some high-level officials of Nigeria and Cameroon. The BBC referred to Mallam Hassan Tukur, the Principal Secretary to President Goodluck Jonathan, as saying:

"They have assured us they have the girls and they will release them. I am cautiously optimistic."

Reconnaissance reports revealed that the deal with Boko Haram insurgents actually began during the previous visit of President Goodluck Jonathan to Chad. It was gathered that at the instance of President Idris Derby, the President had a meeting with some representatives of the sect. At the conference, it was reported, some terms for the swap contract between the sect and some mediators working for the Federal Government were discussed.

The Chad talks thus paved the way for the current efforts by facilitators of the dialogue with Boko Haram. One of the sources close to the negotiations said:

"The swap deal gathered more momentum when the President visited Chad. This is why President Derby is playing a critical role in facilitating the conclusion of negotiation with Boko Haram."

The 19 Boko Haram commanders slated to be released in a simultaneous prisoner swap include Awwal Albani Sultaniya, Mallam Abdullahi Damasak, Mallam Bashir, Baa Malam, Mallam Tijjani al Barnawi, Mallam Musa Moby, Mallam Awara, Mallam Zindar Zindawi, Baa Alhaji, Bana Mongono, Baraa Mallami, Sheikh Umar ibn Mustapha, Mallam Jabir Al Jjihad, Tanko al Kurd, Mallam Aradu, Abidina Janzila and Mallam Aboul Kaka. Prior to the latest cessation of hostilities agreement there had been powerful talks between Boko Haram and some negotiators from the Federal Government who were coordinated by the President, Civil Rights Congress of Nigeria, Comrade Shehu Sani.

In September, the negotiation was observed by some officials of the International Committee of the Red Cross (ICRC). The last talks in Abuja were attended by Shehu Sani, ICRC officials, a former Minister of Information, a Geneva-based Human Rights Activist, a two-man delegation of Boko Haram, two others close to the sect's leadership, and a PDP leader.

However, the ceasefire agreement announced by the Nigerian CDS seemed to have collapsed as Boko Haram insurgents on Saturday, October18 attacked villages in

Adamawa and Borno States causing carnage of over 100 people and destroying properties. There were allegations of disharmony among splinter groups of Boko Haram with respect to the ceasefire. Some 25 suspected Boko Haram rebels were Sunday night killed in clashes with Nigerian soldiers in Damboa, Borno State. Five civilians were also killed in fighting elsewhere in the northeast, a military source and residents revealed on Monday. [33]

RESPECT CEASEFIRE DEAL, OBAMA WARNS FG, BOKO HARAM

The United States of America President, Barack Obama, on October 21, 2014 urged both the Nigerian Government and Boko Haram to honour their ceasefire agreement reached four days earlier. The statement from the White House followed continuation of hostilities between the Nigerian Army and the insurgency sect. Speaking through the Deputy Spokesperson of the State Department, Ms. Marie Harf, in Washington, DC, President Obama said that it would be a thing of delight for the American government if the Nigerian government and members of the Boko Haram sect turn in and maintain such a ceasefire. The report was relayed by Abiodun Oluwarotimi from New York. According to Ms. Harf:

"We confirm reports that a ceasefire has been announced and it appears to have been put into place. We would welcome that ceasefire, call on all parties both to implement and maintain such a ceasefire, and hope that such a ceasefire would herald the return of peace to the northeast. This is a region that has had far too little of that. It's our understanding

that negotiations about a deal to release the girls continue. Obviously, would join the world, I think, in hoping that these girls would be reunited with their families as soon as possible, but it's our understanding those negotiations do continu."

On the prospect of the United States participating in the mediations, the State Department designate asserted that there was no kind of American involvement in the ceasefire talks or other deliberations. She said:

"I don't believe so, but let me check. Not that I know of. But never say never, I will check"[34]

#BRING BACK OUR GIRLS WINS CASE AT HIGH COURT

The FCT High Court, Abuja sitting in Maitama and presided over by Justice Abubakar Talba in October affirmed as legitimate peaceful assembly and protests by members of the Bring Back Our Girls. The group had gone to court on June 3, 2014 to demand enforcement of their fundamental human rights to freedom of expression and peaceful assembly as enshrined in the constitution of the Federal Republic of Nigeria 1999 as amended. That was sequel to an announcement by the Nigerian Police banning them from further demonstrations for the rescue of over 300 school girls kidnapped by Bokko Haram. The court, on the 30th of October 30, 2014 in a landmark judgement, confirmed their demands as constitutional.

Addressing the camp at the Unity Fountain, Abuja after the ruling, defence counsel, Mr. Femi Falana SAN, revealed to the crusaders that the Federal Government wanted to use the court to stifle their campaign. He stated that the plan was thwarted by the superior arguments of defence. Members expressed gratitude to the erudite lawyer and human rights activist for standing behind them to uphold justice, equity, the constitution and the Rule of Law. [35]

BRING BACK OUR GIRLS RISES TO ALARM DEMONSTRATION

Monday November 3, 2014, the Bring Back Our Girls group took their crusade to the level of alarm by staging a hands-on-the-head protest. Wearing customary red shirts, members clutched their hands over crowns to express critical dissatisfaction with the government over the rescue of the Chibok girls in Boko Haram captivity. The assembly walked round the Unity Fountain in a mood of despondency, emphasizing that it will reposition itself to seek answers to many unanswered questions in government.

Addressing the campaigners at the solemn ceremony leader of the group, Mrs. Oby Ezekwesili, her voice eloquent, her language commanding, her pyrotechnics rapid fire and her analysis replete with niceties, said:

"We are demonstrating because of the level of falsehood we have witnessed from our government. Our girls' continuous stay in the hands of their abductors means that there is a lot to be done. We have too many unanswered questions. We want to search for the truth."

On the new tack of their movement she revealed thus: *"We are repositioning the movement as truth seekers. We are asking for the truth. We want answers about governance, about the military, about the Chibok girls and many other things about the country."*

She hinted of a possible alignment with other movements or camps to propel a wider campaign. According to the former Minister of Education:

"We will continue our quest for the truth and we will be looking for coalition partners for seeking the truth. We will have an umbrella of truth seekers. If we can establish the truth, the truth can set us free. If we have gotten to the point of a third promise and fail, we must adjust ourselves for our quest for truth from our government."

The group thus implored Nigerians to stand up and speak out against insurgency and mal-governance in the country. [36]

BOKO HARAM ASSERTS KIDNAPPED GIRLS HAVE BEEN MARRIED OFF

In a new video sent to Agence France Press on November 1, 2014 Boko Haram leader, Abubakar Shekau, said he had married off the abducted Chibok school girls to his members thereby foreclosing the prospect of their rescue. More than 500 women and girls aged from infancy to 65 had been kidnapped by Boko Haram and held in militant camps since 2009, Human Rights Watch said this week, including 60 reportedly kidnapped from two towns in north-eastern Nigeria the previous week. On the fate of the Chibok girls Abubakar Shekau said in Hausa language with a malevolent laugh:

"Don't you know the over 200 Chibok schoolgirls have converted to Islam? They have now memorized two chapters of the Qur'an. We have married them off. They are in their marital homes. If you knew the state your

daughters are in today, it might lead some of you ... to die from grief."

Referring to the collapsed ceasefire talks he seared:

"We have not made ceasefire with anyone...We did not negotiate with anyone... It's a lie. It's a lie. We will not negotiate. What is our business with negotiation? Allah said we should not. You people should understand that we only obey Allah; we tread the path of the Prophet. We hope to die on this path ... Our goal is the garden of eternal bliss."

He gruffly stated that Boko Haram is interested only in: *'battle, hitting, striking and killing with the gun, which we look forward to like a tasty meal.'*

Human Rights Watch said in a report published within the week that Boko Haram was holding upwards of 500 women and young girls and that forced marriage was commonplace in the militant camps. [37]

CHADIAN EMBASSY RESCHEDULES BBOG GROUP'S VISIT

The Chadian Embassy cancelled its meeting with members of BBOG citing security engagements. In a communiqué sent to BBOG the embassy requested a re-conference with five delegates from the group instead, as their premises would not accommodate a large crowd. The BBOG, however, affirmed that their planned protest of December 3 would still hold and the five delegates sent to the embassy.

BBOG had expressed serious dissatisfaction over the allegation of involvement of the Chadian Government in the Boko Haram insurgency and the continued incarceration of the abducted Chibok school girls and other women. The camp referred to the botched ceasefire deal between the Federal Government of Nigeria and Boko Haram brokered by the Chadian President, Idriss Derby, and now the report of missiles purchases by Mr. Mahamat Bichara Gnoti – a close acquaintance of the Chadian leader.

Mr. Gnoti was reported to have been apprehended on the Chadian-Sudan border with 19 SAM2 missiles, allegedly bought from the Sudanese army to boost Boko Haram arsenal. Sahara Reporters quoted a Cameroonian reconnaissance journalist, Bison Etahoben via his Twitter, saying that Mr. Gnoti claimed that President Derby gave him the funds to buy the weapons. He also reportedly said he waived a Presidential pass issued to him by Mr. Idriss Derby's office in order to freely pass through road check guards who searched and found the deadly missiles on him. Nevertheless, the BBOG was seeking clarifications on the latest development in the catastrophic rebellion.[38]

ONE YEAR ANNIVERSARY OF THE ABDUCTION

On Tuesday 14 April 2015 the Bring Back Our Girls celebrated one year anniversary of the kidnapping of over 276 school girls writing West African School Certificate examinations in Government Secondary School, Chibok in north eastern Nigeria. That was the climax of the series of events which commenced on April 8. On Thursday (April 9), the group marched from their Unity Fountain Abuja assembly ground past the Federal Secretariat to the Police Headquarters. They were chanting their usual solidarity songs to compel rescue of the girls in captivity. Along the expressway red ribbons were tied on trees, poles and rails as a reminder that the girls were still languishing in the wild.

At the police head office Mrs. Oby Ezekwesili informed the numerous gun-brandishing policemen that reports came to the BBOG from some wives of police officers that their husbands (numbering about 56) serving in Gwoza were missing for more than six months. They had not got reasonable explanation regarding the whereabouts of their husbands from the Nigerian government, and thus had been abandoned with their children in despair and quandary. Ezekwesili entreated the police to cooperate with the BBOG in the humanitarian work of pushing for the rescue of the Chibok girls. She equally demanded that the case of the missing policemen be thoroughly investigated.

Day of Sadness and Despair

Events kicked off at 11a.m. with a march by 100 plus Chibok Ambassadors—young girls aged between 3 and 18—to the Ministry of Education at the Federal

Secretariat, carrying placards with various inscriptions. It was all tears as the teens sang solidarity songs, demanding to see the Minister for Education. They expressed their disgust at the non-release of their Chibok counterparts to continue their education. Thereafter they read their demands to officials of the Ministry.

There was a mammoth crowd at the Unity Fountain. Journalists came from all over the world and around Nigeria to cover the occasion. Later in the afternoon the Chibok community in Abuja addressed the press on the fate of the girls in distress. With heavy hearts, they enumerated their agony and trauma in the hands of brutal insurgents. Hence, they called for rescue and return of the abducted girls to their parents, the return and resettlement of all Internally Displaced Persons, and the rehabilitation of all destroyed structures in Northern Eastern Nigeria.

At about 3p.m. the leadership of BBOG also presented a press statement read by Maureen Kabrick and signed by Mrs. Oby Ezekwesili and Hadiza Bala Usman. In the briefing, she thanked all persons and countries that have worked in one way or the other across the world to compel rescue of the abducted Chibok Girls. She highlighted that:

*"Among the special commemoration activities today will be the **lighting of the Empire State Building in New York City** with the colours, red and purple; red being specifically for our Chbok girls, purple for violence against women.... Our Chibok Girls are the global symbol for defence of the dignity and sanctity of human life; of the girl child, women, for all those oppressed, repressed, disadvantaged, hurting, unsafe persons everywhere. As long as they stay missing, it means*

nothing is as yet working. We must all prioritize their safe return."

The daily sit-out of the BBOG took opened as usual by 4p.m. In attendance were members of the Chibok Community. There were discussions on the journey so far in the delivery of the girls and need to continue the pressure. It was really a solemn moment.

Two hours later there was a candlelit procession by the BBOG around the Unity Fountain. The symbol was to reignite the compulsion for the safe liberation of the distressed girls back to the hands of fellow patriots. Glowing candle lights were made to keep alive the hope that the girls would soon be released to rejoin their families.

In an open letter to mark one year anniversary of the Chibok Girls abduction, Pakistani teenage rights activist and Nobel Peace Price Winner, 17-year old Malala Yousafzai wrote:

"Like you, I was a target of militants who did not want girls to go to school. We can not imagine the full extent of the horrors you have endured. But please know this: we will never forget you. Today and everyday, we call on the Nigerian authorities and the international community to do more to bring you home. We will not rest until you have been reunited with your families."

Same day United States Representative, Carolyn Maloney (D-NY 12th District), addressed a large crowd in New York City to draw global attention to quickly rescue the Chibok Girls from the hands of terrorists. Nations of the world and personalities have expressed shock at the continued languishing of the Chibok Girls in the den of terrorists. Elsewhere, campaigners from New Zealand to the United Sates posted online solidarity messages using the hash tags #365DaysOn, #ChibokGirls NeverToBeForgotten.

The same way, Multi-talented Grammy Award winning artist, Alicia Keys of the 'We Are Here Movement' joined a large throng of protesters outside the Nigerian Consulate in New York to recharge the Nigerian government to rescue school girls held by Boko Haram Gordon Brown, former British Prime Minster and now the UN special envoy on global education, wrote in The Guardian newspaper that the girls were kidnapped 'simply because they wanted to go to school.' According to him:

"The campaign was the most iconic fight of a freedom struggle. The fight will be won some day. No injustice will can last forever. But for the sake of these girls, it must be won soon."

In his solidarity speech the UN Secretary-General, Ban Ki Moon, said:

"One year ago, over 200 girls were abducted by Boko Haram from their school in Chibok, Borno State in north eastern Nigeria. While some of the girls were fortunate to have escaped, the fate of many still remain unknown. We must never forget the kidnapped Chibok girls, and I will not stop calling for their immediate release and their safe return to their families."

On the humanitarian situation in northern Nigeria, he said:

"Over the past 12 months, Boko Haram intensified its brutal attacks on boys and girls in Nigeria and neighbouring countries. Hundreds of thousands of children have been displaced from their houses, and deprived of their rights to live and grow up in safety, dignity and peace. Boko Haram's killing, abduction and recruitment of children, including the use of girls as suicide bombers is abhorrent. The legitimate response to Boko Haram attacks must be fully consistent with international law and not creat additional risks for the protection of children. On this day, I reaffirm my support to the governments and people of the region in the fight against Boko Haram. I stand in solidarity with the families of all abductees, especially children, their communities and society at large."

ActionAid also lent voice for the immediate recue of the Chibok girls. The Deputy Country Director, Ifeoma Charles-Monwuba, in shared aims with the BBOG said:

"At present, Nigeria does not have schools that are safe. We need to put in place appropriate facilities that do not allow girls to be molested."

In a disheartening mode former Director of Lagos Business School and Presidential Candidate, Prof. Pat Utomi, stated that:

"For one year, our conscience has been held hostage. Anyone whose conscience has not been held hostage is not a human being. Terror is not something we can tolerate in our society. It is something we must stamp out. We are not going to stay in our house and fold our arms. We must stand up to those whose way of life is terror

because we are much more than them. Today is also not just about to sing Bring Our Girls Back but to stay together to fight for what is right."

Convener of the Lagos campaign and President of Woman Arise, Mrs. Joe Okei-Odumakin, said they had assembled to remind the government that the girls were still suffering in the bush and required urgent salvation. She came with a series of rhetorical questions like this:

"Where are the girls? Didn't the government say they sighted the girls already? That's months ago. So, why are we still here asking for our girls' rescue? This government has one inescapable assignment before the end of this regime. Otherwise, it would have failed us altogether. The assignment is compulsory rescue of Chibok girls."

Literary icon and Nobel Laureate, Professor Wole Soyinka, while addressing the Lagos event, voiced:

"We must make sure that such assault on our humanity doesn't happen again. The survival of humanity and of the nation must remain paramount."

In an interview published in THE SUN of April 14, leader of BBOG, Mrs. Oby Ezekwesili, enraged that the Chibok girls have not been found and brought back home, said:

"It is bringing the girls back that will be the priority of every leader. No matter who concocted the plan, if at all it is true, it is our school girls who innocently went to school and are not where they are supposed to be, that should be."

The UK and EU stated on that Chibok Girls Day that they would work closely with the incoming administration of Muhammadu Buhari to restore peace and security in communities 'blighted by conflict'.

The UK Minister for Africa, James Duddridge, in a statement read by the Press Secretary in the British High Commission, Edward Dunn, declared:

"We must not forget the brutal abduction of 270 school girls from Chibok one year ago today (Tuesday). My thoughts are with the victims of this terrible crime, their families and the thousands of other men, women and children abducted by Boko Haram in North-East Nigeria. There can be no justification for these abductions. The UK is supporting Nigeria and its neighbours in efforts to end the conflict and find those abducted. And we will work closely with Nigeria's new government to restore security and prosperity to areas blighted by conflict."

Elsewhere, the EU in a statement by its spokesperson, Catherine Ray, expressed solidarity with the families of the girls held hostage by insurgents, and the Bring Back Our Girls campaign group. Her speech read:

"A year has passed since 287 school girls from Chibok in North-Eastern Nigeria were abducted by Boko Haram. Though some girls escaped, others have since been taken and more than 300 girls are still missing. We express our solidarity with the plight of the families and with the Bring Back Our Girls campaign. All efforts must continue to be made to rescue and reunite the girls with their families, and bring the perpetrators of this terrible act to account." [39]

OBY EZEKWESILI URGES BARACK OBAMA TO RESCUE CHIBOK GIRLS

On the 21st of April 2015, leader of the Bring Back Our Girls group, Dr. Mrs. Obiageli Ezekwesili, was lionized by Time Magazine. Speaking at the Time 100 Gala in New York City, Ezekwesili who was named by the magazine as one of the world's most influential people, urged US President, Barack Obama, to get the abducted Chibok school girls the way he got Osama bin Laden. Mrs. Ezekwesili was honoured alongside Rosemary Nyirumbe who runs a school for former child solders in Uganda. Samantha Power, the US Ambassador to the UN, also graced the occasion. In her address to the gala, Ezekwesili said:

"If he could get Osama bin Laden, he could get our girls. It is time for someone as powerful as Barack Obama to compare the girls of Chibok to his daughters These girls are a symbol of own message to girls, that they should be educated, that we should go beyond the call of duty for you."

Accentuating on the need to rescue the languishing young women, she declared:

"There is nothing that the God I believe in cannot do. But the same God has given man and woman the power of choice. Whatever we choose to do we can accomplish. Let us choose to bring back our girls."

On her part, Nyirumbe said the meeting with Mrs. Oby Ezekwesili reminded her of 'the power of women'. According to her:

"I would like to see a lot of people involved in practical solutions to practical problems. Women have got to the point where we can turn the world upside down."

Power hinted that the US was surveying ways to bolster the fight against Boko Haram which has snuffed thousands of lives and rendered millions homeless in Northern Nigeria. In his message, he said:

"We have been looking at how to throw our weight behind an international force."

Other Nigerians who were celebrated at the occasion included Muhammadu Buhari, rising author, Chinamanda Adichie and Boko Haram leader, Abubakar Shekau.[40]

MORE HOSTAGES RESCUED TO REFUGEE CAMPS

Associated Press (AP) on May 3, 2015 reported the suffering of captives in the hands Boko Haram terrorists at the approach of the Nigerian troops to their hostage camps in the dreaded Sambisa Forest. The tragic stories were broken by young girls and mature women evacuated to the refugee camp in Yola, Adamawa State. According to Lami Musa, 27, one of the first refugees to be transported to the Malkohi refugee centre, a dust-blown deserted school on the outskirts of Yola:

"Boko Haram came and told us they were moving out and said that we should run away with them. But we said no. Then, they started stoning us. I held my baby to my stomach, bending over to protect her."

Another survivor said several girls and women were killed, but they did not know the number. The Nigerian

Army's 23 Armoured Brigade in Yola had on May2
handed more than 275 women and girls rescued from
Sambisa Forest to the National Emergency Management
Agency for rehabilitation. The victims comprised 69
women, 14 girls, 26 male children aged 6-12 years, and
49 male children aged five years, 48 female children aged
0-5 years and 69 females aged 5-12 years. 21 injured
victims were on admission at the Federal Medical Centre,
Yola. Those included cases with bullet wounds and
fractured limbs.

The freed refugees were scrawny with obtrusive
rib cages and shoulder blades. They looked despondent
and terrified—their eyes retreated into hollow sockets.
Some highly malnourished babies were placed on
intravenous fluids while other children received packs of
protein concentrates. Through interviews NEMA officials
had established that most of the displaced persons came
from Gumsuri, a village near the beleaguered rustic town
of Chibok. On Sunday, May 3, the Nigerian Army
rescued another 260 women and children, fleeing from
insurgents in Adamawa State, bringing the number of
salvaged hostages to about 800. Information received
from NEMA which was thereafter rehabilitating over one
thousand rescued women and children stated that 214 of
the women were at various stages of pregnancy.[41]

EUROPEAN UNION VISITS BRING BACK OUR GIRLS

On the 19th of June 2015, an EU delegation had a brief solidarity conference with the Bring Back Our Girls group at their Unity Fountain sit-out camp in Abuja. At the occasion, the EU said that more than 200 girls abducted by Islamic rebels on 14 April 2014 from Government Secondary School, Chibok deserve justice. Thus, the EU member states would not relent in supporting the rescue of the girls held in the wild by insurgents.

Addressing the group, the EU Commissioner for Humanitarian Assistance, Mr. Christos Stylianides, said his recent visit to Yola, the Adamawa State capital, confirmed the terrible state of the Boko Haram insurgency and its hideous human displacement effects. In his empathy speech, the envoy said:

"I have been to Yola and saw for myself the situation of damages caused by the Boko Haram sect. I assure you that the EU will not rest until our girls are rescued. The girls are no longer yours alone but are now our girls too."

Leader of the Bring Back Our Girls campaign, Mrs. Oby Ezekwesili, in her welcome address thanked the EU for supporting efforts to rescue the kidnapped school girls. She stated that the group had earlier written to the new Government of Nigeria led by President Muhammadu Buhari for an engagement to effect immediate release of the Chibok girls. The former education minister implored the EU to assiduously work with President Buhari at diplomatic levels to achieve the deliverance of the young women in distressed captivity. A member of the camp and Chibok native, Dr. Allen Manasseh, gave a sorrowful account of IDPs in and across Nigeria, and emphasized the need to rescue the girls, stanch the rebellion, rehabilitate displaced persons and rebuild ravaged towns and rustics in north-eastern Nigeria. [42]

BRING BACK OUR GIRLS FINALLY MEETS WITH PRESIDENCY

On the 8th of July 2015, the Bring Back Our Girls crusade group at last had a meeting with President of Nigeria, Muhammadu Buhari, on the fate of 219 Chibok school girls still languishing in the lair of Boko Haram terrorists. Previous attempts to engage the past government were outrageously rebuffed. That conference marked the 450th day of abduction of the young girls and 435 days of the Bring Back Our Girls campaign, subsequent to an invitation by the Presidency in response to their earlier application for an meeting.

At 9 a.m. members gathered at their Unity Fountain sit-out camp, had instructions and proceeded on a march to the Presidential Villa under security escort. At the second gate of the Villa the group (numbering about 400) had to wait for conveyance to the State House. Later they were ushered into the reception and screening oval room.

From there they were further driven to the Council Chambers, and again screened before admission. About 12 p.m. President Buhari entered the hall and said, 'welcome ladies and gentlemen'. After reciting the first stanza of the National Anthem the business of the day commenced. Dr. Mrs. Oby Ezekwesili opened session by greeting Mr. President and subordinates, the BBOG group, press and other attendees. In her introductory speech, she said:

"Our Chibok girls have stayed away beyond an acceptable amount of time in the hands of savages. It is now time for their government to bring them back. There is no time left."

She accentuated that the rescue of the Chibok school girls would be 'the strongest statement government would make for having respect for the sanctity and dignity of every Nigerian life.'

One of the founding mothers, Mrs. Mariam Uwais, in her narrative about the Bring Back Our Girls group, articulated the humanitarian circumstances that led them to coalesce to press for the immediate rescue of the abducted Chibok Girls. She emphasized that her group would continue their campaign nationally and internationally until the girls are brought home to the bosom of their parents. In their 13-Point ABC of Our Demands Agenda, the group asked among others that:

"The Federal Government should spare no resources in urgently rescuing our 219 Chibok Girls as promised by the President and the National Security Adviser of the President at various times. Our Federal Government has the constitutional duty to give justice to our Chibok Girls by ensuring their immediate rescue. The rescue of Our Chibok Girls will amount to the strongest statement that our Government has respect for the Sanctity and Dignity of Every Nigerian Life.

"An apology for the failure of governance that led to the abduction

"An apology for the failure of governance that caused failure to rescue our girls for over 400 days

"Strategies for curbing the emergence, and growth of curious sects

"Immediately set up a structured feedback and communication system that is composed of the Federal and Borno State Governments through designated security and ministerial authorities, the parents of the abducted girls, the Chibok (KADA) community, and citizens, through the BringBackOurGirls group. The feedback mechanism, so the Parents and the public can have regular updates on efforts to rescue our 219 Chibok Girls.

"The National Security Adviser, Leaders of the Counter Insurgency Task Force, the Department of State Security on one hand; and State Governments of Adamawa, Borno and Yobe, aided and supported by Local Authorities and Traditional Leaders, on the other hand and the representatives of abduction victims on the other hand. The Team should be tasked with credible implementation of the VARS. The primary task of the Team shall be to work with every abducted victim's family and community to accurately ascertain the true identity of such individuals and following their accurate identification to make available the comprehensive program for Recovery, Rehabilitation Resettlement and Reintegration to the rescued citizens. We advise that this system should be adopted for the 200 girls and 93 women rescued on the 28th April 2015.

"The rehabilitation, resettlement and reintegration following their authentication should be implemented by both the Borno State Government and the Federal Government that make up the VARS Team and supported

by development partners, NGOs and public-spirited Nigerians. Our movement, BringBackOurGirls, stands ready to support this initiative. Furthermore, grant access for BBOG to Chibok girls when rescued; thereby accepting our offer to support re-unification of rescued Chibok girls with their families as well as their rehabilitation and reintegration."

Afterwards Mrs. Oby Ezekwesili introduced two leaders of Chibok community, a cleric and Mr. Dauda Iliya, chairman of Chibok Area Development Association. Both men spoke on the need to rescue the adducted girls from the den of insurgents, quell the rebellion, resettle displaced persons and rehabilitate destroyed towns and rustics. Mr. Iliya was emphatic that the Federal Government should take care of parents of the kidnapped young women, build more schools in the community and provide essential infrastructure (roads, electricity, portable water, etc) in the area. Convener of the first Bring Back Our Girls protest in Abuja, Hadiza Bala Usman, gave a concise account of their crusade so far and vowed that the group would continue to mobilize until the girls are released.

The Bring Back Our Girls delegation asked the Federal Government to immediately set up a **Missing Persons Bureau** and formally re-affirm the legitimacy and relevance of the # Bring Back Our Girls campaign as a purely citizen contribution. They also presented President Buhari with three documents: **Citizens' Solution to End Insurgency, Verification, Authentication and Reunification System (VARS) and # Bring Back Our Girls Accountability Metrics.** This presentation was led by Bukky Shonibare, a member of the Strategic Committee.

Two women, parents of the abducted Chibok Girls, were invited by Mrs. Oby Ezekwesili in turn to make submissions. They pleaded with Mr. President to help them locate and bring back their daughters. One of them--distraught ebony--heavily shed tears; grouching and gesticulating helplessly to return their children to them.

While the group was presenting their demands, Mr. President conscientiously put down notes. Then it was time for him to respond. With equanimity, he said:

"Nobody in Nigeria or outside could have missed your consistency and persistence, demonstration of the injustice meted on you, the parents, the community and Nigeria. "Representing the government of Nigeria, I cannot rationalize the government's incompetence in dealing with this issue. We only ask for your patience.

"I'm impressed with the presentation of BBOG by Mrs. Uwais, which is comprehensive enough and the leadership of the Chibok community has made a comprehensive representation as well as leader of this group, the cleric that represents the group.

"It's unfortunate that the security and federal government conflicting reports initially presented the government and its agencies in a very bad light both nationally and internationally because the law enforcement agencies and the government were conflicting each other sometimes within hours or within weeks. That is not very impressive.

"The delayed and late reaction by former government and its agencies was very unfortunate as I said. And I thank the leader of Chibok Community for the articulated priorities he has drawn about welfare of the families, of the communities and rehabilitation of infrastructure. I think government should provide these infrastructures as a matter of right.

"I think you will agree that the present government takes the issue very seriously. Within a week of being sworn in,

I visited Niger, Chad and would have visited Cameroon but for the invitation of the G-7 to go to Germany and listen to them. I'm very impressed with the leadership of this important group (G7) other than the United Nations itself. They are very concerned about the security in Nigeria led by abduction of the Chibok girls by the terrorists. When the terrorists announced their loyalty to ISIS, the whole attention again was brought squarely to Nigeria. And now we are rated with Afghanistan, Iraq and Syria, this is very unfortunate.

"After Ramadan, I will visit Cameroon to see the President there and then Benin Republic. But on the efforts, we have been making, we will not disclose some of them publicly because it will not be consistent with security. But I assure you that under the Lake Chad Basin Commission, the military have met. The ministers of defence have met. We the presidents have met here in Abuja except the President of Cameroon who was represented by his Minister of Defence.

"Strategy and tactics have been drawn. Multinational taskforce has been put in place with headquarters in Ndjamina with a Nigerian General as Commander. The troops delegated by each of the countries are to be put in place by the end of the month. And Nigeria, I assure you, will do its best because we as I said are the battle ground and we are being helped by our neighbors.

"It is paradoxical what the Nigerian military has achieved from Burma to Zaire to Liberia to Sierra Leon to Sudan. But Nigeria has now to be helped by Niger, Chad, and Cameroon. How have the mighty fallen!

"We will do our best to restore the respectability of our country and its institutions. And with you, your steadfastness and your seriousness, we will do what we

can do. We will accommodate all your observations including the negative ones about the performance of the government and its agencies.

"At the G7, the leadership there asked us for our shopping list which I'm still compiling. The military has submitted theirs and I'm waiting for the governments of the front-line states to submit their local government by local government in terms of infrastructure, schools, health care, roads, markets, churches, mosques and so on."

In addition, on the calamitous rebellion in the north east, President Muhammadu Buhari stated thus:

"We are pleased that in the excesses of the terrorists, they have blown up themselves. I think they should change their names from Boko Haram to something else because no religion will kill the innocents. You can't go and kill innocent people and say 'Allahu Akbaru'! It is either you don't believe it or you don't know what you are saying. So, it has nothing to do with religion. They are just terrorists and Nigeria will mobilize against all of them."

After the Presidential address, all stood up for the first stanza of the National Anthem to end proceedings. However, in line with their tradition, the BBOG continued with the second stanza to the fascination of the meeting. Then Aisha Yesufu set in motion the watchwords of the BBOG:
"What are we demanding...?" At each verse members responded correspondingly. They group took photo shots with Mr. President. As he was leaving, yours truly also

had a warm handshake with him. He asked me: how are you? And I replied, fine Mr. President! [43]

AGAIN, BOKO HARAM OFFERS TO SWAP DETAINEES FOR CHIBOK GIRLS

In the second week of July 2015 a Nigerian activist who has been negotiating with Boko Haram for more than one year, Fred Eno, stated that the terrorist group had once again offered to free more than 200 Chibok Girls kidnapped from their school on 14th April 2014. The new initiative, according to Eno, reopened an offer made last year to former President Goodluck Jonathan to release the 219 students in exchange for 16 Boko Haram members incarcerated by the government. He quoted a man that was close the past botched deal and is involved in current deliberations. Eno said the man spoke to him on circumstance of anonymity because he was not allowed to speak to the press. According to the activist:

"Another window of opportunity opened in the last few days"

In response to that development, Presidential Media Adviser, Femi Adesina, on July 4 said the Nigerian Government 'will not be averse 'to talks with Boko Haram. He stated that:

"Most wars, however furious or vicious, often end around the negotiation table."

While executing a two-month cease-fire and prisoner swap deal last year; Fred in September travelled to the rugged north-eastern country where the captive exchange was to take place. The crucial arrangement at the last minute foundered on discord between Boko Haram and Department of State Security. [44]

BUHARI AGREES TO NEGOTIATE RELEASE OF CHIBOK GIRLS

In a meeting with Nigerians in the Diaspora Organization mid 2015, President Muhammadu Buhari stated that he was ready to negotiate with credible Boko Hram representatives to facilitate safe recovery of the abducted Chibbok school girls. Accentuating the need to rescue the distressed young women the President said:

"Our objective is that we want the girls, alive and returned to their families and rehabilitated. We are working with neighbouring countries, if they will help".

He said he was ready to negotiate the demands of genuine Boko Haram leaders. While addressing the US Institute of Peace, Buhari declared that the United States Leahy Law which forbids military assistance to countries the army of which violate human rights, has tremendously hampered the war against Boko Haram and consequently boosted the assaults of the terrorists in the north east. He called on the US Government and Congress to reconsider the unsubstantiated allegations against the Nigerian Army and thus provide enough redoubtable support to efface the insurgency. [45]

On Thursday, 30 July 2015, Nigerian Army spokesman, Colonel I.T. Gusau, stated that the military had recued additional 71 girls and women following firefights with Boko Haram insurgents. The victims were delivered from the den of terrorists in the rustics about 40 Kilometres from Maiduguri, some having been fettered for as long as a year. One young woman, Yagana Kyari, nervously told the Associated Press news agency that she was just "waiting for death" because the group had constantly threatened to kill their captives. [46]

US CONGRESS VISITS BRING BACK OUR GIRLS

On the 4th of August 2015, a contingent of the United States of America Congress paid a solidarity visit to the Bring Back Our Girls camp in Abuja. Among the mission were: Wilson Frederica, a represesntative from Florida, born in Miami and Jackson Lee Sheila, a Congresswoman from Texas, born in Queens County, New York. Anchor of the reception, Maureen Peter, welcomed the guests and informed them that it was 477 days since the Chibok School Girls were abducted and 462 days of indefatigable vigil at the Unity Fountain, pressing for the rescue of the young girls back to their parents. She deeply lamented that up till then the girls had not been found.

In her presentation to the group, Frederica said:

"We are looking at the President to train the army, bring back the loot, bring employment and save the nation. We are standing and we will continue to stand with you. Put pressure on your elected officials! You put them to work! This is a new day in Nigeria. You should make the elected to be accountable. Keep pressuring them."

Frederica deprecated the absence of Chibok elected representatives at the meeting. She said the frontline reps should attend the daily standing as a show of concern and unity. Her catchword to Nigerians to make the government effective is: pressure, pressure, pressure! She entreated more Nigerians to join the BBOG to fight for the return of the kidnapped girls and wiping out of the terrorism in Northern Nigeria. According to her:

"Everyone, from Senators, representatives and governors, every elected official should join in the fight. It should not be left just for the activists. Everything must be done to win this war. We tweeted so much about the BBOG. We are supporting you."

Earlier at a gathering with BBOG representatives, the United States of America contingent described the missing Chibok girls as Nigerian heroes, declaring that without them the world would not have known the profundity of the plight of the people in the north east. Addressing a press conference organized by the US Congressional delegation at the American Embassy in Abuja to discuss regional security, counterterrorism, Boko Haram and kidnapped and displaced persons, Congressman Darrel Issa said negotiating with the insurgents for the release of the girls was the exclusive responsibility of the Nigerian government which the US government could not meddle. At the occasion congresswoman Frederica was direct that:

"Rescuing the Chibok girls is a top agenda for both US and Nigeria. We however call on Nigeria and all concerned persons globally to keep tweeting about the Chibok girls. Finding them will break Boko Haram, make them less powerful and bring an end to extremism in Nigeria."

To Boko Haram she cautioned:

"Bring back our girls or we will come and find you." [47]

BRING BACK OUR GIRLS COMMEMORATES 500 DAYS OF ABDUCTION

It was all grief and profundity in August 2015 as the Bring Back Our Girls campaign group celebrated the Global Week of Action (GWA) marking 500 days since the Chibok Girls were ruthlessly hijacked from their school on 14 April 2014. The Nigerian Army had till date rescued over one thousand two hundred women and children. Although many women had been reported to still be languishing in the den of the insurgents, the advocates held the remaining 219 girls as a symbol of pressure for the release of all prisoners in terrorists' captivity. There was a sequence of solemn events. For that sober GWA the camp adopted the social media hash tags: #GWA #500DaysOn #ChibokGirls #CryingToBeRescued #NeverToBeForgotten #BringBackOurGirls.

Friday 21 August: Islamic Session of Peace and Unity

The sermon was delivered by Mallam Nura Khalid—the Chief Imam of Apo Mosque. In the earnest and thoughtful message, the Muslim cleric called for unity among all Nigerians despite their ethnic, religious or philosophical affiliations. When asked the question that Western education has provided the means of treasury looting and profligacy, probably justifying Boko Haram, he said the fact that a few people misapply erudition for egocentricity did not mean that the system was blemished. Amazingly both Christians and Muslims were the students of the session.

Sunday 23 August: Christian Lessons and Thoughts

The Christian meeting was led by the Senior Pastor, Strong House Church, Abuja, Pastor Polycarp Gbaja. He also preached peace, harmony and unity among Christians and Muslims. Applauding the struggle of the group to continue the campaign till date, he advised them to stop crying as there was hope for the safe rescue of the abducted girls. He urged them to be prepared for the greater task of rehabilitation of ravaged areas, resettlement of IDPs and helping the government to build a prosperous Nigeria. Speaking after the prayers Dr. Oby Ezekwesili said they hope that the visit of the UN Secretary General to Nigeria then would fortify his support for the group's advocacy. Referring to the UN Chief, Dr. Ezekwesili said:

"We have maintained contact with the secretary general. He has written letters of solidarity to us and we are hopeful that he will visit us before he leaves. We need a global actor for collaboration to end extremism and violence against women which has also brought about the abduction of the girls. We need intelligence gathering to get the whereabouts of the girls. How can 219 girls vanish in this age of technology? There is a way to gather information and we hope that with the UN's help that will be achieved."

On Monday 24 August, the crusaders planted botanical trees in Abuja to keep the hope for the rescue of the Chibok Girls alive. The trees would equally mark the tragedy. Tuesday 25 the group had an engagement conference with the Chief of Defence Staff of the Nigerian Army at the Defence Headquarters.

Thursday 27 August: The Climatic Show of Solidarity

Thursday was the culmination of the GWA events. Members of BBOG in red as usual at about 3p.m. assembled at the Unity Fountain. In attendance were Bishop of Abuja Catholic Diocese, Cardinal John Onaiyekan and Mallam Nura Kalid. Some parents of the abducted school girls and the Abuja Chibok Community represented the devastated rustic. Together with the clerics the group marched along the streets of Maitama District, the young girls—Chibok Ambassadors leading procession with placards and banners.

At strategic positions members of the parade, including the clerics, tied red ribbons on trees and beacons to remind the public that the girls had not been found. Thereafter the troupe marched back to the Unity Fountain singing: 'Solidarity forever' and 'All we are saying; bring back our girls, now and alive'. At the Fountain the coordinator of events, Maureen Kabrik, jubilantly stated that the successful inter faith March demonstrated that the abducted Chibok girls had united Nigeria Christians and Muslims in the war against insurgency.

Leaders of the Chibok Community thanked the Bring Back Our Girls group for relentlessly standing by them to demand the return of their children and an end to the Boko Haram massacre. Striking was a woman in her forties who spoke in fluent English, asking for the blessing of the Almighty God on the BBOG advocates. She was emphatic that but for the BBOG the whole world would have forgotten about the kidnapped girls.

The newly elected Chairperson of the group, Aisha Yesufu, flanked by other members of the Strategic Committee, read a press statement. She narrated the events of the abduction, prompt reaction by the BBOG, inadequate response of the Nigerian Government, the travails and successes of the group over the 500 days period. In her address, she equally declared that the group would continue to put pressure on stakeholders and the International Community until the remaining 219 school girls and other persons in the lair of terrorists were delivered. Subsequently Campaign for the rehabilitation of destroyed territories and resettlement of IDPs would be intensified. After her speech the trio of Mrs. Oby Ezekwesili, Mallam Khalid and Cardinal Onaiyekan proceeded to speak to journalists on the need for unity among Nigerians.

Later in the evening the camp conducted a candlelit procession around the Unity Fountain. Speeches of encouragement and unity were made by members. The candles were raised in solidarity songs; that the earlier unity of Christians and Muslims achieved had kindled hope for the eventual release of the Chibok Girls. The session ended with usual solidarity slogan and songs of the group:

Solidarity forever, Solidarity forever, Solidarity forever; we shall always fight for our girls. X 2
All we are saying; Bring back our girls, now and alive. X3
What are we demanding? Bring back our girls now and alive!
What do we want? Our girls back now and alive!
What are we asking for? The truth, nothing but the truth!
When shall we stop? Not until our girls are back and alive!
When shall we stop? Not without our daughters!
Who are we? Chibok girls!
Who are we? Nigerians!
Where are we from? Chibok!
Where are we from? Nigeria!
What are our core values? HUMANITEEDS!

What are we fighting for? The soul Nigeria!
The fight for the Chibok girls is the fight for the soul of
the Nigerian state and the world!

In another development, on the 27th of August 2015, the primate of the Church of Nigeria (Anglican Communion), Most Rev. Nicholas Okoh, averred that the long stay of the Chibok girls in captivity has injured the integrity of the country. In a sermon, the cleric said:

"The story of the Chibok girls is a bad story, bad story in the sense that the parents are not happy, the government is not happy and the public is baffled. From what the president is saying, you can sense that he is not happy about the inability of government to bring the girls back. But here we are, some have said that the Chibok girls have been married off, some said they have been distributed to various places, that they are not together as a group, or they have been used as suicide bombers.

"We don't know exactly. It complicates the situation. We are hoping that the military will be able to do more. All those areas that they have captured and rescued people, where are the Chibok girls? We have not really solved the problem. We have not reached them."

He appealed to the Nigerian government thus:

"We appeal to government to seek a more advanced way of doing it in terms of technology which can help us locate their whereabouts. As it is now, the soldiers have searched the Sambisa Forest and have not been able to see them. It will continue to be a festering sore in our lives if we are unable to find these girls. We plead with our government, the US, EU, UN and anybody who can help us to come out and help us find the girl.s."

Likewise, the Chairman, Chibok Community in Abuja, Tsambido Hosea-Abana, was sad that the abducted girls' whereabouts were still unknown after 500 days. He painfully asserted:

"We are feeling very bad. It is not only that the girls were abducted; the pitiable thing is that we do not even know their whereabouts. We were accusing the past administration of not doing something visible. We were hoping that by now, we are under three months of the new administration; this administration would have established that these girls are in a particular place and they are working on ways to bring them out. We don't know where they are, so we feel so sad. Even the parents at home, if you want to talk to them, some of them decide not to talk because of sadness and annoyance."

He entreated the government thus in this way:

"Our call on government, not only Nigerian government but also the world over, because this is a slap on the face of the whole world that up till this moment, the girls have not been rescued; 500 days now and the Chibok girls are still in the hands of their captors. It is unbelievable. I am calling on the leaders of the whole world to rise up and do something. As for me, I am saying that they are not serious about our girls.

"We receive different visits from the international community; they would just say nice words and when they go, we won't see anything. If they will come together, with air and ground armies, I believe they will track the girls. Everything has become political. There is no statement followed by action towards this issue. Right now, it is like only in the first week, we knew the girls were in a place. Now, we don't even know where they are."

Resilient activist and leader of the group, Aisha Yesufu, stated that members of the group were celebrating with heavy hearts. In a mournful mood, she said:

"We are having heavy hearts. For me right now, it is like there is a heavy load on my chest. I think the mood is throughout. People are just down that the girls are not yet back. None of us thought that at day 500, we would still be here. We didn't know when we started this advocacy that we would stay for more than two weeks. It is saddening. It is a shame that the abduction of over 200 girls couldn't bring us close as a nation."

To the government she implored:

"The government should ensure that the girls are rescued. As far as they are still with their captives, nobody is safe in Nigeria. We are failing our children and we are telling them that if they are kidnapped, nobody will do anything about it. We are sending a wrong signal to would-be terrorists that if any one of our citizens is abducted, nothing will be done about it. The primary responsibility of government is to protect the lives and properties of its citizenry.

"Right now, people don't feel safe in the country. The government should wake up and do all it can. It is not only about talking; we need action, doing the right thing and ensuring that the girls are back home. They are a symbol of all those that were abducted before and after them. We have so many people in captivity and they need to come back home."

She emphasized the resoluteness of their advocacy thus:

"We are not tired. We can never be tired. We have a slogan and we always ask ourselves, 'when will we stop?'

and we reply, 'until our girls are back and alive'. How do you live your life and move on when your daughters are with monsters who can do terrible things? We have seen people who have been rescued, how they are; some are pregnant while others are HIV positive. Some of them are mentally deranged; they have gone through hell and the type of stories they tell are terrible stories. We won't stop until the 219 girls are accounted for."

Co-founder of the group and activist leader, Dr. Mrs. Oby Ezekwesili was extremely depressed that the girls were not yet back. She said:

"The activities of the Global Week of Action are to remind the world that we are still standing for the abducted girls. Some people never knew that the advocacy for the girls continued. We want our government to rise to their responsibility. It is their responsibility to bring back the girls and we won't get tired of telling them that. The government needs to find the people who have our daughters and we need to get them back."

On the Campaign group and the President's statement she said:

"It has been tough on us. If anybody had told us that we would be here beyond day 50, we would not have believed them. But we are now in day 500. We will not cry any more. We have passed the stage of acting like victims. We should act as victors. We need strength to continue.

"We are going to be strong and we will maintain our point. The president had said that the country cannot say that it has won the war against the insurgency without the girls being back. That statement is important; we lay emphasis on it and hope that the girls will be back soon, "

Her message to Nigerians:

"Some Nigerians genuinely ask us if we are still standing for the girls. Those people need information to know that the group still exists through our twitter handle and everyday coverage by LEADERSHIP newspapers of our activities. But some other Nigerians are people whose mission in life is mockery.

"These people keep asking if the Chibok girls were really abducted. For this category of people, we don't need to bother ourselves about them. I tell you not to waste your time on them. It does not matter what you say. If they ever admit that the girls are abducted, it will make them lose their essence."

Concerning Ban Ki Moon's visit, she declared:

"It was all about organization of time. Ban Ki-moon could not address us because of time constraint. We pleaded with him to pass through and share his words with us. But his time was eaten into and he was to head to the dinner with the President. His not addressing the group was not disrespect.

"At the time, we had a meeting with victims of Boko Haram, they were begging the UN secretary general to help them get a sense of livelihood and what the UN secretary general could say was that he would call on Nigerians who pledged to help them in the Victims Support Fund to redeem their pledges. This buttresses the point that there is nobody outside our government that has the responsibility to rescue our girls. More is expected from our own government. We must continue to insist."[48]

BRING BACK OUR GIRLS ENGAGES NHRC TO ESTABLISH MISSING PERSONS REGISTER IN NIGERIA

On the 2nd of September 2015, the BBOG group marched to the headquarters of the National Human Rights Commission (NHRC) seeking to engage the agency in the setting up of Missing Persons Register across the country, in view of the calamitous insurgency in northern Nigeria where thousands of citizens have been snuffed and millions rendered homeless. The camp led by leader, Mrs. Aisha Yesufu, was worried that there was no record of killed, missing or IDPs in the country. They therefore provided a framework for such data management to the commission.

While introducing the outline, Aisha said:

"We need to know the people missing; if they are rescued, we should know. With will power we can get things done. It is not about money. We are volunteering to be part of this. Nigerians will be happy to be part of it. The country needs to know when anybody is missing, no matter who; the state needs to take care of its citizens. There should be respect for the human life."

Responding, the Executive Secretary of NHRC, Prof Ben Angwe, benignly welcomed the group and expressed sadness over lack of birth and death data in Nigeria , much less missing persons. He kindly said:

"I will give directive to our office to open and maintain missing persons register across the federation. We will lead the campaign. We will write letters to all the

115

governments of the States to begin collation of birth registration and data of all Nigerians.

"This will be one of the legacies of the BBOG struggle. We will insist that the life of every Nigerian must begin to mean a lot. We need to maintain a data and account for the lives of all Nigerians."

Prof Angwe urged Nigerians whose relatives are missing to bring the bio-data of such persons to the offices of the Commission in the country for documentation to facilitate eventual re-unification. He decried the nonexistence of data and identity of Nigerian citizens. Accentuating this deficiency, he said:

"Many Nigerian have nothing to show that they are Nigerians. Many have no birth registration. Many are not being born in hospitals. Many still deliver in their homes with an old woman as midwife: which is responsible for the high rate of still born and they do not have birth certificates.

"Many are in the hands of captives and are unknown because of absence of data. Some do not know the need to talk about their missing persons. We will take it upon ourselves to sensitize Nigerians on the need to not only report when their relations are missing but register them. You have come to strengthen us."

He lionized the BBOG for resolutely campaigning for the rescue of the abducted Chbok school girls despite the manifold obstacles they have had to grapple with. The generations of Nigerians yet unborn, he said: would ever remain grateful to members of the group. He stated that the whole world had recorded their exhibition of humanity. The Almighty God, he implored would reward them in abundance.

While officially presenting the missing persons data plan to the Executive Secretary Aisha assured Nigerians present that the BBOG would continue standing and pressing until the kidnapped women were delivered and re-united with their parents. She said that they had noted the promises of the Executive Secretary and would curiously monitor and compel implementation of this crucial project. [49]

BBOG MARKS 18 MONTHS OF ABDUCTION

Thursday October 14, 2015 marked one year and six months of kidnapping by Boko Haram rebels of over 300 girls taking their final examinations at Government Girls Secondary School, Chibok in north eastern Nigeria. 57 of the young women escaped while 219 were to date languishing in the den of the terrorists. The government of Nigeria said it was negotiating with insurgents for the safe release of the distressed girls. However, while the Nigerian Army was making some progress towards routing the terrorists, the religious extremists continued their attacks and suicide bombings in the three frontline States and even the Federal Capital Territory, Abuja.

Members of the Bring Back Our Girls expressed disappointment that those innocent women were still being mutilated and dehumanized by savages after eighteen months. They appealed to the government to intensify intelligence, reconnaissance and surveillance towards the rescue of the girls. Constructive intelligence gathering and analysis was *de rigueur* to fishing out the captives and setting them free, they accentuated. Despite their having waited for so long, expending their times, talents and treasures, the group vowed to continue standing and putting pressure on related bodies for the delivering of the girls back to the hands of their parents, loved ones and Nigerians.[50]

BRING BACK OUR GIRLS LOSES ONE SOLDIER

According to Dr Martin Luther King Jr., in freedom fighting to change a despicable society, some revolutionaries will lose their lives and there are martyrs that will be sacrificed to set others free and give them peace. So, on the day of solemnization of eighteen months of abduction of the Chibok school girls, 219 of whom were still in the lair of insurgents, one member of the Bring Back Our Girls, Elvis Inyorngurum, died of liver carcinoma involvedness. An erudite scholar, Elvis was a mentor of literature art and syntax, highly revered for his punctiliousness in prose writing. He had taken ill several months to this date but doggedly managed to attend the group's daily sit-out, sometimes unable to keep standing.

Elvis was a great freedom fighter against injustice in country and society, especially ethnic domination in Nigeria. He had been resolute and hopeful that the Chibok girls would be rescued back to the hands of fellow Nigerians. His bald and receptive articulation of views on camp issues would be missed. Next day, 15th October, the group held a funeral session in his honour. Members prayed for the peaceful repose of his soul and the courage for family and friends to bear the irreparable loss.

There were elegiac speeches from the crowd, applauding the humanitarian and selfless virtues of Elvis. In attendance was the Leader of the group, Dr Mrs. Oby Ezekwesili, and Senator Dino Melaye, Chairman, Senate Committee on Information and FCT. The following day a condolence register was opened to mark his death at the Unity Fountain.

51

BBOG MARKS UNIVERSAL CHILDREN'S DAY, 2015

As the Universal Children's Day was marked on November 20, 2015, the Bring Back Our Girls called on the Federal Government of Nigeria to implement the provisions of the Child Rights Act 2003 fully. The complete application of the act, the group averred, would mitigate child abuse and mutilation in a country wrecked by insurgency, female suicide bombing, child trafficking and displacement, and rape. In a declaration appended by leaders: Dr. Mrs. Obiageli Ezekwesili, Hadiza Bala Usman, Aisha Yesufu, the archetypal humanitarian camp urged the government to effectively propagate child rights awareness among the Nigerian populace using various ministries and departments. In a statement released to the press the group said:

"We count on the commitment of Nigeria to ensure these actions are implemented to breed children that can positively impact their society.

"This September the UN included the target to eliminate violence as part of the Strategic Development Goals. Studies prove the connection between a violence-free society for children and economic growth."

On their continued demand for the rescue of the Chibok school girls abducted on 14 April 2014 the campaigners stated:

"Today is 585 days of our #Chibokgirls abduction and 570 days consistent daily advocacy for their rescue and safe return. Our Chibok girls represent the worst of child abuse that can ever be imagined. We call on all this day to continue to stand for them, to raise our voices louder, more so the December deadline to rescue and bring them back is less than 41 days away."

The epochal Declaration of the Rights of the Child in December 1954 was adopted as the Universal Children's Day by the UN General Assembly to protect the rights of the child to survive, thrive, learn, grow and attain full potentials in society. [52]

BBOG ADVOCATES ELIMINATION OF VIOLENCE AGAINST WOMEN

The Bring Back Our Girls group joined Nigerians and the whole world to celebrate in the end of November 2015 the International Day for the Elimination of Violence against Women. Accordingly, at the event held on the 26th, the camp urged the Federal Government of Nigeria to prioritize the education of the girl-child and guard them against dehumanization and mutilation. In a press conference read by its member, Comfort Iliya, the crusaders said negligence of the absolute right of female children to education has resulted in societal discriminations and manifold violence inflicted on them.

The humanitarians, who have been putting pressure on the Nigerian government for over eighteen months to rescue the abducted Chibok school girls, called on the Nigerian authorities to adequately fund education for girls by adhering strictly to the Education for All (Dakar) Framework of Action by objectively increasing the budgetary allocations for education to a minimum of 20 per centum while at the same time guaranteeing judicious application of this revenue. Emphasizing the right of compulsory education for female children, the group said:

"It is therefore of utmost importance to prioritize education as a tool to among others, reduce the spate of gender-based violence in the country while creating room for peace in the home, and by extension, peace in the nation and the world.

"To this end therefore, in the 2015 International Day for the Elimination of Violence Against Women, we call on governments at all levels in Nigeria to ensure implementation of all education-related policies that promote access to safe and quality education for girls.

"We also demand that the government ensures that States comply with the provision of the 2004 Universal Basic Education Act where it was stipulated in section 2(1) that 'Every government in Nigeria shall provide free, compulsory and universal basic education for every child of primary and junior secondary school age, especially in States where education uptake is low."

The BBOG accentuated the inevitability of strengthening the judiciary especially in the States to secure decisive resolution of matters relating to violence against women, be it physical, sexual, psychological, social or economic. Members of the BBOG have always repulsed the fact that the Chibok school girls were kidnapped while learning, to make their lives and society better. On the 219 Chibok girls, still in the lair of insurgents, the camp reiterated:

"The very abduction of our Chibok girls on 14 April 2014, 591 days ago, 219 of them still missing with not one of them found—young women who dared to seek education despite the challenges of going to school in their cultural setting as females, and the unsafe learning environment-- emphasizes the Importance of this year's theme."

The non-profit advocates entreated governments to fortify and enforce all gender-based laws and regulations which safeguard women against battery, and assault, sexual violence, human trafficking, sexual exploitation and slavery, female genital mutilation and induced child marriages. [53]

BBOG ENGAGES NEMA

On the first of December 2015, the BBOG paid a courtesy call to the headquarters of NEMA in Abuja. The object of the meeting was to discuss the state and care of millions of insurgency-IDPs scattered all over the country. There was also the need to find out response efforts to the

vulnerable and new cases of displacement and attacks.
The BBOG group was led by camp head, Aisha Yesufu.
The Director-General of NEMA, Mr. Mohammed Sani
Sidi, at the conference disclosed that over 410 births were
registered while 187 marriages were conducted at
Internally Displaced Persons (IDPs) centres in Borno and
Adamawa States between August and September 2015.
According to the head of the emergency management
unit:

*"Emergency Education for IDPs Children became a
major priority after unprecedented insurgency attacks on
students, teachers, school infrastructure; about 269
teachers lost their lives during the attack. The agency in
ensuring efficient management of camps has trained
personnel in camp coordination and camp management
(CCCM) and deployed to manage various IDP camps in
Borno, Yobe and Adamawa and to provide for specialized
needs of vulnerable people during emergencies."*

He entreated the collaboration of the BBOG thus:

*"I am appealing to the advocacy group to extend their
platform to other issues like unaccompanied minors and
mass childbirths in the camps as disaster management is
multidisciplinary, multidimensional and multitasking."*

Leader of the group, Mrs. Obiageli Ezekwesili, expressed
discontentment over the inability of the government to

rescue the Chibok girls, indicating that day marked the 596th day since they were abducted from their secondary school. She requested the cooperation of NEMA for mobilization to protect and care for the vulnerable in the society—the poor, patsies and Cinderella. Correspondingly, the Chairperson of the BBOG crusade, Aisha Yesufu, affirmed that they were at the agency's office to collaborate in the areas of education, IDP living conditions, security, health and other humanitarian issues, and how their platform could be used to support the rehabilitation of IDPs by the federal government in areas where the agency deemed necessary.[54]

BBOG MOURNFULLY MARKS 600 DAYS OF ABDUCTION

The BBOG on the 5th of December 2015 with profound grief celebrated 600 days of abduction of the Chibok school girls in northeastern Nigeria.The group in a press statement said:

"Today is 600 days since our Chibok school girls were abducted in their school, Government Secondary School Chibok, by terrorists on the night of 14th April 2014. It will also be few days to complete five months since our meeting with the Nigerian President, urging him to prioritize their immediate rescue and return; whereby he reiterated his commitment."

In an interview during the special sit-out and candle light procession at the Unity Fountain by the Chibok Girls Ambassadors, the Chairman of Chibok Community in Abuja, Tsambido Hosea-Abana, regretted that the girls had not been rescued despite successive promises by the government. Their hope in the new administration, he said, had so far been dashed. Expressing sadness Hosea-Abana said:

"It is unfortunate. We are commemorating this moment with sad and heavy heart. It is a sad moment. We never knew that it will ever get to this day. When we joined this advocacy, we never envisaged that it will get to this day. Six hundred days is really a long time for peoples' children to stay in the hands of terrorists. We don't know the state of the girls. We have heard nothing. We are all shedding tears of grief.

"The parents of the girls are also in pain. They don't know what to expect any longer. They had kept their hope alive, thinking that the new administration will do what the past administration didn't do; that is, bringing the girls back. But they have seen no positive result. They are confused. They don't even know what to do and what to ask government any longer."

In a statement signed by leaders of the camp, Oby Ezekwesili, Hadiza Bala Usman and Aisha Yesufu, calling on everyone in Nigeria and around the world to continue to remember the Chibok girls, the advocates expressed hope that the December deadline given by the President for the girls' rescue and return, and annihilation of the terrorists would be achieved.

"This becomes even more important as we all look forward to the 31ˢᵗ December deadline given by the President for their rescue and safe return, and the annihilation of thee terrorists, amidst reports of more abduction," the camp said.[55]

BRING BACK OUR GIRLS STORMS ASO ROCK AGAIN

The BBOG again on January 14, 2016 marched to the State House, Abuja to have a meeting with President

Muhammadu Buhari on the state of 219 Chibok secondary school girls still held by Boko Haram insurgents in Sambisa Forest. Added to the group were over one hundred parents (men and women) of the abducted Chibok girls who came all the way from far Chibok villages to join the protest. It was all crying and grief as the procession arrived at the gateway of the villa by 9.30 am.

The parents were sitting on the road, the women weeping sorrowfully. One of the women fainted out of exhaustion and was taken to the hospital in an ambulance. The rustics looked scrawny and dejected.

The flood of campaigners was received at the Aso Rock conference hall by a contingent from President Muhammadu Buhari that included the Minister of Women Affairs, Aisha Al-Hassan, Minister of Defense, Monsur Dan-Ali; National Security Adviser, Mohammed Monguno, and Chief of Defense Staff, Abayomi Olonishakin. Mrs. Aisha Al-Hassan opened session by welcoming the BBOG group as well as the despondent parents. She informed the visitors that Mr. President was having a crucial meeting with the President of Benin Republic, Boni Yayi, appertaining to latest redoubtable tacks being worked out to secure the release of the Chibok girls and stanch the insurgency. Consequently, she advanced that the President had delegated them to discuss this matter with the crusaders. She thus sought to listen to them.

However, this did not go down well with the alliance of BBOG representation. Leader of the group, Mrs. Obiageli Ezekwesili, replied that their coming was a follow-up to the earlier meeting of July 8 in which the

President gave them firm promise to quell the rebellion and bring home the kidnapped young women. The Chairman of Chibok community in Abuja, Mr. Hosea Abana, concurred with Oby Ezekwesili that the parents that arrived had sold their harvested corn, beans and other farm products to secure transport facilities to Abuja. This indicated that the parents were rather anxious to see Mr. President to know the fate of their daughters before going back home.

A stalemate of silence ensued due to the intransigence of the campaigners. Mrs. Al-Hassan re-opened dialogue by stating that the issue of the abducted Chibok girls and insurgency in the north east was top in the agenda of government. She stated that their secret plans by the government to rescue the girls alive, which could not be made public for security reasons. Thus, she insisted that the visitors should continue discussions with them while arrangement was made for the President to come and talk to them.

Other members of the Presidential delegation took turns to explain the operations of the military in the new administration to rescue the Chibok girls and subsequently stem the insurgency. They appealed for patience and time considering the involvedness of such anti-insurgency operation. Oby Ezekwesili took exception to Aisha Al-Hassan's presentation and accused her of disparaging the camp. She (Ezekwesili) got up and said:

"You have been very unfair to us. I don't understand why you can be chiding the parents and the movement. These parents were triggered by the words of the president who promised to rescue their daughters."

The National Security Adviser, however, moderated situation by saying he would confer with Mr. President to come and see the protesters. Later the President came in and was introduced by Senior Special Media Adviser, Garba Shehu. Mrs. Oby Ezekwesili opened this segment by stating that the group had come to the villa to get an update on efforts to rescue the Chibok girls. She said that the parents of the abducted young woman were worried that the probe panel set up by the former administration of Goodluck Jonathan did not conclude its assignment. In her presentation before Mr. President she said:

"Number two is the matter of investigation of exactly what happened that led to the abduction our Chibok girls is critical. It is consistent with our movement's demand that the General Sabo report, that is the Presidential fact-finding committee report on our Chibok girls which was conducted and delivered during the previous administration, it needs to be disclosed; it needs to be transparently open so that everyone would read what it was that the committee found during their investigation."

In his reply to the demands the President said:

"I assure you that I go to bed and wake up every day with the Chibok girls in my mind.

"The unfortunate incident happened before this government came into being. What have we done since we assumed office? We re-organized the military, removed all the service chiefs and ordered the succeeding service chiefs to deal decisively with the Boko Haram insurgency.

"Despite the terrible economic situations, we found ourselves in, we tried to get some resources to give to the military to re-organize and equip, retrain, deploy more troops and move more forcefully against Boko Haram.

"And you all know the progress we have made. When we came in, Boko Haram was in Adamawa, Yobe and Bornu. Boko Haram has now been reduced to the area around Lake Chad.

"Securing the Chibok girls is my responsibility. The service chiefs and heads of our security agencies will tell you that despite the dire financial straits that we found the country in, I continue to do my best to support their efforts in that regard. God knows I have done my best and will continue to do my best."

After being persuaded by aides to relay his statement in *Hausa* so that the villagers would comprehend him very well, the President stood up and hurried to the exit door. In her post-conference briefing to journalists, Mrs. Ezekwesili said the government explained it had made considerable progress in decimating Boko Haram in the north east and that what remained was to rescue the Chibok girls and other kidnapped citizens, and secure any remaining rustics occupied by rebels. For this, she said, the government had asked for time and the group had agreed to bear with them 'to make that effort'.

The engagement with government this time was a little bit confrontational and unreceptive compared with the July 8 encounter in which the President sounded affable, shook hands and tool photographs with members of the delegation. It would be recalled that the BBOG, a non-political humanitarian movement, was accused of clandestinely working for the APC (by putting fierce pressure for the rescue of the Chbok girls) during the 2014-15 Presidential political campaigns. Consequently, members of the camp were abused and physically assaulted by hoodlums allegedly sponsored the last PDP government.

During this period, there were frequent Intel reports that the BBOG members were to be attacked and snuffed at their Unity Fountain camp. To avoid being killed they continued to change their secret sit-out locations. It might therefore evince ingratitude for the present administration to be rebuffing or antagonizing the group.[56]

DENMARK GOVERNMENT VISITS BBOG

The Denmark government made a pledge on February 23, 2016 to take the crusade for the rescue of the abducted Chibok school girls to the whole world. In his visit to the Bring Back Our Girls camp at the Unity Fountain, Denmark Foreign Affairs Minister, Kristian Jensen, said:

"I will assure you to work towards making the world never forget to always fight, to find the truth and bring the girls back alive."

Accompanied by the Denmark Ambassador to Nigeria, Torben Gettermann, Mr. Kristian stated that the fight for the release of the Chibok girls symbolized the fight for the freedom and education of young woman worldwide. Accentuating the humanitarian angle of the pressure to deliver those languishing young women, he said:

"I have three sons. I don't understand your pain but I understand the fear of what would happen if they were abducted on their way to school. The fear is what makes the world remember. You are fighting for the soul of the world, not just Nigeria. We are fighting for girls' right to education.

"What happen to your girls now affects other girls who are scared to go to school. They don't have a right to choose a life of their own because of fear. Your fight is to allow girls right to education. Denmark has been chosen to be a champion of girls' right to education in the world."

While welcoming the contingent, leader of BBOG, Mrs. Oby Ezekwesili, remarked that it would be unhealthy for the world to move on without a closure on the issue of the kidnapped school girls. In a solemn mood, she said:

"It is remarkable after nearly two years of the abduction a leader of a country will visit us. It is a demonstration that the world still remembers the girls. By visiting us you are telling us that the people of Denmark have not moved on. It is significant to us.

"When the girls were abducted, we had gathered through a common spirit of comradeship because of our girls. We are still persistent with our advocacy because we believe unless there is closure to the issue of the abducted girls; it would be unhealthy for the country to move on. We believe that the world would lose moral credence to advocate for girls to go to schools if there is no closure on the issue of the girls.

"This movement says we will be a voice for the girls that go in search of education. We are talking of the importance of human capital. Our country should spend more in the security of our girls and boys as they go to school."

In her appeal to the Denmark Government the woman activist said:

"The key issue from our last visit with our President is the credibility of intelligence of the whereabouts of the girls. We want to give you a message, not just to Denmark or European Union; we want a global support to obtain credible intelligence in the fight against the insurgents. We believe that the Chibok girls can still be rescued. We are recruiting you as an ambassador of the girls. Please do anything you could so that the world will help in the rescue of the abducted girls."

Rebuking those who doubt the abduction of the Chibok girls, one of the victims' parents, Esther Yakubu, demanded the rescue of her daughter to be re-united with the family. Despondently she managed to say:

"I give thanks to God and the BBOG group. This small group has made our girls not to be forgotten. I have five kids; I can't say my baby is kidnapped when she is not. We want our children back so that we will get our joy and happiness back." [57]

BRING BACK OUR GIRLS COMMEMORATES 2ND YEAR OF BUNI YADI MASSACRE

Early 2016 the BBOG remembered the boys who were slaughtered in their school by Boko Haram insurgents in 2014. In attendance were parents of the slain Buni Yady boys from Yobe and Bornu States who made solemn presentations regarding the horrendous incident, asking the government to rebuild the destroyed school and safeguard students. They expressed gratitude to the BBOG for standing by them.

Pastor Polycarp Gbaja and Nura Khalid were present to give spiritual messages---on the need for peace and unity in the country. Mallam Nura stated that humanity goes beyond religious, linguistic and geographical boundaries. Pastor Polycarp said the Nigerian nation failed the school children by not providing them with adequate security while they went to school, making them vulnerable to assault by kidnappers and rebels.

A commemorative press statement from the group was read by leader, Aisha Yesufu, emphasizing the need to protect school children and provide them adequate education. She reaffirmed the group's resolve to continue standing and putting pressure on the Nigerian Government and the whole world until the 219 Chibok girls were rescued.

Co-founder, Mrs. Oby Ezekwesili rounded up proceedings by thanking the parents for coming all the way from the north east. She accentuated that the right of children to go to school should be unquestionably preserved. Consequently, she declared that the group would continue their advocacy for a closure on the issue of the abducted Chibok school girls. Yours truly urged all

Nigerians to exhibit humanity by coming to the aid of besieged and displaced communities irrespective of religion, tribe or geographical bearings.

There was a candlelit procession later in the evening. This was organized to keep the light shinning that the boys did not die in vain; their death would continue to kindle the struggle for Nigerian children to have laissez-faire and secure education. The occasion closed with solemn prayers by both Christians and Moslems. [58]

BRING BACK OUR GIRLS LOSES ONE MORE WARRIOR

The BBOG suffered grave set-back on 5th of March 2016. One of the freedom fighters, Mubaraka Sani, died in a road traffic accident along Abuja-Kaduna expressway. Mubaraka, in her twenties, was a gentle and affable lady, fully dedicated to the cause to serve humanity vis-à-vis the struggle for the rescue of the abducted Chibok school girls and ending insurgency in the north east. A condolence register was opened in her honour for sympathizers on March 7, 2016.

The day's sit-out was a funeral session devoted to pay tribute to her. Members spoke of her resplendent virtues and contributions to the cause of the Chibok girls, and prayed for the repose of her soul. This brought to four the number of BBOG members who had hitherto died in the struggle, the others being Elvis Iyorngurum, Senator Zana and Bilkisu Yusuf.[59]

2ND YEAR COMMEMORATION--GLOBAL WEEK OF ACTION

The BBOG commemorated two years since the Chibok School girls were kidnapped by Boko Haram insurgents into the tortuous jungle of Sambisa with a 7-day Global Week of Action, starting with Moslem prayers and lectures in mosques around the world on day one (8th April, 2016). At Abuja, the principal celebrant was the Chief Imam of Apo Mosque, Ustaz Nura Khalid, who led the prayers and delivered a lecture titled: *'The importance of girl child education in Islam'*. He emphasized that girl children should have knowledge and for this they have to be educated.

According to him: 'Boko is *Wajib'*—an obligation to learn about life and nature, and God. The girl child, he said, is a human being, has human rights and is supposed to be given equal rights as the male. On the question of whether Islam recognizes human rights, he said:

"No religion is against human rights."

He revealed that one of the teachings of Islam is human rights; as well do other great religions. Thus, he appealed for women education and freedom.

Leader, Aisha Yesufu, gave the opening address on this day 725 of abduction, accentuating that the world has failed the 219 Chibok Girls by abandoning them in the hands of savages for two years. She thanked members of the BBOG for coming out daily for 210 days to stand and demand for the rescue of the girls despite the arduous and grave challenges they had been facing all along. She concluded by urging her comrades to keep hope alive that the girls will come back and will be rehabilitated.

On the 10th of April, there was Christian session featuring renowned Pentecostal preacher and prophet, Pastor Tunde Bakare of the Later Rain Assembly. Expressing revulsion over the continued stay of the girls in the wild, the articulating pastor said:

"We are not convinced that the matter of our daughters has been given the needed thoughtfulness. We do not believe that those who are in position to act have taken sufficient action toward addressing this issue or even toward calming our anxiety as waiting parents. We are not unmindful that the Nigerian state failed to provide security for our daughters as they gathered to write their final examinations despite prior intelligence reports that suggested they were in danger... "[60]

As the world commemorated the second year of the April 14, 2014 horrendous abduction of the Chibok secondary school girls, the CNN relayed a new video clip believed to have been taken on 25 December 2015, showing 15 representatives of the hijacked young women looking healthy in captivity. The CNN said it obtained a video of Chibok girls which had been sent to negotiators by their captors as 'a proof of life'. In the report Rifkatu Ayuba was shown her missing 15-year (now 17) daughter, Saratu Ayuba on the screen of a laptop— 'the closest she has been to her child in two years'. The video was released by someone to show the parents their daughter was alive and motivate the Nigerian government to intensify efforts to rescue them.

Saratu, in the video shown to some family members for the first time in an emotional meeting, was wearing a purple abaya with a patterned brown scarf covering her hair as she stated directly into the camera. On seeing her daughter Rifkatu Ayuba told CNN, desperate to pluck her from the beastly wild:

"I felt like removing her from the screen. If I could, I would have removed her from the screen."

The displayed girls, their hairs covered and wearing long flowing robes, lined up against a dirty yellow wall. As the camera focused on each of the, a man behind the camera fired some questions: What is your name? What is the name of your school? Where were you taken from?

From the clip, one by one each girl calmly stated her name and explained she was taken from Government Girls Secondary School, Chibok. Towards the end of the 2-minute video, one of the kidnapped girls, Naomi Zakaria, made a final—apparently scripted—appeal to whoever was watching, urging the Nigerian authorities to help re-unite the girls with their families.
She said:

"I am appealing on 25 December 2015 on behalf of all the Chibok girls and we are all well."

Her emphasis on the word '*all*' probably meant that the 15 girls shown were representatives of the 219 Chibok secondary school girls languishing in the wild. Recently a 16-yeear old girl, carrying a five months pregnancy for a Boko Haram member who she was coerced to marry in the horrendous camps, said that she saw the Chibok girls in a remote village near the Cameroun border with Nigeria.

Meanwhile Vice President of Nigeria, Prof Yemi Osinbajo, speaking at a roundtable organized by office of the National Security Adviser (NSA) on vulnerable people and conflict situation in Nigeria, said:

"I am sure we will rescue those girls and I hope it will be very soon". [61]

In another development, the Department of State Security (DSS) earlier on April 13 paraded one Bello Danhajiya— a Fulani from Zamfara State and deputy to top Boko Haram leader, Al Barnawi. The DSS had the previous week announced the arrest of Khalid Al Barnawi, a notorious terrorist in West Africa.

On the 13th of April, the BBOG celebrated their 'Walkathon?' and Red Ribbon tying around Abuja streets to keep hope alive for the return of the girls. Later in the evening there was display of manifold arts in relation to the abduction of the Chibok Girls. There were songs, music entertainment and poetry recitations. The modernistic Playback Theatre performed wonderfully at the occasion.

On the seventh and final day of the Global Week of Action (GWA), the BBOG staged another march from their Unity Fountain camp through the Eagle Square to the Presidential Villa. They went to ascertain from the Presidency the latest efforts put in place to rescue the 219 abducted Chibok girls still held by insurgents in the Sambisa Forest. However, the group was prevented from reaching the gate of the Villa by a barricade of police women. The DPO in charge of operations, Grace Lunge, declared that the crusaders were barred from entering for security reasons. Leader, Mrs. Oby Ezekwesili, said the women blockade was unnecessary as her group were law-abiding and responsible citizens. Head of the BBOG Strategic Committee, Aisha Yesufu, in her press statement said:

"It is for this reason that parents of Chibok girls, their community and our movement were devastated by the feedback received from the President seven months into his administration. We are puzzled at the fact that the President in our meeting of January 13, 2016 inferred that that our Chibok girls were not yet rescued because the government lacked credible intelligence on the whereabouts of the girls."

Emphasizing that the whole world has failed the Chibok girls languishing in the jungle, Aisha said that the recent video of some of the girls identified by the parents evinced hope for their return. She appealed to the Nigerian government and other countries to apply hi-tech intelligence and reconnaissance to locate and deliver the girls wherever they may be.

I Share Your Pains, PMB Assures Parents of Chibok Girls

In the meantime, President Muhammadu Buhari, speaking though his Senior Special Assistant, Media, Garba Shehu, on the 2nd year commemoration, assured the parents and relatives of the abducted Chibok girls that he shared with them their pains over their missing daughters. He believed that will the total commitment of the federal government, the Nigerian Armed Forces, security agencies and support of the International Community the girls would eventually be rescued.

Chibok Girls: Senate Summons NSA, other Security Chiefs

Elsewhere the Senate of the Federal Republic of Nigeria, worried by continued suffering of the abducted Chibok girls in the lair of insurgents, on 14 April, 2016 summoned the National Security Adviser (NSA), Babagana Monguno, and other security heads to address them on the latest efforts in the ongoing rescue operation. Commending the BBOG for standing by the girls staunchly till date, The Senate resolved that the security agencies should do everything humanly possible to retrieve the tormented young women. This resolution was sequel to a motion by Senator Deno Melaye (Kogi West) and three others entitled: *'Abduction of Chibok Girls, 2 years after'*. In raising the motion Senator Melaye said:

"The abduction of over 200 girls by Boko Haram has wrongly affected us as a people as could be seen in the international condemnation of the government's slow reaction to this unprecedented outrage committed against us Nigerian womanhood ..Yesterday (13th April) makes it 739 days, 17520 hours and 1051 minutes that our Chibok school girls have been under captivity."[62]

AT LAST TWO OF THE 219 RESCUED

It was an emotion-laden moment when Amina Ali Nkek (now 19) was reunited with her family after she had been rescued from Boko Haram terrorists on May 18. Amina, who is among the 219 Chibok school girls bestially kidnapped over two years earlier, is now mother of a 4-month old baby she got from a forced marriage with an insurgent. The baby is named Safiya.

The rescued girl disclosed the depressing news that at least six of the abducted young women had lost their lives in horrendous captivity. She was allegedly delivered by local security forces known as Civilian JTF when she was discovered hiding in a derelict house at Baale village in Damboa Local Government of Borno State.

A vigilante member who took part in the rescue mission told newsmen in Borno State thus:

"I identified her as soon as we saw her hiding with some other ladies. She was the only girl from Chibok and she carries a baby. We took her to Chibok for identification from her parents, then back to the military in Damboa. She said many of the girls are still alive except for six who have died."

Amina's uncle, Yakubu Nkek, told Associated Press that Amina was reunited with her mother in Chibok. Incidentally, it emerged that 'Commander' Mohammed Hayatu, who claimed to be Amina's husband, was also arrested by the Nigerian Army.

There was rapture in the BBOG camp on May 19 when it was announced that another Chibok school girl,

141

Miss Serra Luka, had been rescued in Borno State. Serra is identified as number 157 in the abducted Chibok girls list. The Acting Director of Army Public Relations confirmed the development at 11: 30 pm.

Meanwhile, Amina Ali Nkek who was earlier found on May 17 shad been presented alongside her 4-month old baby to President Muhammadu Buhari at the State House, Abuja on May 19. Governor Kashim Shettima of Borno State took the freed girl and her family members, and representatives of the Bring Back Our Girls led by Hadiza Bala Usman to meet with Mr. President. On meeting Amina with her baby, President Buhari illustrated fatherly passion by cuddling the infant and directed that she should be taken back to school at the expense of the state. Lamenting the trauma, the abducted girls had gone through in the den of insurgents, the President said:

"Like others all over the world, I am delighted that Amina Ali, one of missing Chibok girls has regained her freedom. But, my feelings are stringed by with deep sadness and horrors the young girl has had to go through at such an early stage in her life. Although we cannot do anything to reverse the horrors of her past, the federal government can and will do everything possible to ensure that the rest of her life takes a completely different course.

"Amina will get the best care that the Nigerian government can afford. We will ensure that she gets the best medical, emotional and whatever care that she requires to get full recovery and be integrated into the

society. Yesterday medical personnel from government and other NGOsexamined her for a total of about five hours; trauma experts from UNICEF also met her.... Continuations of Amina's education, so abruptly disrupted will definitely be a property of the federal government."

On the quest to rescue the remaining tormented girls from the shackles of terrorists, Buhari promised thus:

"Rest assured that this administration will continue to do what it can do to rescue the Chibok girls who are still in Boko Haram captivity. Amina's rescue gives us new hope and offers a unique opportunity to vital information." [63]

PRESIDENCY TO BBOG: DON'T GIVE UP

The Presidency early July 2016 appealed to the officials and members of the BBOG campaign group not to dither in their support to the government in the war against terrorism and continuing efforts to free the remaining Chibok school girls and other captives held by the rebels in the north east. The BBOG had in a previous biting statement said President Muhammadu Buhari had 'broken all promises' made about rescuing the missing girls and that the government had been 'lackadaisical' in the mission to secure the languishing young women.

However, in a Presidential Statement Senior Special Assistant to Muhammadu Buhari on Media and Publicity, Garba Shehu, asserted that in the past one year of the administration the Nigerian military had stepped up operations against the insurgents resulting in the liberation of territories and hostages to normal life. He as well stated that ferocious assaults on the rebels in the Sambisa Forest had drastically reduced their guerrilla capacity, yielding the capture of hundreds of them. Army records, he said, showed rescue of 15,000 captives from February till date. He concluded that:

"President Muhammadu Buhari will never make bogus promises or play to the gallery. It is misleading of anyone to preach that the Chibok girls are within an easy grasp. If the military knew where they are held they will bring will bring them home today. The Presidency is open to renew cooperation with the BBOG group, international bodies, religious groups, social workers and others who are assisting to ensure that those who have so far been rescued get the needed support to make a full recovery and be re-integrated fully with society." [64]

CHIBOL GIRLS WEEPING IN NEW VIDEO
There was great misery among some of the abducted Chibok girls as they were displayed by their captives in a new video on August 14, 2016. In the video released by a splinter group of Boko Haram led by Abubakar Shekau about fifty of the school girls kidnapped over two years earlier were shown wiping their eyes with their *hijabs*. One of them was carrying a scrawny baby of about a year old. A masked Boko Haram fighter in camouflage who introduced the girls in the film in Hausa language said that forty of the adducted girls had been married off to some insurgents, urging their parents to appeal to the Nigerian government to speed up negotiations for their release in exchange for terrorist commanders held in various prisons. A transcription of the entire message read thus:

"This is a message from Jam'atu Ahlis Sunna Lidda Awati Wal Jihad under the leadership of Abu Muhammad ibn Muhammad Abubakar As-Shekau. We are sending a special message to the parents of the Chibok girls and the Nigerian government.

"We thank God for giving us the opportunity to send this message to the parents of the girls. It pleased God to let us have these girls in our captivity for over two years now. Our first message is to the parents of the girls, to let them know that their daughters are still with us, some of them. I also want to tell them to ask the Nigerian Government to release our brethren especially those in Maiduguri, Lagos and Abuja, and other places in Nigeria. They should be released immediately.

"You all know we have the girls but God never allowed you to know their location and you will never know. You keep lying in your media that you will rescue them. They have been with us for over two years yet you can't even know where they are. You have just been lying about these girls; people should know that.

"Also for over two years that we have been with these girls, about forty of them are married; some are dead as a result of airstrike by infidels. We will show you a video of how your own aircraft dropped a bomb that killed some of these girls. Some of the girls have fractures and other forms of injuries as a result of the airstrikes.

"As you can see these are the girls. All we want is for you to release our brethren; otherwise you will never get

these girls, God willing. This, in short, is our message to the Federal Government and the parents of the Chibok girls. As long as the government does not release our people we will also never release these girls. That is our message.

"I specially inform our people in captivity in Lagos that they should be patient and continue with their prayers. God will take us to where no one expects and we will rescue them. All those in Lagos, Maiduguri and other southern parts of the country, keep praying; very soon we will rescue you.

"Let me conclude this message by saying that many people have been coming to us, lying that they were sent by the Nigerian Government to get the girls released. Let the government and the whole world know that we have not sent anyone to negotiate with the government on our behalf over these girls. We have dealt with you in the past before and you know our recommended negotiators. If you need to, you should talk to them. We don't use our own people to negotiate with you. We use your own people such as journalists to talk with you. We have not sent any other persons. You know that we prefer to use journalists known to you.

"Let me say again, release our people and we release your girls; otherwise they will never be released. If you think you have the power to come and rescue them, go ahead and try. President Buhari, your army has been lying to you that they have finished us. Let them try and see if they can rescue the girls alive."

After his speech, the Boko Haram presenter introduced one of the girls who said her name was Maila Yakubu (later identified as Dorcas Yakubu). She started speaking in English and the accent later changed to Chibok language. She explained that she was from Chibok and abducted about two years earlier from Government Secondary School Chibok, pleading with the Federal Government to accept the offer of the insurgents for their release from despair. Her speech translated in English read thus:

"We are not happy living here. I'm begging our parents to meet the government to release their people so that we can be released. We are suffering here. There is no kind of suffering we haven't seen. Tell the government to give them [Boko Haram] their people so we can also come home to be with you. ... There is nothing you, or we can do about this, but to get their people back to them, so we can go home..."

The father of one of the missing Nigerian schoolgirls abducted from Chibok told CNN he was delighted to see her alive on a new video released by the terrorist group Sunday. Dorcas Yakubu was identified by her father, Yakubu Kabu, at Abuja in the presence of Dr. Manasseh Allen, spokesperson of the Kibaku Area Development Association.

The BBOG in a statement signed by Mrs. Oby Ezekwesili and Aisha Yesufu and read at their Unity Fountain camp on Sunday said that identification of the girls by their parents lent strong credibility that they were the real Chibok School Girls kidnapped on 14th April 2014. The declaration of BBOG read thus:

"After listening to the call of Dorcas Yakubu, we demand an immediate action, as well as a result-oriented response plan by the government. The excuse of a split within the terrorists' ranks or a period of validation of the authenticity of their claims will not suffice this time. We shall press these demands with a march to the Presidential Villa in the next few days."

The group expressed disenchantment over the failure of the government to make use of the information it received from the earlier video of the girls in April. On this they said:

"In the aftermath of an earlier video, we repeatedly called on government to treat the information as the missing piece of credible information it was seeking. Not even the return of Amina Ali, a Chibok girl, inspired the sort of response we demanded."

They called on the governments of the United States, United Kingdom, Canada, France, China, Australia, Israel and global agencies like the United Nations and the African Union to re-engage by adopting a strategic rescue position to free the languishing girls.
Co-founder of the BBOG, Oby Ezekweisili, grieved by the sight of the girls, said:

"We are not going to let up until this government acts. Let them get ready because every day we shall be marching to the (Presidential) villa. These girls were kidnapped while getting education, which annoyed me to no end. It is on this basis of education that I became what I am today. If it means marching to the villa everyday to demand the release of our chibok girls, so be it.... Only three choices are available – negotiate to release our girls, use the military operation or a combination of the two. We don't want to see a fourth video."

Also, Esther Yakubu, the mother of the abducted girl that spoke, Dorcas, said she broke down while watching the video of her daughter. She revealed that in addition to her daughter, she recognized about twenty other abducted girls. She averred:

"I recognized Saratu Ayuba, Awa Ishaiya and others. In that video, Dorcas has grown up a little and she is slimmer. I cried when I saw her in the video. That is only change I observe, but I thank God she is alive."

Responding to the new video Nigerian Minister for Information, Lai Mohammed, in a press statement said:

"We are on top of the situation but we are being extremely careful because the situation has been compounded by the girls in the leadership of Boko Haram.... We are also being guided by the need to ensure the safety of the girls."

Consequently, the Nigerian Army declared three Nigerians: Ahmed Salkida (journalist), Aisha Wakil (a lawyer aka Mama Boko Haram) and Ahmed Bolori, also a lawyer wanted for concealing information on the location of the abducted Chibok school girls. The next day (15th August) both Aisha Wakil and Ahmed Bolori presented themselves to the army, claiming there was no basis for the military or the Federal Government to declare them wanted as they had committed no crimes.

Meanwhile Amina Nkek, one of the abducted Chibok School Girls that escaped from the lair of the terrorists, three months after her rescue told CNN she wanted to be re-united with her Boko Haram husband. In

her conversation with newsmen at an undisclosed location in Abuja on Tuesday, August 16 Amina said:
"I'm not comfortable with the way I'm being kept from him."

As if speaking directly to her husband identified as Mohammed Hayatu, Amina who was discovered with a baby, Safiya, said:

"I want you to know that I'm still thinking about you and just because we are separated doesn't mean I have forgotten about you."[65]

BBOG LAUNCHES TWO WEEKS OF GLOBAL ACTION ON CHIBOK GIRLS
March to the Presidential Villa, 22nd August

Consequent on the latest video released by Boko Haram on 14 August 2016 showing some of the abducted Chibok school girls in torment, the BBOG launched a two-week Global Action to compel the Nigerian government and the International Community to intensify efforts for their immediate rescue. The programme commenced with a protest march early morning on 22 August to the State House, Abuja. Coincidentally, they were joined by another oppressed group known as Immigration 2000, protesting their unwarranted dismissal by government some months after recruitment, commissioning and deployment. As usual they were led by principals Dr. Mrs. Oby Ezekwesili and Aisha Yesufu. On reaching the entrance to the Presidential Villa the troop was confronted by a barricade of police men and women, and officials of the NSCD and DSS.

Mrs. Oby Ezekwesili opened dialogue by asking the police why they stopped the march to see Mr. President. The police officer in charge of operations at the gate, CSP Obasi Chuks, said he had acted to prevent the campaign from cascading to violence because the protesters, according to him, had not followed the required 'process' to enter the State House. Although it was explained to him that the notice of our coming was duly submitted to the Presidency, he remained intractable.

As a result, members of the crusaders sat on the Independence Layout road while the leaders arranged the table and chairs to commence the day's crusade there. The anchor was indefatigable freedom fighter, Florence Uzor, inviting speakers from the group to address Nigerians on issues of corruption, the abysmal state of IDPs and relief measures, Boko Haram insurgency, devastated communities, and pressure for the immediate rescue of the suffering Chibok school girls.

Yours sincerely gave a talk on inveterate corruption in government institutions. Mr. Hosea Tsambido— Chairman of the Chibok Community in Abuja, expressed grave anger at the continued languish of the young women in the bush. He declared that if the Federal Government was not ready to help then, they should be granted territorial independence to seek protection elsewhere.

Highlight of the campaign was that the BBOG called on the Federal Government of Nigeria to immediately establish a **Rescue Monitoring Team** for the abducted Chibok girls, which would comprise representatives of the government, parents of the girls, KADA Community and the BBOG group. In her briefing to the press leader, Aisha Yesufu, stated that such a monitoring team would act as a transparent mechanism for feedback on evidence of the President's sustained action towards bringing back the kidnapped girls. She implored the Federal Government to effectively exploit recent videos from Boko Haram concerning the girls in torment. Such information including the 'proof of evidence' video released by CNN on 14th April, she said, should be actionable and utilitarian.[66]

Second March to Aso Rock Blocked by the Police

True to plan, the BBOG again marched to the Presidential Villa, Abuja to confer with President Muhammadu Buhari on the fate of 218 Chibok school girls under Boko Haram captivity and torment. Once more they were barred from entering the State House by cordon of police men and women mounted at the Independence Layout Road Junction. The police could neither provide an answerable squadron leader nor give reasons for the blockade. Consequently, the BBOG arranged their tables and chairs to start the day's event.

As usual proceedings commenced with the second stanza of the National Anthem. Thereafter there were media reports on the Chibok girls, Boko Haram insurgency the condition of IDPs and resettlement of ravaged communities—by Abubakar. There was a depressing report on the attack of Shawa Village in Askira Uba Local Government of Borno State by Boko Haram. Speeches were delivered by members on the worsening economic situation of the country and the exigency to bring the girls back home.

The parents of the abducted girls took turns to address Nigerians on the misery they cope with everyday. Among them was Mrs. Yakubu, mother of Dorcas Yakubu who addressed the world in the Boko Haram video of 14th August. She lamented the continued stay of their daughters in the wild because of government insensitivity. Reverend Enoch Mark, father of two abducted girls and having recently suffered a Cardiovascular Accident because of daily brooding, deplored the delinquency of the Nigerian Government to rescue the kidnapped young women. In his outrage, he said:

"Many Chibok parents voted you because we believed that you would ensure the return of our daughters. You promised us that you are a military man and that you cannot lie. You said the war will not be over until the girls are back.

"Now we hear shouts of victory. And you turn around and say you do not know how to get out daughters. Former President Sani Abacha told us that no country can fight war for up to 24 hours without its government knowing about it. If the president lacks intelligence to bring back the girls let him resign.

In a press statement read by Mrs. Oby Ezekwesili the group reviewed the Chibok Girls debacle and made the following declarations:

We acknowledge the courage and gallantry of our soldiers in the frontlines, the Multinational Joint Task Force and the Civilian JTF, and urge them to remain resilient in the face of attacks as these. Their labour and sacrifices shall never be in vain. The opening of a

Nigerian Air force mobile clinic in Bama, the only functional healthcare centre in the area, is highly applauded.

"However, reports regrettably show our troops at the frontlines complained about their salaries and emoluments. This they say I weaken their morale in the fight against insurgency as the food they are fed is in no way better than that served prisoners. This is unacceptable and we call for an investigation."

While requesting for a 'Special Envoy' for the north east with the critical role of mobilizing the private sector, Nigerian public and the International Community., the group said:

"Reports from former Head of State, Yakubu Gowon, after a meeting with Mr. President, suggest that the Federal Government's position remains a 'lack of credible intelligence'. Coming over seven (7) months since our engagement with Mr. President on January 14 and considering the lack of feedback on rescue efforts, this strengthens the position that there has been no focused, coherent and consistent operation to rescue our #Chibok Girls.

"Having submitted four cogent reasons why it could not be said that there is a lack of credible intelligence during our meeting in January, and three further reasons just three days ago, the discussion must shift from 'credible intelligence' to 'political will' to decide on a line of action and act. This is especially so because Mr. President acknowledged the level of first-person intelligence that was to be obtained from the debriefing of our #Chibok Girl, Amina Ali, while receiving her on May.

"Today, Day 864 since the abduction of our girls; time has completely run out. It is time to take decisive action and bring them home. NO MORE DELAYS!!!

"Another key issue in last seventy-two hours is the military's announcement that Boko Haram leader, Abubakar Shekau, was fatally wounded during air raids. We want it on record that this is at least the fourth time the Nigerian state has triumphantly announced killing this fellow. When will he finally die?

"Our advocacy has remained focused, issue-based and consistent. It has remained administration-neutral. And while government may come and go, we have vowed that if the girls are not back we remain committed to the cause.

"So, we restate our SPECIFIC DEMANDS to Mr. President:
That Mr. President should swiftly make a firm decision for their immediate rescue based on the three available options: -
1. Military operation
2. Negotiation with the terrorists
3. Combination of 1 and 2
Mr. President must access the wealth of information and state resources available to pursue a lowest risk option of these three. That Mr. President addresses Nigerians on the rescue plan and timeline of our #Chibok Girls.

"That Mr. President immediately constitutes a Chibok Girls Rescue Monitoring Team made up of representatives of Federal Government, parents of #Chibok Girls, KADA (the Chibok Community) and

#BringBackOurGirls. This multi- stakeholder's platform should act as a transparent mechanism to for feedback of evidence of Mr. President's sustained action towards bringing back our #Chibok Girls.

"Mr. President should immediately preside over National Emergency in the north-east Conference to articulate a cohesive plan to the Humanitarian Crisis and designate a Special Envoy responsible for the inter-agency collaboration work required. Mr. President should pay attention to the Fulani herdsmen menace ravaging the entire country.

"That Mr. President directs the Attorney-General and EFCC to set up a Special Desk with the responsibility for fast-tracking the trial of the arms procurement fund and providing regular updates. We reject any suspension or termination of any of the trials without reaching a legal conclusion. The BBOG concluded that President Muhammadu Buhari must 'now' exercise redoubtable and dedicated leadership on rescuing OUR #Chibok Girls as they were his own daughters.

"As Nigerians, we join the parents of the abducted girls in saying: #BringBackOurGirls
MR. PRESIDENT: NO MORE EXCUSES!
MR. PRESIDENT: NO MORE DELAYS!
MR. PRESIDENT: NO MORE PREVARICATIONS!
MR. PRESIDENT: NO MORE ASSURANCES WITHOUT FOCUSED ACTION!
MR. PRESIDENT: DECIDE NOW!
MR. PRESIDENT: ACT NOW; WE WANT RESULTS!

Meanwhile, the British Government pledged to do whatever it could to help in rescuing the girls. The UK High Commissioner to Nigeria, Paul Arkwright, declared in a conference with members of the BBOG in Abuja that:

"UK stands in solidarity with the Chibok people; the girls are global citizens; so, we will do whatever we can to partner the Nigerian government to help find the girls."[67]

NIGERIAN GOVERNMENT AGAIN CONSIDERS PRISONER SWAP

Following intense pressure from the Bring Back Our Girls group and the International Community, Nigerian President, Muhammadu Buhari, on 28th August 2016 in far away Kenya agreed to swap the languishing Chibok school girls with Boko Haram leaders held in Nigerian prisons. The President spoke to journalists in Nairobi on the sidelines of the 6th Tokyo International Conference on African Development (TICADA). However, President Buhari gave the following conditions:

1. That the Boko Haram members should appoint an internationally recognized non-governmental organization (NGO) if they do not want to talk to the government directly.
2. Convince the NGO that they are holding the girls.
3. Should identify the Boko Haram leaders they want the Federal Government to release from detention.

He emphasized that his government was prepared to negotiate with bonafide leaders of Boko Haram. According to Buhari:

"If they do not want to talk to us directly, let them pick an internationally recognized Non-Governmental Organization (NGO), convince them that they are holding the girls, and that they want Nigeria to release a number of Boko Haram leaders in detention, which they are supposed to know. If they do it through the 'modified leadership' of Boko Haram and they talk with an internationally recognized NGO then Nigeria will be prepared to discuss their release."

Public analysts had viewed Mr. President's statement as shirking responsibilities and granting powers to Boko Haram to go ahead with every negotiation that might bring the girls home in lieu of employing the utilitarian machineries of government.[68]

Third protest to Aso Rock Barred by the Police
The troop departed the Unity Fountain at 11:10 am led by Dr. Mrs. Oby Ezekwesili and Aisha Yesufu. The demonstration this time was spectacular: members walked in silence, their lips sealed. The entrance to the State House, as usual, was blocked by the police without explanations.

Arriving at 11:45 am barred, members of the BBOG sat on the bare tarred road leading to the Villa in absolute mournful silence for over thirty minutes. At 12:12 am Bukky opened session by announcing to the audience that it was exactly 869 days since the Chibok School girls were abducted on April 14, 2014. While some of them escaped from the insurgents, 218 were still being held captive—their immediate release being the reason for our coming to see Mr. President. She then introduced Mrs. Ezekwesili to read the press statement of the day.

The statement was a follow-up to the BBOG's declaration 72 hours earlier: that it was their 3rd attempt at engaging Mr. President on the plight of the suffering Chkbok girls but unfortunately, they were blocked again.

She stated that their coming to the State House was in response to the plea for rescue video released by Boko Haram. Information available to the BBOG indicated that no evidence of persuasive, dedicated and result-targeted action had been observed from the government.

The group also expressed sympathy with all IDPs throughout the country and called for their thorough rehabilitation and resettlement. This 3rd march coincided with International Day of Disappeared and Missing Persons, being launched in Nigeria by the Human Rights Commission and allied global agencies. It would be recalled that the BBOG had approached the National Human Rights Commission in July 2015 seeking the establishment of a register of missing persons in Nigeria.

After the address, the group quietly marched back to the Unity Fountain. They stopped briefly at the Military Cenotaph at Eagle Square to observe one minute silence in honour of Nigerian soldiers. At the Fountain, the day's event was reviewed as spectacular and productive.

As part of their international mobilization for quick action on the missing Chibok girls, the BBOG at 2:30 am same day visited the Canadian High Commission. The embassy promised to continue to align with global and Nigerian Government efforts to rescue the girls.

Drama as BBOG, pro-Buhari group clash

On the 4rd march to the State House, 6th September 2016 a mild drama ensued between members of BringBackOurGirls and the police who prevented them from embarking on their pacific campaign in Abuja. The redoubtable crusaders, who gathered at their usual Unity Fountain base as early as 6 am, commenced their peaceful procession at exactly 9:30. A police officer, Abiodun Alamatu, approached their leadership, demanding a police permit. Leader of the group, Mrs. Oby Ezekwesili, straight away presented to the police man acknowledgement copies of the letters submitted to the FCT Police Command after which they could progress.

Not satisfied with the letter, the police again stopped the humanitarian troop halfway to the Presidential Villa Junction, insisting that the group did not get police approval to conduct the demonstration. Under the headship of Mr. M.D. Garba, a Deputy Commissioner, the police barricaded the road thus forcing the BBOG members to surge through the blockade of riot policemen and officers, and eventually got to the entrance of the Villa. The march brought about grave traffic jam.

As the police were busy preventing the BBOG from having access to the Aso Villa, another group allegedly hired by the government as claque, identifying themselves as 'With Buhari We Stand', had already passed through the junction, singing and rebuking the BBOG's, constant demand for the release of the Chibok girls. Not minding the pervasive mission of the pro-Buhari group, the BBOG went ahead to paste the photographs of each of the missing 218 Chibok girls on the walkways and pavements.

In her address, Aisha Yesufu said:

"It is not a privilege to bring back our girls; it is not right. "The option of do-nothing, unfortunately, is what the government is doing."

The #BBOG group decried that the police allowed Mr. Buhari's praise-singing protesters to go close to the villa gate but refused to allow the #BBOG camp to exercise their fundamental human rights. Leader of #BBOG, Oby Ezekwesili, said the day marked 871 days since the Chibok girls were abducted. She condemned the counter-protest, which she said was aimed at undermining their campaign, insisting they would not allow the president to rest until the girls were rescued.

Mrs. Ezekwesili said:

"There is nothing to be cheerful for. We have sat with the President two
times and nothing concrete has been done. The
government has decided to curtail the freedom of
movement of the people by stopping us from exercising
our fundamental human rights."

Addressing Nigerians, leader of the pro-Buhari group, Idris King, described the kidnapping of the Chibok girls as a scam. He however paradoxically, stated that the Buhari administration was doing everything to rescue the girls alive. The two contending groups were prevented by the police from attacking each other.

When contacted to explain why the police prevented the BBOG from embarking on their peaceful march which they had been carrying out for some time, the Police Public Relations Officer (PPRO), Anjuri Mamzah, denied the assertion. He insisted the police did not prevent members of the group or any other group from embarking on protest.

Nevertheless, the FCT Police Command had earlier on September 5, issued a statement advising individuals and groups wishing to carry out any demonstration to notify the Commissioner in writing and secure approval. The statement issued at about 9 pm in the night read:

"The FCT Police Command has observed with serious
concern the flagrant disregard for the law some
individuals and group of persons who lay siege to the
Federal Capital City in the form of protests and
demonstrations. These indiscriminate actions which are
carried out in disorderly and sometimes riotous manner,
create unwarranted tension and apprehension among
law-abiding citizens and in the process, obstruct
legitimate business activities. The command hereby

advises any person or group of persons who wish to embark on any demonstration to notify the Commissioner of Police FCT in writing and secure approval." [69]

FEDERAL GOVERNMENT REVEALS ATTEMPTS TO RESCUE CHIBOK GIRLS

On the 15th of September 2016, the Federal Government of Nigeria announced that the security agencies had made three failed attempts to rescue the languishing Chibok school girls from the lair of insurgents. The Minister of Information and Culture, Lai Mohammed, made this disclosure at a press conference to keep informed the public on efforts of government to freeing the girls. He disclosed that the moves were thwarted by a contact group and the division in the ranks of Boko Haram. Narrating he said that in July 2015, a contact group was in touch with government with credible facts confirming that some of the girls were alive. According to Lai Mohammed:

*"Precisely on July 17, 2015, the DSS opened negotiations process with the group holding the Chibok girls.
However, in return for the release of some of these girls, the group also made some demands. These included the release of some of their fighters arrested including some involved in major terrorist actions, resulting in several fatalities, and others who were experts in manufacturing of locally assembled explosives. This was difficult to accept, but appropriate security agencies had to again inform Mr. President of these demands, and its viewed implications. Again, Mr President gave his assent believing that the overall release of these girls remains paramount and sacrosanct.*

Mr. Lai Mohammed further divulged that the government and the security departments fashioned out the modalities of the hostage swap which included creating the neutral haven or expedient venue of swap and working out the logistic details; the first step for the swap agreed to start on August 1, 2015. He said:

"On 4th of August 2015, the persons who were to be part of the swap arrangements and all others involved in the operation were transported to Maiduguri. This team, with the lead facilitator, continued the contact with the group holding the Chibok girls. The Service was able to further prove to the group its sincerity, as it established communication contact between it and its detained members.

"All things were in place for the swap which was mutually agreed. Expectations were high. Unfortunately, after more than two (2) weeks of negotiation and bargains, the group, just at the dying moments, issued new set of demands, never bargained for or discussed by the group before the movement to Maiduguri. All this while, the security agencies waited patiently. This development stalled what would have been the first release process of the Chibok girls."

He additionally stated that on November 13, 2015, another fresh bargain process with the group was commenced. Concerning the new deal, he averred:

"This time, there was the need to discuss a fresh component to avoid issues that had stalled the former arrangement. There were, however, some problems that many may not discern, but should be expected in this kind of situation. Some critical persons within the group who played such vital role in August 2015 were discovered to be dead during combat action or because of the emerging rift among members of the group then.

"These two factors delayed the process. In spite of these, negotiation continued on new modalities. By November 30, 2015 it was becoming glaring that the division among the group was more profound. This affected the swap process."

The Minister equally disclosed that as at December 10, 2015, another negotiation line was in place but it was likewise futile because of the capricious demands of Boko Haram. Concerning latest efforts to bring the girls back home, he said:

"Officers and men have sacrificed their time and energy, and some have already paid the supreme price since the abduction of the Chibok girls, fighting for the safe release of the girls. Many friendly countries and organizations have equally been very forthcoming in providing their human and technological resources to assist in the process. They are still doing so. We cannot as a nation ignore these sacrifices."

Mohammed appreciated the tenacity of Nigerians in the war against terrorism. He appealed to the parents of the Chibok girls for patience and time while the government intensifies effort to free the girls. To the mournful Chibok parents, he said:

"We are with you; we feel your pains and shall not relent until we succeed in bringing home our girls and every other citizen abducted by the group."

He urged those who had shown concern in resolving the matter (indirectly referring to the Bring Back Our Girls and other humanitarian Nigerians) to continue their trust on the efforts of government to deal with the catastrophe. However, the government failed to give information on IRS, fresh swap negotiations and establishment of location of the girls since January 2016. On their part, the BBOG welcomed the development and asked for facts on latest efforts by the government and military to deliver the abducted girls.[70]

BUHARI INVITES UN TO MEDIATE CHIBOK GIRLS RESCUE
President Muhammadu Buhari on 21 September 2016 in New York, United States emphasized his administration's readiness to swap the abducted schoolgirls with captured Boko Haram insurgents. He therefore called the UN to help as mediators in the crisis. Buhari gave the heart-felt invitation at the bilateral meeting with the United Nations Secretary-General, Ban Ki-moon, on the sidelines of the 71st UN General Assembly in New York. Re-iterating his resolve to rescue the girls, Buhari said:

"The challenge is in getting credible and bonafide leadership of Boko Haram to discuss with. The split in the insurgents group is not helping matters. Government had reached out, ready to negotiate, but it became difficult to identify credible leaders. We will welcome intermediaries such as UN outfits to step in."

The President underscored that the teachings of Boko Haram were not Islamic, since neither Islam nor any other religion advocates hurting the innocent. According to the President:

"The fact that they kill men, women, children, and other people wantonly, and shout Allahu Akbar (God is great) shows that they do not know that Allah at all. If they did, they would not shed innocent blood." [71]

BOKO HARAM AT LAST RELEASES 21 CHIBOK GIRLS

In the early hours of 13 October 2016 Islamic Jihadist group, Boko Haram, released to the Nigerian Government 21 of the remaining 218 Chibok School Girls abducted on April14, 2014. The deal for the freedom of the young girls was mediated by Switzerland and the ICRC. The insurgents transported the girls to the northeastern Nigerian town of Banki, near the border with Cameroon from where they were picked by Nigerian security agents. They were first presented to the Governor of Borno State, Shema, before being flown to a DSS reception facility in Abuja. A child born to one of the girls and believed by medical experts to be about 20 months old was also freed, according to sources from the State House, Abuja.

The names of the released girls as confirmed by the government and the Bring Back Our Girls include: Mary Usman Bulama, Jummai John, Blessing Abana, Lugwa Sanda, Comfort Habila, Maryam Basheer, Comfort Amos, Glory Mainta, Saratu Emannuel, Deborah Ja'afaru, Rahab Ibrahim, Helen Musa, Maryamu Lawan, Rebecca Ibrahim, Asabe Goni, Deborah Andrawus, Agnes Gapani, Saratu Markus, Glory Dama, Pindah Nuhu and Rebecca Mallam. In his address to journalists after meeting the girls, Vice President Yomi Osinbajo, said:

"I met them about an hour ago and I can confirm they are in good health. In the next few days or months we will be able to negotiate the release of more of the girls."

He denied the speculation of ransom payment or prisoner swap thus:

"Absolutely, there was no exchange of any kind."

In his tweeter handle he wrote:

"Dawn, dusk, almost a 1000 day. Twenty-one of our girls are back. It is my joy to welcome you home. The nation has been waiting for you."

In a press statement confirming their release Minister for Information, Lai Mohammed, said their release is *"a result of the round-the-clock efforts by the administration to put a closure to the sad issue."* He further told reporters that:

"We see this as a credible first step in the eventual release of all the Chibok girls in captivity."

The BBOG which has been standing for the girls daily for over two years in a joyful statement signed by leaders Oby Ezekwesili and Aisha Yesufu welcoming the release of the girls on Thursday, said:

"This wonderful development confirms what we have always known about the capacity of our government to rescue our #ChibokGirls.

"While awaiting further details, we take this opportunity to salute the work of our security services at the front lines – the commitment, resilience and tireless efforts of our members of the Multi-National Joint Task Force and the civilian JTF.

"We also thank the International Committee of the Red Cross, the Swiss government and all negotiators involved in securing the release.

"Following this development, we trust that our government will continue to work to keep the safety, security, and well-being of the other girls a high priority.

"We further urge the international community to continue to support our government's effort to rescue all other abducted Nigerians, so that parents, the Chibok community, the nation, and the world can finally put an end to this nightmare once and for all"[72]

CHIBOK GIRLS: WE STAYED WITHOUT FOOD FOR 40 DAYS

It was a moment of tears and happiness when the released 21 Chibok girls were re-united with their parents at a thanksgiving church service on Sunday, 16th October. The event held at the DSS facility in Abuja was attended by: Minister of Information and Culture Alhaji Lai Mohammed, Minister of Women Affairs, Hajiya Jummai Alhassan, Chairman of Chibok Local Government Council, Mr Yaga Yarakawa, Chairman of Abducted Chibok Girls' Parents Association, Mr Yakubu Nkaki, and a member of the Chibok community in Abuja, Mr. Hosea Tsambido.

Gloria Dame (being Number 139 on the BBOG movement's list of abducted girls) who spoke in Hausa on behalf of the girls after the service, said:

"I did not know that a day like this will come that we will be dancing and giving thanks to God among people.

"For one month and 10 days we stayed without food. I narrowly escaped bomb blast in the forest.

168

"We are praying to God to touch the heart of Boko Haram to repent and we are calling on Nigerians to pray and fast for the release of our remaining ones in captivity."

Tears flowed freely as parents arrived and took turns to identify their daughters, while one woman simply carried her daughter on her back in ecstasy. Unfortunately, some leaders of the BBOG who came to welcome the girls were shut out of the event. They expressed amazement at "some people" being too desperate to make political gains out of the entire situation. According to a staunch BBOG member, Dr. Emman Shehu:

"Our eyes are on the goal and not the glitz of photo opportunities." [73]

ONE MORE CHIBOK SCHOOL GIRL RESCUED
Troops of 121 Battalion, Nigerian Army, deployed at Pulka, Gwoza Local Government Area, Borno conducting *Operation Lafiya Dole*, on 5th of November rescued another kidnapped Chibok girl, Maryam Ali Maiyanga. A statement issued by the Army Spokesman, Colonel Sani Usman Kukasheka, in Abuja revealed that the girl was discovered while the troops were screening some escapees from Boko Haram terrorists' hideout in Sambisa forest at about 6 a.m. In the press release, Col Usman said:

"She was discovered to be carrying a 10-month-old son, named Ali. She has been taken to the unit's medical facility for proper medical check."

Confirming the rapturous information, the BBOG through their public relations officer, Sesugh Akume stated thus:

"We welcome news of the return of another of our abducted #ChibokGirls. Reports from the Acting Director of the Army Public Relations, Colonel Sani Usman Kukasheka, state that Maryam Ali Maiyanga was found amongst a group of fellow escapees by troops of 121 Battalion, Nigerian Army, deployed at Pulka, Gwoza Local Government Area, Borno State.

"Preliminary investigations on our part, show that Maryam Ali (Number 198 on our list), a school prefect, is from Askira Uba and was abducted along with her twin, Halima Ali (Number 197), who is yet to return. We shall update the public with more details as necessary.

"We applaud the federal government under President Muhammadu Buhari, the military and other security formations working day and night to rout the terrorists and rescue all Nigerians in captivity.

"The news of the death of the Commanding Officer of the 272 Task Force Tank Battalion, Lieutenant Colonel Muhammed Abu Ali, a highly-rated young officer, and 4 other members of his team in a separate incident at Mallam Fatori, is unfortunate and saddening. We send our heartfelt condolences especially to their families, and the Nigerian military."

With the delivery of Maryam Maiyanga, the BBOG had still to press for the rescue of the remaining 196 girls in the hand of insurgents, yet to regain their freedom.[74]

ANOTHER CHIBOK GIRL FOUND WITH BABY

The Nigerian Army announced on 5th January 2017 that its troops named *Operation Lafia Dole*, fighting the Boko

Haram insurgents, rescued another Chibok school girl, Rakiya Abubakar with her six-month old baby in the Alagano area of Damboa Local Government of Borno State. With the delivery of Rakiya the number of Chibok shool girls still in the hands of the terrorists (according to the record of the BBOG) remained 195.Preliminary investigations revealed that Rakiya, sent for medical examination, was the daughter of Abubakar Gali Mulima and Habiba Abubakar of Chibok. President of Nigeria, Muhammadu Buhari, welcomed the abducted girl, praised the gallantry of the Nigerian soldiers and gave hope for the rescue of the outstanding young school women kidnapped since April 14, 2014.

While relaying the rescue of the girl the Director of Army Public Relations, Brigadier-General Sanny Usman, citing information from the Commander of *Operation Lafia Dole*—Major-General Lucky Irabor said the army had within one week arrested over 1,400 Boko Haram insurgents in Sambisa Forest and other places.

In another development, the Red Cross revealed that refugee women in the Lake Chad Basin were forced into prostitution to survive. It ascribed this ugly trend to the Boko Haram rebellion which had evacuated about five million people out of their homes. According to **Simon Brooks**, head of ICRC's delegation in Cameroon:

"It is extraordinary to see a woman and her family and they have nothing other than what they have been given. The children are clearly malnourished and it is just hopeless. When you don't have the means to survive, you will go begging for it. It is loss of dignity when you have to resort something to like that (prostitution) just to keep

your children alive—fraternizing with people who have money."[75]

GLOBAL WEEK OF ACTION: BBOG MARKS 1000 DAYS OF ABDUCTION

It was a daily sit-out standing for their release. The event commenced on Sunday, 8th January 2017, with a march to the State House. The protest was planned to show appreciation to the government and the Nigerian Army for rescuing so far 24 of the abducted young women, and to press for the delivery of the remaining girls. It was a lugubrious occasion as the BBOG observed 1000 days of the kidnap of the Chibok girls and 985 days of daily demanding the delivery of the remaining 195 young women still languishing in the lair of Boko Haram insurgents.

Members of the indefatigable BBOG as usual at 3 p.m. assembled at their Unity Fountain camp to the siege of unprecedented number of truck loads, pick-ups and buses of manifold species of police men and women armed to the teeth. Their object was to prevent the group from proceeding to the State House. However, the camp played a fast one on the police by surreptitiously arranging to re-assemble on the road beside Transcorp Hilton Hotel in lieu of marching straight from the Fountain.

Being outsmarted, the security agents drove fast to block the entrance to the Presidential Villa. The BBOG group chanted their solidarity songs to a welcome barricade of beefy police. They continued with their catchphrase:

What are we demanding?

Bring back our girls now and alive!

At this juncture leader, Dr. Oby Ezekwesili, demanded to know why they were blocked. The head of police on duty explained that they had order to restrain the group to the Villa entrance. He appealed to the camp to comport themselves so that they would not be seen as attacking 'the system'.

Being law-abiding, the BBOG started the day's programme with recitation of the first and second stanzas of the National Anthem. Coordinator, Aisha Yesufu, read the press statement of the BBOG, chronicling the events of the Chibok girls' abduction since April 14, 2014, the number (24) of the girls rescued and the need to secure the remaining 195 from the hands of savages. She concluded by stating the schedule of the Global Week of Action which would include protests in support of the military, the fight against fabric corruption, revamping the Nigerian decadent education system, etc. Members pasted photographs of the remaining missing Chibok girls on the road side rails with police permission. They closed with the National Anthem and proceeded back to their assembly ground.[76]

Subsequent marches to the Presidential on which the BBOG were, as usual blocked by security personnel took place as follows:

Monday January 9: Internally Displaced Persons—the condition of refugees in the north and the urgency of their proper rehabilitation and resettlement

Tuesday January 10: March for the welfare of our military including the soldiers that assiduously and arduously prosecute the war against terrorists at the frontlines. We accentuated the expediency of adequately equipping them and motivating them to carry out the operations. There should be proper documentation and resolution of cases of soldiers who had died or were missing during the war.

Wednesday January 11: March against endemic corruption in Ministries, Departments and Agencies in Nigeria. Yours truly delivered a speech on the need to forcefully curb fabric corruption to buoy economic growth in the country.

Thursday January 12: Endangered Education—the need for effective education of children especially the girl child. Education at all levels should be a programme of 'read with your brain and pass with your brain' instead of passing examinations with sex and money.

Friday January 13: Girl-child Vulnerability—the need to care for and protect the girl-child against moral and material neglect, and abuse in line with section 17(3f) of the Nigerian constitution.

Saturday January 14: Insecurity in Zamfara, Zaria, Jos, Enugu, Agatu, Southern Kaduna, etc. There is the exigency to arrest inter-ethnic clashes and wanton destruction of lives and property in those areas.

VISIT TO SAMBISA FOREST: WHAT WE SAW, WHAT SHOULD BE DONE – BBOG

INTRODUCTION

Today is Day 1012 of the abduction of our Chibok girls, taken from their school, Government Secondary School, Chibok by terrorists on 14 April 2014, Day 602 under President Muhammadu Buhari's watch, and Day 997 of consistent daily advocacy for their return as 195 of them remain missing, Day 1000 of our <u>Chibok Girls</u> abduction.

On January 8, 2017, our movement held a Global Week of Action (GWA) with seven days of twenty-four hourly marches to the exit into the Aso Villa office and residence of the President of Nigeria. On the fifth day of our GWA, being 12th of January 2017, we received a letter from the Federal Government inviting #<u>BBOG</u> to a "Guided Tour of the North East" commencing the following two working days. The invitation came as a surprise considering the history of adversarial actions against our movement over the last one year by the Federal Government.

Nevertheless our <u>BBOG</u> movement responded by welcoming the opportunity to explore a tour of Sambisa with our Military but on the prior condition that a pre-tour meeting would hold to help clarify various issues of concern to us. In its response to that demand, the FG pleaded that due to operational and cost constraints, it could not delay the tour date, urging us to reconsider and join with local and foreign journalists that were on the delegation to observe the air component of the counter insurgency war by Nigeria Air Force.

OUR DELEGATION
The #*BBOG* team was led by Dr. Oby Ezekwesili (Co-
convener), Aisha Yesufu, (Chair, #*BBOG* Strategic
Team), Ibrahim Usman (Member representing our Sit-
out), and Dr. Manasseh Allen (Representative, Chibok
Community and uncle to some of the abducted Chibok
Girls).

THE FEDERAL GOVERNMENT DELEGATION
The Federal Government was led by the Minister of
Defense and the Minister of Information and Culture and
included the Chief of Air Staff. Several Journalists from
both local and international news media were also on the
Guided Tour.

BBOG STATEMENT OF OBJECTIVE FOR ACCEPTING
TO PARTICIPATE IN THE FG GUIDED TOUR

In consideration of the FG's inability to reschedule the
tour, we reviewed our original position and decided to
join the "Guided Tour". We thereafter framed our
objective for the tour as "an opportunity to directly learn
from our Military the operational objectives, successes,
failures and constraints involved in its effort to rescue our
Chibok Girls and other abducted citizens even as it
secures and defends our national territorial integrity in
order to empower our advocacy for the rescue of our
remaining 195 ChibokGirls and other abducted citizens.

BBOG ALWAYS HAD CONFIDENCE IN OUR TROOPS
IN   THE   FRONTLINE   OF   BATTLE
Even as we framed the Objective for our movement's
participation in the Guided Tour of the war zone, we
consider it important for the records to reiterate that our

176

movement was never in doubt that our troops at the frontlines of the counterinsurgency war are giving their best effort to the task of searching for and finding our daughters. We were never in doubt that our troops are doing their utmost to finding and rescuing all other citizens we as a nation never even knew were in terrorist captivity. We were never in doubt that our troops were sacrificing with their lives to secure and defend the territorial integrity of our country. Indeed, like most Nigerians, members of our movement individually and collectively take pride in the capacity and commitment of our troops fighting in the frontline of battle.

Our advocacy is entirely directed at the leadership of the federal government and the military establishments which have the strategic responsibility to adequately resource our troops with the appropriate tools, equipment, guidance and decisions that they must have in order to be effective and achieve results. Evidently, since our ChibokGirls were abducted and our movement began advocating for their rescue, what the public sees— especially in the early years of the terrorist insurgency–is failure of leadership to appropriately prioritize, resource, guide troops and make strategic decisions for their rescue. It is for this reason that our movement defined our advocacy as a Demand for Good Governance from those who have the constitutional mandate to ensure the security and welfare of citizens like our Chibok Girls.

ACTIVITIES AND BRIEFINGS OF THE NIGERIA AIR FORCE LED GUIDED TOUR OF SAMBISA GENERAL AREA WAR ZONE 16-17 JANUARY 2017
On Monday 16th January 2017 at 8.53 am our

movement's four-member team, the Minister of Information and Culture, local and foreign journalists on the delegation, departed the Air Force base at Nnamdi Azikiwe International Airport, in the Nigeria Air Force (NAF) Hercules C130 aircraft. On arrival at the Yola Air Force base at 10.35 am, the delegation was received by the Chief of Air Staff, Air Marshal Sadiq Abubakar. The Minister of Defence, Mr. Mansur Dan-Ali, and the representative of the Chief of Defence Staff arrived concurrently and the full delegation was ushered into the briefing room of the holding room of the Nigerian Air Force.

The Guided Tour was a combination of briefs and search flights into the war zone called 'The Sambisa General Area' by the military. The briefings were categorized into segments with Air Force officers and experts led by the Chief of Air Staff. They made technology-powered presentations on various aspects of the counter-insurgency war as well as basic general routines of the Command. The delegation was given access to the analysis and technical war room of the Nigeria Air Force. Crucially, two members of our _BBOG_ Team were on the two Sorties — Flight Searches — that took place at day and at nighttime during the Guided Tour.

THE KEY HIGHLIGHTS OF THE _BBOG_ PARTICIPATION IN THE FEDERAL GOVERNMENT-LED GUIDED TOUR OF SAMBISA GENERAL AREA HOSTED BY NIGERIA AIR FORCE:

We had interactions with the leadership and the officials of the Nigerian Air Force that enabled our movement to *assess the quality of the personnel in the establishment. We can confirm that the air component of the counter insurgency war is being prosecuted by a highly professional, capable, motivated and committed team of the Nigeria Air Force. Furthermore, the presentation by the Chief of Air Staff on the training and human capital development strategy of the <u>NAF</u> enabled us to appreciate its plans.*

We saw that Data, Knowledge and Information Analysis play a major role in the strategy of the Nigerian Air Force prosecuting the air component of the war. Our exposure to the Intelligence, Surveillance and Reconnaissance (ISR) platform and the technical room of <u>NAF</u> indicated the level of adoption of technology in the prosecution of the war. We were presented data on the growing fleet of ISRs, fighter jets, Helicopter Gunships and other tools and equipment available to prosecute the air component of the war by NAF.

We observed the Coordination between the <u>NAF</u> and the Nigerian Army which prosecutes the ground component of the war was demonstrably strong as we saw evidence of the manner in which they share information toward achieving results.
We were provided data and imagery evidence to show that the search for our <u>Chibok Girls</u> and other abducted citizens is a daily activity by <u>NAF</u>. The data sheet showing the summary of all search operations was displayed with the following key data points over the last eighteen months by NAF:

Total Missions to Sambisa General Area–2,105
Number of Sorties— 3,534
Time/Hour of flight— 6,323
Fuel Cost: Over N2.4 billion

The Day Sortie *— that is, the 3 hours search flight on the ISR platform in which we participated on Monday 16 January had us being flown at as low as 15,000 feet. It enabled us to see the theatre of war in Sambisa and to clearly observe activities on the ground via the technology platform within the aircraft. We observed cases of human movement and saw a woman running with a child. When our Day Sortie report was later analyzed, it showed that 14 women were gathered around a suspicious location which the NAF designated as the "Tree of Life" because it has been suspecting enemy around that spot. The Nigerian Air Force (NAF) stated that they would probe the result further with their army colleagues in order to determine the appropriate response.*

The Night Sortie
At 2.41am on Tuesday, we participated in the Night Sortie which involved a similar flight search of the theatre of war like we did during the day. We were told by the NAF that until the acquisition of more equipment by our military since July 2015, the terrorists used to be most active at night time as darkness offered them advantage. It was usually during the night that they moved their captives who are mostly women, girls and children across locations. Interestingly, our Night Sortie only revealed one movement on the ground–an animal foraging for food.

The searches enable the _NAF_ to also sight enemy activities and to determine appropriate response jointly with the Nigerian Army. The Air Force presentation revealed its missions in which it sighted Boko Haram terrorists (BHT) as well as abducted persons running, fleeing from their captors especially during the operation that led to the capture of Camp Zairo. For example, some dates on which sightings were made are Kangarwa: 1st and 6th January, Dogon Chiku: 6th January and Chikun Gudu: 8th, 10th, 12th and 16th January. Data trends like level of equipment of _NAF_ and their direct impact on volume of observed enemy activities within the Sambisa General Area proved the correlation between adequate resourcing of the troops and results. Our flight into the Sambisa General Area on the ISR platform showed low suspected enemy activities compared to the data of previous year.

Better understanding of a key military language like the celebrated "capture of Camp Zairo" which previously to our movement and the larger public meant that capture of the entire vast land of Sambisa General Area. We now also know that the capture of Camp Zairo is significant because it used to be the operational base of the terrorists. With its capture, the military has achieved a major degradation of the capacity of the terrorists to launch attacks on our country.

We became aware that our troop must remain in Sambisa General Area which the _NAF_ data presented as 60,000 square kilometers and equivalent to 18 times the size of Lagos. (There is currently a public contention and debate *over this data and so our movement calls on the <u>NAF</u> in the promotion of transparency to clarify the accuracy for everyone's understanding. The legitimate fear of regrouping of the enemies to re-launch new attacks means that our military on air and on ground operations must continue.*

There is no contradiction in the fact of the recovery of Camp Zairo by our troops and yet our <u>Chibok Girls</u> not having been recovered at that same time. This is because, in view of the vast land of the Sambisa General Area, our <u>Chibok Girls</u> could have been taken to a new base into which the terrorists relocated when they fled Camp Zairo. Signed:
For and on behalf of#BringBackOurGirls

OBY EZEKWESILI
AISHA YESUFU
MANASSEH ALLEN
IBRAHIM USMAN

BBOG MARKS THREE YEARS OF CHIBOK GIRLS ABDUCTION

The Bring Back Our Girls movement once again scheduled resplendent activities in the Global Week of Action to commemorate the 3rd year since the Chibok School Girls were hijacked by terrorists from their dormitory on 14 April 2014. The occasion commenced on Friday, April 7, 2017 with Islamic lessons and prayers led by the Chief Immam of Apo Mosque, Sheik Nura Khalid. On Saturday, 8 April members moved around the Unity Fountain to tie ribbons on trees and sign posts to remind Nigerians and the whole world that 195 of the girls were still languishing in the lair of insurgents. They also planted a symbolic *Moringa oleifera (Zogele)* tree at the centre of the Unity Fountain in honour of the missing girls. This is the press statement signaling the beginning of the event:

"Today is Day 1089 since schoolgirls of Government Secondary School, Chibok were abducted in their school by terrorist; 57 escaped, 24 returned, 195 of them remain missing. It is Day 674 of their captivity under President Muhammadu Buhari's watch. It is Day 1074 of our movement's daily advocacy demanding that the Federal Government discharges its constitutional duty and rescue the abducted girls from terrorist captivity. In another 7 days, it will be 3 years since the tragic events of that night. Tragically, 195 of our young women whose only sin was their quest for knowledge are left by their government to remain in terrorist enclave.

"We are utterly disappointed at the Government of Nigeria's abysmal handling of this historical tragedy and are at a loss at the obvious emotional disconnect and insincerity that have defined the actions and words of the President and his government on this matter. None of the commitments made by the government concerning the rescue of our ChibokGirls has been followed through. These days, we have observed a coldness, ominous silence and irritability of key officials whenever the government is reminded of its constitutional duty to rescue ChibokGirls and all other abducted citizens.

"Our movement, BBOG fails to understand why this is so but one thing definite for us is that we shall not stop keeping the President and the administration accountable we remain undeterred in our demand. That is why even though filled with excruciating pain at the protractedness

of this tragedy, we have today commenced our 8-Day Global Week of Action with diverse activities to mark 3 years of our ChibokGirls abduction and their continued captivity by terrorists. This tragic third year of Global Week of Action has the theme hash-tagged as: 3YearsTooLong: #NoMoreExcuses.

"We enter the third year of our Girls being left in terrorist captivity with the constant shock that the Presidency which last October (2016) told the world that 83 more of our ChibokGirls were on their way out of captivity "very soon", has since adopted deafening silence as a tool of avoidance of accountability. What reason can the Federal Government have for never providing progress reports on the status of its rescue operation for our Girls? Except for cursory remarks made by the Minister of Information in January, the Federal Government has acted in manner that suggests that rescuing our ChibokGirls is a matter of lowest importance on its agenda. We denounce this posture that is indicative of lack of respect for the dignity of the life of the Nigerian Girl Child of which our ChibokGirls are symbols.

"We also recall that President Muhammadu Buhari had on 14 January 2016 authorised the set up of yet another investigation into the abduction. It is extremely pathetic that nothing has come out of that pronouncement. The situation is worsened by the fact that the federal government shockingly denied our Movement's use of the Freedom of Information (FOI) to request to access the report of the Presidential Committee that investigated into the abduction (General Sabo Committee) in 2014.

"Furthermore, regarding the 24 ChibokGirls that are back, the media reports of sparse information from the government on their wellbeing almost only touches. On

the 21 it negotiated release, we ask: where are the other 3 ChibokGirls? The poor and rather opaque communication by the FG on its rehabilitation program for the 24 Girls keeps even families in the dark leading to some asking for updates from our movement.

"The Government had woefully disappointed the Nigerian public on the entirety of its shoddy handling of our ChibokGirls and their tragedy. This Global Week of Action is a time that our Movement loudly declares, 'Enough is Enough', No More Excuses, Bring Back Our Girls! Now and Alive!! Close to 2 years ago during our Global Week of Action to mark Day 500 of the abduction, our theme was '500 Days is too long'. Today, sadly we are reiterating on the third year of the abduction, we have no intention of repeating this. #3YearsTooLong: #NoMoreExcuses #BringBackOurGirls.

"This Global Week of Action shall be marked in cities in Nigeria (Lagos and Abuja), New York, Paris, etc; and shall run for 7 straight days as usual. Kindly view website www.bringbackourgirls.ng to see details and to participate. In Abuja where activities commenced today with Asr (Islamic) prayers, we shall have duo marches by different sets eminent personalities, celebrities, Chibok mothers, et al from Unity Fountain to the State House every day with the theme #IMarchForChibokGirls.

"Other events include tree planting, a workshop on the Missing Persons Register, an initiative of our movement which is being worked on in collaboration with the federal government and her relevant agencies: The National Human Rights Commission, Nigeria Police Force, and others. The events will be capped on Friday 14 April with the Inaugural #ChibokGirls Annual Lecture: 'Where Goes the Girl-Child there Goes the Nation' to be delivered by His Highness, Muhammad

Sanusi II CON, a well-recognised advocate for girl-child liberation/ empowerment and education.

"The event shall be eminently chaired by Professor Grace Alele-Williams, the first Nigerian female to receive a doctoral degree, first Nigerian female professor of mathematics education, and the first female to be a vice chancellor of a university in Africa. (Kindly find details on our website).
Kindly make plans to participate. #3YearsTooLong: #NoMoreExcuses #BringBackOurGirls. Would you be silent if your daughter went missing for 3 years?"

"MR PRESIDENT, NO MORE EXCUSES!'
'MR PRESIDENT, NO MORE DELAYS!!'
'MR PRESIDENT, DECIDE NOW!!!'
'MR   PRESIDENT,   ACT   NOW,   WE   WANT RESULTS!!!'
Signed: For and on behalf of #BringBackOurGirls
AISHA YESUFU
OBY EZEKWESILI

Sunday, 9 April 2017
The day was a Christian session to continue to demand for the release of the girls. In attendance were: co-founder, Dr. Mrs. Oby Ezekwesili, his husband, Pastor Chidi Ezekwesili and Pastor Polycarp. Pastor Ezekwesili deplored the continued languishing of the young women in the den of savages and the inability of the government to rescue them. There were prophetic messages that the girls would soon be released and members of the BBOG would welcome them with joy. Subsequently, prayers were offered for the save return of the abducted school girls and the unity and stability of the Nigerian nation.

Charley Boy Protests to State House to free Chibok Girls

Weird musician and entertainer, Charles Oputa aka Charley Boy on Monday, 10 April, joined the league of humanity demanding for the release of the remaining Chibok girls 195 Chibok girls in terrorists' captivity. He marched all the way from the Unity Fountain to the Presidential Villla to the admiration of numerous road users and onlookers. Wearing a red Bring Back Our Girls T-shirt, Charles Oputa displayed a placard as he walked aggressively towards the Villa.

Tuesday 11 April 2017

On Tuesday Christian and Islamic clerics campaigned for the return of the Chibok girls. Present were the Archbishop of Abuja diocese, His Eminence Rev. Dr. John Onaiyekan; the chief Immam of Apo Mosque, Sheik Nura Khalid; lead pastor of the Redeemed Christian Church of God, Pastor Chidi Ezekwesili. They were followed by reverend fathers and sisters of the Catholic Church. As they marched from the Unity Fountain to the State House gate with their placards which read: 'I march for Chibok Girls', they raised their hands and proclaimed: 'Bring Back Our Girls now and alive'. At the Presidential Villa gate, facing the world press, Archbishop Onaiyekan said:

"Life is important. We have still almost 200 girls out there missing for about three years. So, I feel concerned not only about the remaining Chibok schoolgirls but also maybe running into hundreds of other Nigerians who are missing, carried away by kidnappers.

"Their families are languishing. We came to draw the attention of the whole nation. We are glad that we are able to carry out this simple exercise of walking down the streets from the Unity Fountain to here. And we thank government for making police available to protect us.

"This is not the first time I am joining in this kind of walk. I was here a year ago. At that time, most of the Sambisa forest was still under the control of Boko Haram and when we were marching, we were hoping that our girls were somewhere in the hands of the Boko Haram within those premises", he added.

"Today, the situation is different. We have been told that the whole of the Sambisa forest has been completely cleared. The question we are asking now is: Where are our girls? They cannot disappear.

"Those who are responsible for taking away these girls, whether they are Boko Haram or not, they have the first major responsibility to tell us what has happened to our girls and then whether they are alive or they are dead, whether they are around or they have been sold off. They have the responsibility to tell not only the parents and the family of the girls but the rest of Nigerians.

"And we believe too that the government ought to step up action in this direction. That is what is bringing us here and I believe the rest of the world has been waiting to hear and they can't understand that we lose people like that and nothing seems to be happening.

"One of the major reasons why I came too is because this matter concerns me personally, and that is why I brought my brother here. The Holy Ghost father was taken away by kidnappers over a year ago and up to now; we have had no information about him.

"Now that touches me and I am sure there are many Nigerians who are suffering the same thing from the loss of members of their families. And so, this march is not just about Chibok girls, it is about the whole idea that Nigerians can just disappear, missing and we are not able to trace them, either dead or alive."

The Islamic cleric, Nura Khalid, told journalists at the event that, as he had been doing, he allied himself with the position expressed by Onaiyekan. He declared:

"I joined this action because I want to equally send the message that His Eminence is sending to Nigerians and to the government that we can never allow terrorists to win the war. If they get away free with those girls; then they have relatively won the war. That is what we can't afford. And, we are tired of having Nigerians kidnapped, abducted and just like that. We want more actions from our government.

"It is true that some clerics like myself have been killed in the course of the insurgence of Boko Haram. We are not saying that the government is doing nothing, we are telling them to do more."

Pastor Chidi Ezekwesili concurred with his colleague, demanding the immediate rescue of the girls who have overstayed in rebels' custody.

Inaugural 14th April BBOG Lecture

The BBOG rounded up the GWA with spectacular inaugural lecture on the morning of April 14 marking the day of abduction of the Chibok girls. The event took place at Transcorp Hilton Hotel and featured eminent personalities like Professor Grace Alele Williams, first

Nigerian female Vice Chancellor (University of Benin), Archbishop John Onaiyekan and the Emir of Kano represented by his daughter to deliver the key-note address. Prof Alele Williams deplored the continued languishing of the Chibok girls in the wild. She called on the government, the military and other security agencies to fortify intelligence and operations to rescue those young women she said had been held for so long.

There was a 6-minute display of the Chibok Girls Video which narrated the events from the April 1, 2014 when the girls were kidnapped, the rescue efforts and delinquencies of the government and daily persistent protests of the BBOG. Poetic recitations on the Chibok girls were conducted by invited artistes.

CHIBOK GIRLS' PARENTS MARCH TO ASO ROCK
As the BBOG concluded its GWA the aggrieved parents of the abducted Chibok girls commenced their own protest on Monday 17 April, 2017. The community resolved to continue their peaceful campaign to the Presidential Villa until they obtained from the government information about the latest efforts to rescue their daughters. On the first and second day of the march to the State House gate the government deplorably ignored them.

However, on the 3rd day they created some fracas on reaching the first gate. The parents sat on the road daring oncoming vehicles and insisting that they wanted their daughters. Minister for women affairs, Hajia Alhassan, at last came to rescue the situation after a brief conference at the Villa. She said that she was directed to take them inside the Villa to the Vice President (VP), Prof

Yemi Osinbajo. At the meeting with the VP the parents complained of negligence over their devastated rural area where they groan under hunger and malnutrition occasioned by scarcity of food. They criticized what they called silence of the government over their daughters languishing in captivity and lack of information regarding their rescue.

The VP contended their assertion by stating that the government was working arduously for the release of the remaining girls and has indeed been briefing the Ministry of Women Affairs on developments in this respect. He assured them that in future briefings the parents of the Chibok girls and the Chibok community would be invited as stakeholders. Mr. VP revealed the impenetrable nature of the negotiations with the rebels who capriciously renege on agreements. None the less, he said, operations and mediations would continue to secure the remaining school girls. Prof Osinbajo rebuked the Defence Minister's earlier statement that the Chibok school girls might not be rescued in the next ten years. [77]

82 MORE CHIBOK GIRLS RELEASED

The Global Week of Action of the BBOG to mark the 3rd year of abduction of the Chibok school girls yielded a magnificent result on May 6, 2017. That day the Federal Government of Nigeria announced the release of 82 kidnapped girls by Boko Haram rebels. It was overwhelming rapture at the Unity Fountain camp of the BBOGon May7 as members were seen hugging each other in joy, and thanking God for the liberation of the young women. They were happy they had not suffered in vain.

The deal to free the girls was said to have been brokered by Mustapha Zanna, a barrister who is currently the manager of an orphanage in Maiduguri. He was once the lawyer of <u>the late founder of Boko Haram, Mohammed Yusuf</u>. The negotiations also involved the Swiss government and the International Committee of the Red Cross. The girls were picked up at Banki—a Nigerian border rustic with Cameroon in Red Cross vehicles and given the agency's branded T-shirts to wear. The Red Cross conveyed them to Maiduguri where they boarded military helicopters and were flown to Abuja to be received by President Muhammadu Buhari who shifted his medical trip to England for some hours to make the ceremony. In press statement on 6th of May Senior Media Assistant to the President, Garba Shehu, said:

"The President is pleased to announce that negotiations to release more of the Chibok Girls have borne fruit with the release of 82 more today.

"After months of patient negotiations, our security agencies have taken back these abducted girls in exchange for some Boko Haram suspects held by the authorities. The girls are due tomorrow in Abuja to be received by the President.

"The President expressed his deep gratitude to security agencies, the military, the government of Switzerland, the Red Cross, local and international non-governmental organizations for the success of this operation."

Lengthy negotiations on the release of the girls took place in Switzerland and Sudan, according to Shehu Sani, a Nigerian senator. Sani told the Guardian that he introduced Zanna, the chief negotiator, to the government and came up with a workable trajectory for the talks. Two of the 82 girls were physically injured; one had a wrist injury and the other on crutches.

President Muhammadu Buhari, in receiving the freed girls, thanked both local and international organizations that facilitated their rescue. By Monday, 8th May, the names of the released girls had been made public by the government. The list concurred with the authentic record of the Bring Back Our Girls. In a statement issued Sunday morning by spokesperson, Sesugh Akume, the BBOG expressed appreciation to the government; the security agencies as well as international organizations that made the girls' rescue a success. In the declaration, the BBOG said:

"We are exceedingly delighted by this good news that has been long awaited following last October when upon the release of our 21 #ChibokGirls, our federal government promised that; "another 83 was being negotiated to be released very soon. We are also glad in view of the remaining 113 of our #ChibokGirls that are still captives of terrorists, the statement from the Presidency reiterated the President's and his government's commitment to continue to earnestly pursue the release of all our Chibok girls."

Amnesty International welcomed the development as a big relief. The agency's Nigeria Director, Osai Ojigho, emphasized the expedient to give the freed girls 'adequate physical and psychosocial counseling and support so that they can fully reintegrate in their communities.[78]

ITALIAN PARLIAMENT SPEAKER VISITS BRING BACK OUR GIRLS

It was a historic moment on the evening of May 8 when the Speaker of the Italian Parliament and President of the

Chamber of Deputies, The Honourable Laura Boldrini, visited the BBOG at their Unity Fountain camp to congratulate them on the release of 82 Chhibok school girls by Boko Haram insurgents, and to fortify their spirit of struggle. The tall, slim, jovial lady with a soft accent and her entourage ignored the prevailing rainstorm in Abuja to interact with the BBOG. On arrival, she was admitted with an embrace by BBOG leader, Aisha Yesufu.

Mrs. Aisha welcomed her to the sit-out ground of the BBOG: informing her that we had been standing there for over three years, putting pressure for the rescue of the abducted Chibok girls and all other persons missing as a result of the crisis in the north east. She cheerfully revealed that additionally 82 girls were released the previous day, leaving a balance of 113 girls to be rescued. The redoubtable leader appreciated Boldrini for coming to express solidarity with the group and Nigeria.

In her speech, the Italian Chief legislator demonstrated gratitude to the BBOG for welcoming her consort. She exhorted us to continue to put pressure on the government and other stakeholders to release the remaining school girls in captivity. The Italian lady extended thankfulness to the national government for their punctilious efforts in the rescue operations.

Boldrini accentuated that young women in Nigeria must be educated because, according to her, 'if they are educated they cannot be intimidated'. One of the BBOG members, Hajia Fati, decorated the Speaker with their Bring Back Our Girls badge. Other members of the contingent gratefully accepted the memento, wishing that the tragic incident would never happen again. The occasion was concluded with exchange of pleasantries between the BBOG campaigners and visitors; group photographs in front of the BBOG banner; then chanting of BBOG slogans and solidarity songs. Both visitors and hosts chanted:

What are we demanding?
Bring Back Our Girls; Now and Alive! Etc.

From my discernment and evaluation of events, it is unquestionable that the respectable and patriotic BBOG, nobles who uphold national ethics, the constitution and the rule of law, the very stone the builders of deceit, debauchery and squander mania of the Nigerian State reject, shall be the corner stone of cohesion, peace, stability and prosperity of the Federal Republic of Nigeria.

DAY 1205: BBOG STORMS ASO VILLA AGAIN

On the 1st of August 2017, the BBOG staged another momentous march to the Presidential Villa, Abuja, demanding the immediate rescue of the remaining 113 abducted Chibok secondary school girls and other recently kidnapped persons. The procession commenced with briefing by leader Oby Ezekwesili at the Unity Fountain by 10: 30 am. Thereafter the troop marched on under the escort and guard of many policemen as usual, chanting 'solidarity forever' and 'bring back our girls, now and alive'.

At 11:20 am the crusaders arrived at the junction leading to the State House confronted, as before, by a barricade of police men and women. Leader Oby

Ezekwesili (with her bandaged accidentally-fractured right leg) opened proceedings at the Villa Gate by welcoming members of the public present, the press and BBOG members. She then read the press statement of the BBOG on this historic day.

She started by recalling the fateful14th of April, 2014when the 276 Chibok School Girls were abducted. 57 escaped on the way while the federal government had so far rescued 106, remaining 113 girls to be delivered from the den of insurgents. The indefatigable freedom fighter reminded the government of the promise to Nigerians at its inauguration: that the war against Boko Haram would not be said to have been won without the rescue of all the Chibok school girls missing.

Mrs. Oby Ezekwsili said the BBOG members were worried that there had not been any information from the government since the past three months regarding efforts to bring back the remaining girls. Deploring the seeming delinquency and lethargy of the government over the girls, she emphasized that the parents of the girls in captivity wanted them to be returned like the others. She therefore declared the catchphrase of the BBOG: 1205 years too long, no more excuses!

She likewise informed the government that relatives of 16 police women kidnapped on 20th of June 2017 while traveling to bury a dead female colleague, wrote to the BBOG demanding immediate rescue of their family members. Unfortunately, the Nigerian government had, like the abduction of the Chibok school girls, failed to acknowledge that the police women going for a funeral were actually kidnapped despite the fact that Boko Haram leader, Abubakar Shekau, released a new video days after their abduction claiming that the women and other security agents were in his custody as 'slaves'. The BBOG deplored the inertia and negligence of the government over the abducted security operatives and called for their immediate rescue. Rescue of kidnapped citizens, Mrs. Oby said, is part of the social contract between the government and the people under section 14(2b) of the 1999 constitution of Nigeria as amended.

The BBOG statement also recollected the case of NNPC oil exploration workers and research scholars from the Geology Department of the University of Maiduguri. They were ambushed by the Al Barnawi faction of Boko Haram on their way from oil exploration work in the Lake Chad Basin region of Borno State. One of the hostages, a lecturer speaking on behalf of the others on SOS, appealed to the Nigerian government to fulfill the 'demand' of the terrorists so that they could be released. Hence the BBOG called for immediate rescue of the lectures as well as other persons captured in the ugly incident.

The BBOG appreciated the federal and state governments that facilitated the release of the Ekpe secondary school boys that were kidnapped about two months earlier. They expressed sadness over the aggravated spate of suicide bombings and other attacks on territories in the north east. Tagging this as unacceptable, they demanded the re-assessment and fortification of the IRS capacity of the military and other security components to effectively combat the menacing insurgency.

Mrs Ezekwesili took some time to explain the patriotic and humanitarian citizens' activities of the BBOG at the sittings and the Strategic Team (ST), the old and new officials, transfer of ST Chair from Aisha Yesufu to Florence Ozor while Sesugh Akume remained the BBOG spokesperson and director of publicity. She heartily thanked the press and other Nigerians who had been expressing solidarity with the group all along. If not for the press, she said, the issue of the abducted Chibok girls would be kept in the cooler and the noble work of the BBOG would be extremely impenetrable to be broadcast to the whole world.

Surprisingly, this time around the BBOG was received by a delegate of the federal government, unlike past engagements when they were fiercely snubbed and rebuffed at that State House entrance by security cordon. The government contingent was led by Babafemi Ojodu, Senior Assistant to Acting President, Prof Yemi Osinbajo, on political affairs. He said the Acting President (AP) would have received the BBOG himself but was having a meeting with Ghanaian President. However, he said the AP had been observing the BBOG activities and is with them in their struggle. According to him groups like the respectable BBOG are important for the vibrancy and growth of democracy and thus foster national development.

The AP therefore urged other Nigerians to emulate the productive citizens' participatory crusade of the BBOG over the past three years. He said that he strongly identifies with the BBOG, having taken part in similar democratic struggles during the hideous Sanni Abacha regime. Mr. Babafemi informed the BBOG that the government was not silent on the matter of the remaining Chibok girls as being suggested.

Rather, the government was heightening efforts to get them released. In the weeks to come, he said, a considerable number, if not all will be rescued. The BBOG expressed gratitude to this unusually receptive gesture from the government. The encounter was devoid of the typical cat and mouse game of the government and BBOG. **CIT79**

BBOG STORMS ASO ROCK FOR REMAINING 113 CHIBOK GIRLS

On the 14th of November 2017, the BBOG commenced another sequence of daily protests to the Nigerian State House to demand the immediate rescue of the remaining 113 abducted Chibok school girls as well as other kidnapped persons in north east. Members started gathering at the Unity Fountain camp by 9am. They were joined by relatives of the missing persons: those from Chibok, a contingent that stood for the Lassa police women and representatives of the abducted University of Maiduguri lecturers who were earlier kidnapped while returning from a crude oil exploration mission in the Lake Chad Basin.

At about 10: 30 am the combined large crowd of campaigners started the march to the Presidential Villa under heavy security escort. They were chanting solidarity songs like:

'Chibok Girls......Never to be forgotten'
'Lassa police women....They must come home'

'Lassa police women.... Bring them back now'
'UniMaid Lecturers.... They must come home'
'UniMaid Lecturers...... Bring them back now'
'What are we demanding...Bring back our girls now and alive'

On reaching the entrance to the State House the crusaders were oncee more disgracefully blocked by the police and other security agents. Members tried to no avail to push their way past the human barricade. The police officer in charge of operations at that point told enquiring Mrs. Oby Ezekwesili that the order of their assignment was that the protesters must not pass that junction to the Villa first gate. Infuriated by this development Ezekwesili informed them that one of the reasons for the campaign was to demand the immediate release of Lassa police women that were previously abducted by Boko Haram insurgents on their way to bury one of their dead colleagues.

One of the Strategic Team members, Aisha Yesufu opened session by announcing to the press and public why the group came again to the Villa. She accentuated that despite security threats and harassment they would continue to demand the rescue of all kidnapped Nigerians. The press statement of the BBOG was read by leader of the Strategic Team, Florence Ozor, as follows:

FOR IMMEDIATE RELEASE
Promises made must be kept – Where are our #ChibokGirls?
14 November 2017

A. INTRODUCTION
"Today marks 1, 310 days too long since the tragic abduction of our #ChibokGirls from
Government Secondary School, Chibok, on the 14th of April 2014.

While we appreciate the return of 106 of our #ChibokGirls, we accept no justification for the continued captivity of the 113 #ChibokGirls that are yet to return for 880 days under the watch of President Muhammadu Buhari. It has been far too long without any further progress or tangible evidence that sustained and result-focused effort is being made to rescue them.

It does sadly appear as though the Presidency considers the return of the last batch of 82 #ChibokGirls as the conclusion of the #ChibokGirls tragedy. We vehemently oppose any such stance and impression the public is reading from the absolute detachment of the President and the Federal Government (FG) to the pain of the families of the remaining #ChibokGirls.

All remaining 113 Girls and all other known victims of terrorist abduction must be rescued immediately by the Federal Government. As a movement, we have continued to keep our promise and commitment to advocating for our #ChibokGirls. We continue to sit daily at the Unity Fountain and in Lagos for all of 1, 295 days as at today. The government cannot rest from its own pledge to rescue our #ChibokGirls with even greater urgency and results.

B. NEW ABDUCTIONS UNDER THE ADMINISTRATION OF PRESIDENT MUHAMMADU BUHARI.
There are two other major abductions that have happened under the administration of President Muhammadu Buhari and the victims like our 113 remaining #ChibokGirls remain in captivity. Those two notably traumatic tragedies are:

1. 14 missing Lassa women and others abducted from Lassa on the 20th of June 2017 on

Maiduguri – Damboa road en route to bury fallen police personnel.

2. Members of the NNPC exploration team which included staff members of the NNPC and the University of Maiduguri on the 25th of July 2017.
Shockingly, neither the President nor other officials of the Federal Government seem to
have learned anything from the poor handling of the families of the #ChibokGirls.

Our movement concluded as such because of the appalling and heartbreaking stories of
abandonment by the families of the Lassa women and the UniMaid lecturers. These families have from the moment their relations were abducted contacted us to advocate for the rescue of their relations. We did. We wrote at least two letters to the President on the two cases and specifically to the Inspector General of Police on the Lassa women. We
marched to the Villa Gate in August for both these latest victims and our remaining ChibokGirls.

It is inexplicably tragic that despite all these efforts, none of these families were reached
and updated by any officials of the Presidency and Federal Government. Today, some of
those terribly disappointed families of the Lassa women and the UniMaid Lecturers have
joined us to DEMAND IMMEDIATE RESCUE OF THEIR FAMILY MEMBERS that are captives of terrorists. We support their DEMAND. We DEMAND URGENT ACTION with TANGIBLE RESULTS OF RESCUE by the Federal Government. It is the Constitutional duty of the Federal Government to be responsive to citizens by fulfilling its primary responsibility of protecting the lives of all Nigerians.

Today, we reiterate the specific demands that we have consistently and constantly
communicated to the Federal Government on several occasions, including during our most
recent march on the 1st of August 2017. At our march in August, Mr. Babafemi Ojudu,
Special Adviser to the President on Political Affairs appeared, avowing that he was
designated to address our members on behalf of the FG. He gave what he called a strong
assurance from the President and the Federal Government that our #ChibokGirls and other
victims of abduction will be retrieved shortly.

Our movement received the message of the representative of the President which he delivered, and resolved to await to see the Federal Government take actions necessary to making the assurances meaningful. Most regrettably, we note with dismay that we there is still no evidence of any verifiable actions taken by the Federal Government regarding the very specific demands we have repeatedly made concerning the urgency needed to end the
tragedies of continuing captivity of our #ChibokGirls, the Lassa men and women as well as the NNPC exploration team. Not even the simple matter of reaching out to the affected
traumatised families of abducted victims was acted on by the Presidency and the Federal
Government.

C. BRING BACK OUR GIRLS SPECIFIC DEMANDS FOR #ChibokGirls, LASSA WOMEN AND UNIMAID LECTURERS.
We therefore again reiterate our DEMANDS as a Citizens Movement to the President and
Federal Government as follows:

1. The Federal Government must demonstrate a fierce sense of urgency in efforts to
immediately rescue or secure the release of our remaining 113 #ChibokGirls. Whatever
it chooses to do to bring back the rest of our girls cannot be further delayed and any
relapse to inertia, complacency and indifference is unacceptable to our movement.

2. The FG must immediately send a high-powered delegation to Chibok to reassure
disconsolate parents of our remaining girls that are still in captivity. The obvious and
painful empathy-deficit approach in which the parents have thus far been managed is
undesirable. It must end NOW!

3. The FG and the Nigeria military should immediately provide the public with factual and
accurate details on the missing Lassa women and the NNPC exploration team. The
opaqueness surrounding these two tragedies has created room for unhealthy
speculations and must be urgently addressed.

4. The FG should immediately invite the affected families of the victims of the Lassa
women and the soldiers, NNPC-University of Maiduguri lecturers and staff killings and
abduction for a full briefing on the tragedies that befell their relatives. The FG should
have already taken full ownership of the tragedies and presented families with
persuasive and comforting plans for the immediate rescue of their relatives.

5. The FG, as we have constantly and consistently demanded, must now set up the
structured systems of public reporting on each specific abduction case, the general
management of our IDPs as well as the entire prosecution of the counter insurgency
war. Citizens have a right to know. Even more so, families of victims of abduction have
an immediate right to know status of their missing relatives. The FG alone cannot
successfully win the counter terrorism war. It must mobilize the citizens and this is only
possible when it trusts the people with factual updates relevant enough to build public
support.

6. Finally, we call for an urgent revamping of counterterrorism operational strategy by the
Nigeria military. We also urge the military to overhaul its communication approach and
strategy to become more transparent and engaging with immediate communities and the citizens at large.

D. TROUBLING DEVELOPMENT ON THE HEALTH CONDITION OF SOME OF OUR RELEASED CHIBOK GIRLS
We have received reports of one of our returned #ChibokGirls' illness and the shameful
trade in blames between the FG and her school. She is reported to have said that had she
known that she would be mistreated this way she would have preferred to stay back with
the terrorists. The government of President Muhammadu Buhari ought to be ashamed of
this.

OUR MARCHES SHALL BE DAILY
From today, we will raise the level of our advocacy by conducting daily marches to jointly
express our displeasure in the prior mismanagement of the issues outlined and press
demands that they be addressed immediately. We continue to demand BringBackOurGirls
until all our 113 #ChibokGirls return and advocate for all in captivity while we await swift
responses from the Federal Government of Nigeria. The FG must keep the promises it has
made.

E. GRATITUDE TO THE NIGERIAN PUBLIC AND MEDIA
We are grateful to the Nigerian and global media for remaining steadfast in their critical role to pursue and reveal the truth on the cause of our #ChibokGirls. Thank you for amplifying our voices and ensuring that our #ChibokGirls are not forgotten. We thank members of the Nigerian public and friends of #ChibokGirls around the world who have never ceased to advocate for the rescue of our girls. We urge everyone to keep their voices strong calling on the Federal Government to act decisively and effect their rescue.

F. GRATITUDE FOR OUR UNIFORMED MEN AND WOMEN IN THE FRONTLINE OF BATTLE AND THE CIVILIAN JTF.
We salute and appreciate the commitment of our men and women in uniform including the
Civilian JTF: to restoring peace and normalcy to our nation. We especially honour those who have paid the ultimate sacrifice in the line of duty and pray that their sacrifices shall never be in vain."

Signed: For and on behalf of #BringBackOurGirls

FLORENCE OZOR
AISHA YESUFU
OBY EZEKWESILI [80]

CHAPTER 2
THE BOKO HARAM INSURGENCY

While contributing to the 3-Day Symposium on Current Economic, Social and Security Challenges Facing Northern Nigeria in Washington D.C., organized by the US Institute of Peace, March 17-19, 2014, former Governor of the beleaguered Adamawa State, Murtala Nyako asserted that there is a political scheme sponsoring armed groups to attack and destabilize the region. According to the Governor:

"The Boko Haram itself has not helped matters since it has never come out by its actions to define what type of war it is fighting.
It has bombed facilities of the United Nations and those of all and sundry. It has destroyed churches and mosques and targeted and killed many Muslims and Christians irrespective of the ethnicity of their victims.

"It is therefore most unfortunate that despite professional advice to the Presidency including two Memos submitted by my humble self, it does not seem to know what it is facing and the type of war it should be fighting. Is it a war against terrorists, insurgents or as people are coming to believe, a nurtured war against the people in Northern Nigeria?"

Exculpating the people of Northern Nigeria from fomenting the crisis, Nyako avowed:

"It is now clear to all and sundry that there is an unhindered coordination between the activities of Boko Haram cells and some strategic commanders sitting in some high offices in our national defence system. The security situation we are facing in Nigeria today could be sponsored, financed and supported by evil-minded and

ambitious leaders of government and the society for political gains.
There is simply no person in north-eastern zone rich enough to foot the financial and logistic bills on Boko Haram activities."

He went further to describe Boko Haram as 'a tool by some evil-minded conspirators to kill key traditional and political leaders of Northern Nigeria and cause the disintegration of Nigeria'. [81]

The Islamic sect, Jama'atu Ahlis Sunna Lidda Awati Wal Jihad (Congregation of Followers of the Prophet for the Religion of Islam and the Struggle) aka Boko Haram, launched violent attacks in Northern Nigeria in 2009. Till date, more than 50000 lives have been lost. It has also wreaked extreme injury on socio-economic activities in Nigeria. [82] The August 2011 bombing of United Nations Building in Abuja is a milestone of such assaults.

Reprisals by government security agents have yielded fruitless results because Nigerian army or police can not fight against fellow citizens; [83] we are not at war. The former Military Commandant of Course 34 Study Group at the Armed Forces Command and Staff College Jaji, Air Vice Marshal Ibrahim Kure, had emphasized that best solution to the Boko Haram crisis is for the Federal Government to dialogue with the group.[84] Hence it is

imperative to engage in constructive and wise dialogue with dissenting groups.
85, 86

The root for the existence of Boko Haram is in the constitution of the Federal Republic of Nigeria as amended.[87] Section 38 guarantees freedom of thought, conscience, ideology and religion. The caption, 'Boko Haram' [Hausa language] translates to 'Book or Western Education is an abomination or forbidden', which is a thought. Boko Haram is a religious organization, so they have the right to practice. Section 40 also stipulates freedom of association. Boko Haram members have the freedom to associate and even canvass for membership. The only problem with the group is the attendant violent activities--bombing and killing.

A fascinating facet of their cause is that they want knowledge without engaging in Western Education which is, of course, is food for thought as well as an appealing research work. Is it possible to have knowledge without reference to Western education? Recall that before the advent of white man's education Africans were writing hieroglyphics and cuneiform in papyrus and reed.

Boko Haram is likewise fighting against the canker called corruption in Nigeria. Aliyu Tishako, a Boko Haram leader who the Nigerian Police admitted they detained and handed over to a 'sister' security agency for interrogation from where he gained his freedom, had this to say in an African Independent Television (AIT) interview:

'How can you cut off the hand of a man who stole a goat and leave he who steals billions of Naira with a pen to go free?'[88]

Governor Sule Lamido of Jigawa State, while admitting members of the Bauchi State House of Assembly in his office on 28 February 2012, said that he agrees entirely with the connotation, Boko Haram if:

"It means one going to school to acquire Western Education that guarantees one to steal public funds."

He noted that there is lack of trust between government and the governed where elected politicians use their positions to amass wealth. In his remarks:

"Even if you are in their miserable situation, you would do same."[89]

This updates the message by Rasta man Bob Marley that in a corrupt and fraudulent society:

"Them belly full but we hungry. A hungry man is an angry man."

211

Two expatriate workers of Stabilini Visinoni Construction Company were abducted from their residence in Birnin Kebbi on May 12, 2011 by an insurgent group in north western Nigeria. They were Christopher MacManus, a Briton and Francesco Lamolinara, an Italian. An attempt by Nigerian and British Armed Forces to rescue them on 10 March 2012 was futile because they were met already murdered by their captors. The question is; before this fiasco, why were the foreigners abducted and kept in custody for as long as ten months? [90]

Ex-Military Governor, Major General Lawrence Onoja, had stated that he would have joined Boko Haram if it had not started to kill innocent people. Onoja, while contributing to measures to ensure peace in Nigeria especially the north, in November 2012, said:

"If you look at it from the beginning, they (Boko Haram) have a genuine case. I have told people that I would have been a member of Boko Haram before they started killing innocent people. But if they had started going after those who carry ballot boxes to their houses, thump-print and start announcing fake results the next day, which is what most people are doing; if they go after such people, I will join them." [91]

Leader of the Islamic Movement of Nigeria, Sheik
Ibrahim el Zazzakky revealed that the Boko Haram crisis
is being instigated by people who have selfish interests in
Nigeria. In his presentation at the Christian/Muslim
Alternative to Conflict inaugural ceremony held in
Kaduna on 9 January 2013, el Zazzakky warned those
inflaming the crisis to retreat or be devoured by the
resultant calamities. According to him:

*"If you create a monster, it will eventually consume you.
The same people that instigated ordinary Nigerians
against each other are only digging their own graves for
themselves.'* [92]

 He thus admonished politicians and the elite behind the
crisis to refrain or face the consequential nemesis.

On May 14, 2012, while addressing delegates of
his former Congress for Progressive Change Party,
Nigeria's President, General Muhammadu Buhari said:
*"Except there is justice in the conduct of elections, blood
will flow because there will be bloodshed between the
dogs and the baboons... There is a storm of awareness
and God willing, by 2015, something will happen."*
Deploring the current insecurity in the country, he stated
thus:

"I will like to quote Professor Ango Abdullahi who said that there are three Boko Harams including the original one led by Mohammed Yusuf who was killed and his supporters tried to take revenge by attacking law enforcement agencies and politicians. There is another developed Boko Haram of criminals who steal and kill and the biggest Boko Haram is the Federal Government."[93]

Nevertheless, while airing his repugnance over the April 14, 2014 Nyanya bomb blast as guest columnist of the DAILY TRUST, the ex-military dictator said:

"These acts have no place in Nigeria. Those who commit them have no place in our country. The perpetrators may look like human beings. They may have limbs and faces like the rest of us but they are not like us.

"In killing innocent people, they have become inhuman. They live outside the scope of humanity. Their mother is carnage and their father is cruelty. They have declared war against the people of Nigeria. They have shown that they do not want to liberate the people. They want to kill them." [94]

On the 5th of December 2012, while speaking at the maiden north-eastern Alliance for Transformation

Summit held in Yankari Resort Bauchi, Borno State Governor, Kashim Shetima, voiced that:

"Beneath the Boko Haram, terrorism and other insurgency in the sub region, lies the extreme poverty of the region which the Federal Government has refused to address." [95]

While delivering his homily in a Mass at St Theresa's Catholic Church Madalla on Sunday February 3, 2013, the Bishop of Maiduguri Diocese, Rev. Dr. Oliver Dume, said that Boko Haram is caused by injustice and corruption in Nigeria. He deplored the gravity of treasury looting in Nigeria which has kept the masses in wretchedness, hopelessness, abject poverty and insecurity. According to the Bishop:

"If the resources of this country are equitably distributed, every youth will be employed." [96]

The sermon was an exhortation on Christians to condemn all acts of corruption and deceit in government and society for Nigeria to survive and grow. In his thesis to Nigerians released 15 January 2012, the radical Catholic Bishop of Sokoto Diocese, Rev. Dr. Hassan Kukah posited that:

"The inability of the State to punish criminals as criminals has created the illusion that there is a conflict between Christians and Moslems. Nigeria is changing

because Nigerians are taking back their country from the grip of marauders. Christians and Moslems together in solidarity are protesting against bad governance and corruption beyond the falsehood of religion. It is this poverty that produces jealousy and hatred which leads to violence. "[97]

Nigerian Nobel Laureate and literary icon, Professor Wole Soyinka, had in July avowed that the Islamic insurgency group, Boko Haram, could not cause breakup of Nigeria despite the ferocity of its attacks. Wole Soyinka spoke to Reuters at his country home in Abeokuta on July 2, 2014. He insisted that fatal offensives by the terrorist group had shown Nigerians that working together would be the only way to avoid greater ethnic carnage.

Analyzing the trend of events in the country today, the erudite scholar said:

"We have never been confronted with butchery on this scale, even during the Civil War. There were atrocities but we never had such a near predictable level of carnage, and this is what is horrifying."

Debunking the predictions that the Boko Haram attacks will eventually lead to breakup of Nigeria, Prof Wole Soyinka declared:

"I think ironically it's less likely now. For the first time, a sense of belonging is predominating. It is either we stick together now or we break up, and we know it would not be a pleasant war."

He stated that:

"The Boko Haram forces that would like to see the nation break up are the very forces which will not be satisfied having their enclave. (We) are confronted with an enemy that will never be satisfied with the space it has." [98]

Reacting to the twin bomb attacks in Kaduna on July 23, 2014 in which himself and former Military Head of State, General Muhammadu Buhari were targeted and survived by a whisker, renowned Islamic scholar, Sheik Dahiru Bauchi revealed on 25 July that insurgency in Northern Nigeria is supported by government officials who have personal interest in the phenomenon. In an interview on the Hausa Service of the Voice of America, monitored in the Plateau State capital – Jos, Sheik Bauchi accused the Federal Government of having a 'hidden agenda' in the insurgency. According to the Sheik:

"Government officials are behind Boko Haram. There is no doubt about it and that is why it (government) refuses to end the insurgency. There is no doubt that there is a strong hidden agenda in the whole thing."

The Islamic cleric further indicted the Federal Government of deceit in the effort to negotiate with members of the Boko Haram sect. He said he got government guarantee to start talks of settlement with Boko Haram, culminating in the signing of an agreement between the two parties which later failed. The accord, he divulged, was signed when the 'real Boko Haram was operating, insisting that the current rebellion is a new

Boko Haram. Recounting the events of his foundered mediation initiative, the Moslem teacher said:

"The government is not sincere in its effort to bring an end to insurgency in Nigeria because it has refused to sign the agreement. When I was asked to intervene, I thought the government was sincere about it. Unknown to me, the whole thing is deceptive and all this was when real Boko Haram was existing."

On Wednesday 23 July, Dahiru Bauchi was attacked by insurgents on his way home after he had closed the year's Ramadan Tafsir (sermon) where many were killed and scores wounded. Almost at the same time General Buhari narrowly escaped death as his convoy was bombed by the insurgents which resulted in grave fatalities.[99]

Rebuking the idea of negotiating with the Boko Haram insurgents, former Nigerian Military president, General Ibrahim Babangida, cautioned the Federal Government against engaging in deliberations with hiding and unidentified rebels. He stated that:

"But you need to go into negotiations with the people you know and which you can identify; but in the case of the Boko Haram sect, whom do you negotiate with? That is the problem. I do not believe that the Federal Government or Mr. President should throw open his doors to continue to negotiate with people who have gone into hiding and have not identified themselves. So, who do you talk with?

"You can only negotiate with identified persons who, for one reason or the other, everybody knows them and they

*are fighting for a particular cause by saying this is what
they are doing, and I think that is fair enough. But we
don't know these guys, so we have to be fair to the
Federal Government about this conflict. Let them come
out and say this is the leadership, this is the structure, this
is our grievances, that is what we want and then they can
sit down and talk. But so far, it has not happened."*[100]

Former Canon Emeritus at Coventry Cathedral UK, Dr.
Stephen Davis, who had assiduously worked in Nigeria
and across for the release of the incarcerated Chibok girls,
affirmed the sponsors of the Boko Haram sect to the
global media on August 30, 2014. In an Interview with
Sahara Reporters, the Australian negotiator insists Modu
Sherriff – former Governor of Borno State and Lieutenant
General Azubuike Ihejirika – past Chief of Army Staff
(COAS) -- sponsor Boko Haram insurgency in Nigeria. In
the press report, Dr. Davis also accused an unnamed
senior official of the Central Bank of Nigeria (CBN) as
well as a man based in Cairo, Egypt whom he claimed
operates as Boko Haram's bagman. He said both men, in
addition to Mr. Sheriff and General Ihejirika, were major
players in the funding and continued existence of the
deadly Islamist sect. Specifically, Dr. Davis said;

*"Boko Haram commanders and some connected with
them told me on several occasions Ihejirika was one of
their sponsors."*

Mr. Davis stated that:

*"One of the biggest of suppliers of arms and military
uniforms to the JAS (Jama'atu Ahlis Sunna Lidda'awati
wal-Jihad, aka Boko Haram) currently lives in Cairo,
Egypt. He is the receiver of money sent by political
sponsors from Nigeria. The funds pass through the*

CBN's financial system and appear to be
a legitimate transaction. Meanwhile, the CBN official
who handles the funding is an uncle to three of those
arrested relating to the Nyanya bombings."

Mr. Stephen further divulged that President Jonathan has
been weakened by lack of military loyalty and a history of
security negligence and ineptitude. He cited the example
of repeated attempts to bring the growth of Al Qa'eda
associated cells to the attention of National Security
Advisers (NSA) since 2006 only to have them dismiss
such reports as baseless. According to the Australian,

"By the time Goodluck Jonathan became President Boko
Haram had become a potent weapon with a command
structure embedded in 16 northern states fanned by
support from corrupt politicians."

The Australian mediator also revealed that his years
working with Nigerian Presidents on matters of terrorism
had shown that, even when some prominent individuals
are known to be involved in criminality, the Presidents
are just too afraid to bring them to book. He referred to
the example of the Niger Delta region. At the conference,
he stated that he and former President Olusegun Obasanjo
found out that Abiye Sekibo, who was then Mr.
Obasanjo's Transport Minister, had contracted the
assassins who killed a prominent politician, Harry
Marshall. He tried to persuade Mr. Obasanjo to no avail
to prosecute Mr. Sekibo. Obasanjo refused, adducing that
such a venture could bring down his government.
On the activities of the Boko Haram sect, Dr.
Stephen avowed that he was quite well-informed about
the sect's actions. He told Sahara Reporters that Boko
Haram runs about six major camps in the northeast and
neighboring countries, 700 fighters inhabiting each camp.
Additionally, there are a range of smaller camps within

Borno State, which are often temporary and to which kidnapped girls are taken to be raped by the insurgents.

Dr. Davis revealed that earlier this year Boko Haram was a loose alliance of three Islamist militant groups that worked with one another. However, in the last four months the sects had merged into 'one single entity, become more cohesive, strategically effective and powerful.' He related that:

"They are now linking with other terrorist groups in the region and will soon be very difficult to dismantle. If these political sponsors think they can turn these groups off after the 2015 elections they are going to be surprised to find it is out of their control."

He tagged former National Security Adviser, Owoye Andrew Azazi, as 'utterly corrupt.' Mr. Azazi, a retired Army General, he disclosed, was planning to buy into the Hilton Hotel chain in London to the tune of $100 million before he died in a helicopter accident on December 15, 2012.

Dr. Davis deplored the porosity of Nigeria's various intelligence units as operating in silos that refuse to share information that could tame terrorist groups. The Australian cited the instance of the State Security Services. According to him; months after the SSS won the extradition from the Sudan of Aminu Ogwuche, a suspected terror mastermind of the deadly bombing of an Abuja bus station, the intelligence agency had yet to interrogate the arrested kingpin about his links with the three young men he reportedly contracted to carry out the bombing.

The terrorism negotiator said the three young bombers lived in the home of a CBN official who also carried out banking transactions for Boko Haram through the CBN. Dr Davis, who said he did not want to mention the name of the CBN official - currently working in the bank's currency operations division - as this may affect investigation by Nigeria's security service, maintained that his allegations were informed by discussions he had with several Boko Haram field commanders over a long period of time. Two other young collaborators in the Nyanya Motor Park bombing remain at large.

On August 28, it was relayed that Dr Stephen had revealed Boko Haram sponsors and their plans declaring that:

"These politicians think that if they win power they can turn these terrorists off, but this has mutated. It's no longer a case of Muslims purifying by killing off Christians. They are just killing indiscriminately, beheading, disemboweling people – men, women and children and whole villages."

Davis spent four arduous months in the North-East; his life was subject to extreme danger while he tried to negotiate rescue of more than 200 school girls kidnapped by Boko Haram on April 14. He returned with extraordinary footage of the tough fighting in the region. Mr. Davis said he decided to come out to speak now because the Nigerian authorities were not acting fast and he was heart-broken by the evils being done to the kidnapped Chibok girls and many other girls and boys being kidnapped. The feisty Australian said;

"I have three daughters. I just cannot stand the thought of what those girls are passing through. I have spoken to an escapee who described how she was being raped for 40 days by militants. I can't stand it. It is heart-breaking. Nigerian authorities must act decisively now."
Stephen Davis, 63, who holds a PhD in political geography from the University of Melbourne, Australia,

said he spent 'days and weeks' with commanders of Boko Haram in the north-east during his time in Nigeria.[101]

Meanwhile on September 2 the national leadership of the oppositional All Progressives Congress (APC) called for the prosecution of former Borno State governor, Ali Modu Sheriff over his alleged role in funding of insurgency in the north-east. During a press briefing in Abuja, APC National Chairman, Chief John Odigie-Oyegun, called on the government to hand over Sheriff and General Ihejirika to the International Criminal Court (ICC) for investigation and prosecution. The party chairman fumed that:

"The die is cast. The truth is finally out! Boko Haram sponsors have been exposed. They are within the ruling PDP. They are friends of President Jonathan. He cannot pretend not to know who they are and what they have done and are still doing. His myriad of intelligence agencies, including the DSS and the DMI, cannot pretend they do not have any information on these men."

"Now that the cat has been let out of the bag and the real sponsors of Boko Haram have been exposed, we hope President Jonathan will summon the courage to do the right thing: Hand over the identified Boko Haram sponsors to the International Criminal Court (ICC) for investigation and prosecution. There is no doubt that Boko Haram has committed crimes against humanity in its scorched-earth campaign against unharmed citizens, and the most appropriate body to investigate and try the sect's sponsors is the ICC. Nigerians can rest assured that the APC will not allow this issue to be swept under the carpet."[102]

In an interview with the NIGERIAN PILOT Newspaper relayed on September1, 2014, leader of the Niger Delta Volunteer Force (NDVF), Mujahid Asari Dokubo, ascribed the persistent calamitous insurgency to the political power greed of those he called 'Gambaris of Northern Nigeria with Guinea descent.' In the report Asari Dokubo avowed that:

"In Nigeria, the insurgency is that Goodluck is an Ijaw man. He is a southerner and must not rule. They are going to make the country ungovernable. So, they now apply Islamic sentiment which is nowhere; there is no compulsion in religion. That is what the Quran says. To you, is your faith; and to me is my faith!"

On President Goodluck Jonathan's bid to contest the 2015 election, the riparian war lord seethed:

"Good Luck represents the freedom of you and me from the hands of the colonist Gambari people from Guinea who have foisted their hegemony on us. A lot of people will not understand the spiritual dimension Goodluck's emergence as President of the country. He is the first to become President without the north's approval and he is completing his tenure. It is the sacrifice that Abiola, Dokubo Asari made that brought GoodLuck. GoodLuck represents something greater than himself, and that is the freedom and dignity of you and me."

He declared that the Boko Harm insurgency is a plus to his struggle for an independent Nigeria Delta State. According to the former militant leader:

"So, for me I say kudos to Shekau; you are doing my duty. He is doing what I am supposed to do. I am relaxed. Let them be doing it; let the enemy be running everything that is happening. It is to my own good. It is to the good of my people because we have less people to fight when the time comes."

He re-affirmed his unbelief in the Nigerian state thus:

"Among Nigerians it is believed that because of the corruption, as it were, it is difficult to prosecute the anti-insurgency war. The enemy of my enemy is my enemy. That question is not meant for me. It's meant for the people who believe in Nigeria. I do not believe in Nigeria. I have gone up to the Supreme Court denouncing Nigeria. If my enemy is dying, if Nigeria is dying; why should I bother?" [103]

Early October 2014 previous Head of State, General Yakubu Gowon, offered to mediate between the Federal Government and Boko Haram to end the ruinous insurgency in northern Nigeria. General Gowon, now Chairman of Stakeholders' Dialogue on Peace Development, agreed to serve in this capacity on 9th October 2014 at a Stakeholders' Dialogue/Peace Forum on north-east zone, organized by the Nigeria Security and Civil Defence Corps (NSCDC), in collaboration with United Nations Development Programme (UNDP) and other relevant security agencies, held within the banquet hall of Government House, Gombe State. In a statement communicated by the Hausa Service of the BBC, the former Nigerian military ruler said:

"I am begging them (the insurgents), to please, because of God, stop this carnage; if it entails myself meeting with

them personally. I am willing to mediate on behalf of the government, even if it means going as far as China, just to bring an end to this rampant killing of innocent civilians by the sect in the north."

He decried the alarming insurgency, insisting that issue of the 'killings by the sect is everybody's business'. Gowon affirmed that for us to win the war against terror all Nigerians have a collective responsibility to protect our destiny and there is the need for us as a nation to cooperate with one another irrespective of our religion, ethnic group, socio-economic and political bearings.

January 1967, an accord in Ghana between rebelling Biafran leaders from the south east headed by Lt. Col. Odumegwu Ojukwu, and the Federal Military Government of Nigeria led by Lt. Col. Yakubu Gowon, foundered on interpretation of agreed issues. The calamitous civil war which subsequently broke out between the two dissonant sides in July ended in January 1970 with colossal loss of lives, property and grave retardation of national economy. Amongst the disastrous consequences of that unwarranted war is the current sanguinary rebellion. Hence, the retired General still has a conundrum to decipher: why is it that Nigeria, 47 years after the civil war, the people flounder in abject poverty and the country as a whole is drifting into abyss?[104]

Nigeria cannot defeat Boko Haram alone – UN

Addressing AFP in Addis Ababa on 28 January 2015, the United Nation's envoy for the Sahel region, Hiroute Guebre Selassie, said Nigeria must accept it can not singlehandedly defeat the Boko Haram insurgents ravaging the north east. She emphasized that Nigeria should work with regional armies in a new multinational force. That statement rebuked an earlier assertion by the Nigerian National Security Adviser-- Sambo Dasuki--

that his country can overcome Boko Haram independent of foreign assistance.

According to the diplomat:

"Nigeria cannot handle the problem alone. Boko Haram is not only confined in Nigeria."

She spoke at the Ethiopian Capital where she was preparing the 54-member African Union Leaders (AUL) summit. Warning of a possible training camp in northern Mali, Guebre Selassie said:

"We see a flood of refugees to Niger, Cameroun and even Chad. The Sahel is increasingly affected."

The AU leaders were expected to discuss a proposed regional force of 3,000 troops that would include contingents from Nigeria, Niger, Benin, Chad and Cameroun. Selassie insisted that:

"It is time to take action and to be aware of the danger of Boko Haram for the entire African continent." Boko Haram insurgents have overrun some territories in north eastern Nigeria which they declared as part of 'Islamic Caliphate State."

AU scribe, Nkosazana Dlamini-Zuma, on 27 January said she was 'deeply worried' at the rise of Boko Haram, considering that the group is 'not just a threat to some countries but a threat to the whole continent'. She had proposed 'renewed collective African efforts' to deal with the rebels. Consequently, The AU on 30 January recommended a multinational army of 7,500 troops to eradicate insurgency in the Chadian region.

At the occasion UN Secretary-General, Ban Ki Moon, reiterated the need for a transnational force to stop the spread of insurgency in Nigeria and the entire Sahel. International groups including the New York-based Christian Association of Nigerian-Americans (CANAN). Amnesty International and Human Rights Watch have also called for a concerted action against Boko Haram. [105]

In a 2-minute video released July 2016, the son of slain Al Qaeda leader, Osama Bin Laden, threatened to attack the United States of America in defence of Muslim nations in the Middle East and Africa. Hamza Bin Laden, then in his mid twenties avowed:

"We will continue striking you and targeting you in your country and abroad in response to your oppression of the people of Palestine, Afghanistan, Iraq, Yemen, Somalia and the rest of the Muslim lands that did not survive your oppression." [106]

Abubakar Shekau, dreaded sectional leader of Boko Haram, resurfaced in early August 2016 in a new video vowing to carry out more ferocious attacks on Abuja. In the video delivered in rapid fire Hausa and Arabic accent, Shekau insisted that he was still the leader of Boko Haram and that he had no intention of attacking Muslims. However, the Nigerian Army led by Lt, Gen. Tukur Buratai at the same time claimed Boko Haram had been defeated.

Pledging loyalty to Abu Bakr al-Baghdadi, leader of global terrorist organization—ISIS, Shekau said he would never recognize Abu Musab Al-Barnawi, factional leader of Boko Haram who has ISIS recognition. Al-Barnawi's appointment had earlier been made known in the latest issue of ISIS-managed magazine but Shekau totally rejected the development, charging that ISIS sabotaged him because he opposed their principles. In the 24-minute video Abubakar Shekau said:

"I, Abubakar Ash-Shakawi, the leader of Jam'atu Ahlis Sunna Lidda Awati Wal Jihad, made it a duty for myself to fight Nigeria and the whole world. We have no desire to fight our Muslim brethren. I'm alive by the permission of Allah. Let the Government of Nigeria and West Africa not celebrate or gloat over the division between us and our bothers…We will shock them with attacks never seen before in no distant time…"

Shekau condemned Western countries including the United States, France, Germany and the 'tyrants of the United Nonsense' (UN). As recorded in the Vanguard Newspaper of 5th August 2016, the Niger Delta Revolutionary Crusaders declared as follows:

"If Boko Haram kills Christians and burns down churches, we will slay Muslims and raze down mosques. We want to warn them that the Niger Delta youths in this 21st century will not accept the killing of innocent Christians or the burning of churches. That if they try it in the north or any part of Nigeria, we the Niger Delta youths will not see any Muslim or mosque in the Niger Delta."

This was sequel to an earlier statement by new leader of Boko Haram, Abu Musah Al Barnawi, who apparently had the backing of ISIS: that he would henceforth target only Christians and burn down all the churches in Nigeria. [107]

There are intellectual people in the Boko Haram group. So, it is wise for government to explicitly bring them to reason by dialogue.[108, 109] Utilitarian negotiations had been conducted by the Nigerian government with insurgents in the Niger Delta under the shade of 'amnesty' as highlighted by Nasir el Rufai.[110] In 1945 when America bombed Hiroshima and Nagasaki with nuclear weapons killing about one million people, peace treaties were signed with Japan to end the Second World War. That was another form of dialogue.

It is true that terrorism is ever-present in the world as stated by President Good Luck Jonathan when he visited the bombed UN buildings. What then is the cause of global terrorism of which Nigeria has become a disastrous beneficiary? Whether it is Boko Haram in Nigeria, Al-Shebab in Somalia, Al-Qaeda in the Islamic Maghreb (AQIM) or Al-Qaeda in the Arabian peninsular (AQAP), their grievances are centered on: Zionist (Western) occupation of Arabian lands especially Palestine.

In his speeches, Osama Bin Laden 'doggedly' advocated Jihad against Zionist occupation. On March 21, 2012, while reflecting on global build-up of lethal

arsenals to annihilate human species, Comrade Fidel
Castro of Cuba said:

*"..... The odious policy of those who deny the Palestinian
People their right to exist is repugnant...... If we do not
learn how to understand, we shall never learn how to
survive."*[111]

It is distressing and shameful that world leaders
have failed to establish a two-state arrangement for Israel
and Palestine based on UN resolution 181 of 1947 which
guaranteed independence for the two countries. President
Barack Obama had made a bold attempt to broker peace
by proposing the same two states existence based on the
pre-1967 parameters. Prime Minister Benjamin
Netanyahu accused him of trying to achieve peace 'over
night' and as such a 'Daniel came to judgment'. Since
then, Obama retreated to Washington.

Unfortunately, while terrorism springs from Israeli
occupation in the Middle East, the whole World is
bearing the brunt of its ferocious and catastrophic spread.
America alone had spent more than one trillion dollars in
the past 10 years fighting terrorism, the solution of which
is at its backyard. It is high time US eliminated dubious
equations in dealing with the Israel and Palestine issue.
How do you want Israel and Palestine to exist as
independent state when you veto the declaration of

independence of the later at the United Nations Security Council?

While visiting Jerusalem on the 22nd of October 2012, former US President, Jimmy Carter, stated that the prospect of Israeli-Palestinian peace settlement 'is vanishing.' His contingent christened 'The Elders' (former Prime Minister of Norway and past President of Ireland inclusive), held talks with Israeli President Shimon Peres and Palestinian President Mahmud Abbas. Deploring the degeneration of the peace process, Carter said:

"We have reached a crisis state. The Two-State solution is the only realistic path to peace and security for Israel and the Palestinians." [112]

It is hoped that the observer status granted Palestine by the UN on 29 November 2012 will eventually lead to full independence. World leaders should boldly and unequivocally resolve once and for all the scourge of global terrorism by working out a functional territorial formula which will guarantee independent Palestine and Israeli states.   Regrettably Western leaders who claim they are developed and industrialized are still barbaric: they have assembled nuclear weapons of mass destruction worth trillions of dollars of global wealth and they cannot solve the territorial dispute of Israel and Palestine which is the root cause of global terrorism. Former Nigerian Minister of Foreign Affairs, Ojo Maduekwe, had emphasized in 2009 that for peace to reign in the middle east, which will of course, consequently retard terrorism; Israel must vacate Palestinian lands it seized since 1967.

Sadly, while the government of Nigeria is struggling to end the Boko Haram crisis, top government officials in various strata, politicians and sycophants are smiling to the banks with funds siphoned from the treasury under the pretext of finding solutions. This was corroborated by Boko Haram which stated that previous dialogue it had with government failed to yield fruitful results because state representatives reneged on agreement. [113] The vices of treachery and deceit in government cannot be employed to dialogue with Boko Haram.

After the December 25 Christmas bombing at St. Theresa's Catholic Church Madalla, the leadership of the Nigerian Senate begged Boko Haram members to come and make their demands known--- a clear manifestation of naivety pertaining to the phenomenon. Deploring the suicide bomb attacks at a Kano bus park on March 18, 2013, which claimed the lives of more than 100 people, Senate President David Mark said:

"This act is condemnable. It is inhuman and barbaric. This is certainty not our culture. We cannot live like this. Something serious has gone wrong in the land."[114] Unfortunately, it was then he understood something serious had gone wrong with the land. His statement truly confirmed the earlier assertion that the Nigerian Senate is in the limbo over the Boko Haram crisis.

The United States under Secretary for Political Affairs, Wendy Sherman, has urged the Federal Government of Nigeria to provide jobs for unemployed youths in the north to curb the Boko Haram intrigue,[115] one of the means of dialogue. Former President of Nigeria, GoodLuck Jonathan, promised to implement recommendations of past committees set up to investigate causes of the Boko Haram crisis. [116] Till date reports of these investigations have not been made public. It is our hope that this move and the amnesty [117] will not be derailed or hijacked by sycophants and lip service men at the corridors of power for selfish ends. Meanwhile according to the Nigerian Pentecostal pastor, Boko Haram is 'spiritual cleansing' and 'finger of God' against corrupt leadership and dubiousness. [118]

DESTITUTION BREEDS INSECURITY

The current insecurity and violence are all grist to the mill of underhanded politicians and elite-- the beneficiaries of the resultant confusion. Nigerian tertiary institutions are inundating society with empty-headed graduates -- collecting sex and money from them and giving them certificates. These youths, in their thousands, subsequently rove about the streets searching for jobs in mirage.

Today, it is ubiquitous to see Nigerian youths and children scavenging on garbage to earn their daily morsel. Nigerian teenagers forage on sands, metals, plastics, scraps and derelict house hold appliances in waterways, drainage ditches and rubbish dumps in spite of the accompanying hazards like epidemics, injury and snake bites. The reason behind this deplorable delinquent venture is the crushing poverty propelled by egregious governance in Nigeria.[119]

The Nigerian Telegraph of 15 November 2017 reported hat Nigerian youths were being sold as slaves in Libya. Nigerians were auctioned to prospective buyers at $400 per person. On daily basis, we hear of the unspeakable suffering and deaths of Nigerian boys and girls as they try to cross the Sahara Desert into Libya. More worrisome is the frequent massive death by drowning and ship wreck of these youths making futile attempts to enter Europe by sea for 'greener pastures'.

Jobless youths have resorted to heinous crimes like armed robbery, kidnapping and child trafficking, to make a living. Cases of abduction and child trading are more pronounced in the Niger Delta and south east. The trauma of these crimes to society is unimaginable.

Dissident boys of the Niger Delta, agitating for resource self determination and environmental preservation were settled by late President Musa Yar'adua in a deal camouflaged as amnesty. Some of them had been employed to safeguard oil installations nut later dumped. As poverty and state neglect ravages the Niger Delta the youths spearheaded by the Niger Delta Avengers resumed armed struggle in the creeks after the 2015 general elections, inflicting heavy collateral damage on crude oil installations and output, and demanding a sovereign Niger Delta Republic. After the seismic destruction of key oil facilities with attendant sharp drop in production the Nigerian state was plunged into recession. This devastating recession was aggravated by clueless and ineffective government policies.

Col Umar Opposes Going to War in the Niger Delta

Former Military Governor of Kaduna State, Col. Abubakar Dangiwa Umar (Rtd), on the 30th of September 2016 cautioned President Muhammadu Buhari against deploying troops and military weapons in the Niger Delta to halt the activities of militants. Umar said the Federal

Government's planned use of military force to root out militants, especially the Niger Delta Avengers, was not the best option. He believed the militants were still amenable to dialogue.

President Muhammad Buhari had, in a statement relayed by his Senior Special Assistant on Media Affairs, Mr. Garba Shehu, in Nairobi, Kenya said that he would treat Niger Delta insurgents the same way he dealt with Boko Haram if they refused dialogue. Rebuking the President, Col Dangiwa in a statement entitled, 'War in the Niger Delta: A Most Dangerous Option,' contended that the militants could not be treated like Boko Haram rebels that had murdered over 20,000 Nigerians in the north-eastern part of the country. In his declaration Col. Umar said:

"I am really frightened by the sudden escalation in the Niger Delta Region from where there are some reports of skirmishes between our security forces and the Niger Delta militants. This is happening after the President was quoted as vowing to deal with the militants as he did to Boko Haram. All factors considered the use of military force to resolve the lingering crisis is not a good option and must therefore be discarded.

"As a retired general, Mr. President is aware of the serious and daunting challenges any military will face in its operations in the most difficult and densely populated Niger Delta region. The creeks are so heavily polluted with oil, rendering them highly inflammable. It will take the firing of a few high explosive shells to set the whole area on fire, resulting in the inestimable collateral damage among innocent civilians."

On the inappropriateness of war to solve the problems in the Niger Delta the human rights activist posited:

"It is also difficult to see how an armed conflict can secure our oil and gas assets in the region. Instead, it will aid the destructive activities of the militants and lead to the total shutdown of all oil and gas operations in the area. Besides, the Niger Delta militants cannot be said to be terrorists in the real sense of the word. I believe they are amenable to meaningful dialogue."

Urging the President to reconsider his hostility stance Umar said:

"I need not to remind the President that a war in the Niger Delta will be opposed by most objective Nigerians and the international community as unjust and merely aimed at the control and exploitation of the region's oil and gas resources. I therefore beseech you, Mr. President, in the name of all that is good, to continue to explore peaceful means of resolving the Niger Delta crisis as painful as you may find this. May God direct and guide you on the path of justice." [120]

Comparative Literature Nobel Laureate, Ptrofessor Wole Soyinka, in a press conference with Sahara Reporters divulged the content of his meeting with President Muhammadu Buhari at the State House on August 11, 2016. Soyinka said that their discussion centred on the Niger Delta crisis, the kidnapped Chibok girls, corruption and other 'peripheral issues'. On the matter of the militants for whom he initiated the meeting with President Buhari, Prof Soyinka said:

"My position is that the Delta insurgency and restlessness is an integral part of a certain dissatisfaction with the internal arrangements, socio-political arrangements of the nation.

In other words, for me, I just see this as an aspect of a call for restructuring because of the peculiar history of the Delta region in relation to others, has giving rise to militarism which surges again and again and again.

Soyinka stated that President Buhari was already negotiating Nigeria's sovereignty thus:

"So, I believe we had a very, I believe, positive discussion on that. In fact, I remember telling him that each time you say Nigeria's sovereignty is not negotiable, you or Obasanjo or Gowon or your military people, the world will start talking to insurgents. You are already negotiating Nigerian sovereignty; so, let's move away from the rhetoric and get practical. So, it was along those lines that we had our conversation. Not only on the Niger Delta issue, also talked about Chibok girls, on corruption, on a number of other peripheral issues..." [121]

In 2009 deceitful politicians from north eastern Nigeria recruited some youths as armed guards and claque to enable them win elections with coercion and fraud. After the dubious polls, the boys were abandoned with their arms; they were not settled. Consequently, they reassembled to chart a cause of vengeance. The result is what we are seeing today-- calamitous insurgency, Boko Haram.

The people of Nigeria have been stripped of the right to make decisions concerning their lives and destiny. They are daily being subjected to the authoritarian and sometimes whimsical decisions of duplicitous politicians and select few. According to Dr. Nelson Mandela:

"When a man is denied the right to live the life he believes in, he has no choice but to become an outlaw."

This is a country where over half of the state treasury is frittered away under the guise of petroleum subsidy. The other half goes into State of Emergency and defence, leaving the people, the owners of sovereignty, to swelter in poverty, wretchedness, hopelessness and destitution. It is really a shame!

This sound perception had been buttressed by state security in 2017. In a lecture titled 'Unity in diversity' organized early August 2017 by the Department of State Services (DSS) its Director, Laval Daura, acknowledged that bad governance and corruption are the main factors that trigger ethnic agitations in Nigeria. In his remarks on mal-governance breeding cosmic social insecurity, Daura said:

"These governance failures have been amply implicated in the massive unemployment and very poor socio-economic conditions across the land, which feeds and spread frustrations, anger and agitations, nationwide.

"There is no gainsaying the fact that if we get governance right, we will have more salutary outcome in terms of security and other contemporary challenges."[122]

The masses find it difficult to eat two local meals in a day. They are traumatized, dehumanized and defrauded everyday by their leaders - the imperious demigods that fraudulently pilot the affairs of the State. Their hope in government wanes by day.

When they complain their petitions are treated with contempt and hidden. When they protest persistent injustice, they are bundled into jail on arbitrary charges of public nuisance, incitement and unlawful assembly. This is a vicious scheming with police and judicial complicity aimed at asphyxiating the citizenry.

Why then can't there be insecurity in such a capricious and deceitful nation? If bureaucratic corruption holds sway, insecurity will inexorably be a noose around the neck of Nigerians. Let me use this medium to join Chief Olusegun Obasanjo[123] and plead with all men of benevolence, especially the Boko Haram to disdain violence and allow exchange of ideas and reasoning to resolve this catastrophic and repugnant crisis.[124, 125]

CHAPTER 3

INVASION BY THE NIGERIAN POLICE

On the sunrise of 5th September 2013, campaigners of Anticorruption Revolution in Nigeria gathered at our Anticorruption Square Wuse Market Junction, Abuja for a protest march to the premises of the Economic and Financial Crimes Commission, EFCC. It is a well-known fact by the government that when I climbed to the roof-top of Head of Service building Abuja on 16 July 2012 to protest the gravity of corruption in that department, I was arrested by the State Security Services (SSS), interrogated and released on escort. There after on the 13th of August 2012 I presented a report of the incidence to the EFCC asking that certain grave corrupt practices at the Pension Department of the Head of Service should be clarified and rectified. Mr. Ibrahim Lamorde and his EFCC received that petition, treated it with contempt and hid it from the Nigerian people -a devious proclivity to abet and perpetuate corruption in Nigeria.

Yet again, on the 5th of March 2013 I submitted to the EFCC another set of Anticorruption documents which subsumed the Wuse Market Declaration. Specifically, the Wuse Market Declaration of Anticorruption Revolution contained an 18-point petition on corrupt and fraudulent practices in various Ministries, Departments, and Agencies (MDAs) in Nigeria which we wanted the EFCC to clarify and rectify. Yet they received the documents and kept mute.

Subsequently on the 24th of July 2013 we sent a letter to the EFCC, reminding them of our earlier petitions which have fallen on deaf ears. We gave them two-week ultimatum to respond to those petitions or face court and mass action from the Nigerian people. At the same time the notice was extended to the Headquarters of the SSS on 29 July, 2013).

The lack of response from the EFCC indicated ineptitude, triteness and irresponsibility to the Nigerian People. That was contrary to the dictates of President Goodluck Jonathan who urged citizens to channel their grievances to government institutions through peaceful means and dialogue. But the EFCC turned deaf ears to peaceful petitions from Nigerians.

As a result, the Anticorruption advocates gathered at Wuse to address Nigerians before marching to EFCC to protest Mr. Lamorde's deceit, vacuity and irresponsibility in the Nigerian State. I have to point out here that the protest and gathering was organized in accordance with the following sections of the 1999 constitution of the Federal Republic of Nigeria as amended: -

1.   Section 24b: Help and defence of country

2.   Section 38: Freedom of thought and conscience

3.   Section 39: Freedom of expression, opinion

4.   Section 40: Freedom of association, peaceful assembly.

Just about 10:30am, while we were addressing Nigerians on the need to stop corruption so that our country can survive, grow and prosper (with a display of or 35 posters on corrupt and fraudulent practices), some policemen approached us, asking under whose authority we were operating. We explained that it was in line with the 1999 constitution sections 24b, 38, 39 and 40. They left and another group came and asked the same question. We equally served them the same dish.

They said that we would not make any impact at Wuse Junction. If we wanted to be heard we should go to the National Assembly. We thanked them for that information.

As we were withdrawing into the garden, other police men came in three pick-up vans shooting guns in the air and detonating tea gas canisters all over Wuse Market Junction. Some of them ran into the garden and said we should stop. I instructed the advocates not to run or resist arrest: we are non-violent.

They packed us into one of the police vans, seven of us while at the same time shooting guns. Names of the Anti-Corruption Advocates arrested include: Fatoye Yetunde, Patrick Eguaboh, Gideon Daniel, Achason Friday, Gbenga Bojuwomi, Morison Uwem and Okenwa Enyeribe. Comrade Nyam and one other person were apprehended separately and locked up in Wuse Market Police Post. They were released the following day, Friday.

As they drove from Wuse Junction to Berger, we were shouting; 'One Nigeria, No Corruption' and at the same time throwing the fliers which read: EFCC IS A DECEIT IN NIGERIA to onlookers and passers by along the Road. That was to let Nigerians know why we were arrested.

We were driven to Maitama Police Station Area Command. Before alighting from the van, we said the National Pledge. The police men ordered us in a line. Tear gas canisters were again detonated and placed in betwixt our legs. They continued shooting guns into the air. As we were suffocating to death, I told them that we were not in crime or violence and therefore did not deserve that type of torture.

Then they ordered us into the charge section, seized our phones and other items. We were taken to the cell. It was a 6ft by 6ft room. About one hour later, we were brought out. Some police men from the State Criminal Investigation Department (CID) led by one Mr. Philip (so he introduced himself) had come to grill us.

They asked us our names and other personal information which we readily gave them. Then Mr. Philip asked why we were protesting. I told him that our thought (section 38) is that current endemic and cancerous corruption, if according to continue will lead to collapse of Nigeria which will imperil future generations. As a constitutional duty, we must fight corruption (section 24b, 39, 40) for our country to survive and grow.

Our advocates were given statement sheets and I instructed them to fill in their personal data and adopt my own statement which is our conscience and thought section 38. Mr. Philip then opened his shirt at the back and showed us the scar he had from injuries during his activism in the university. He started displaying his loftiness and bravado by telling us he had his first degree, Master's and was pursuing his Ph.D. We thanked him for his academic attainment.

Right there he told us that he would lock us in Kuje prison. Also, some of his men asked my members 'if they wanted this matter to be settled here or in the court.' What is the meaning of settling the matter there? This question is before the Nigerian people. Then we were asked questions on the exhibits--the caustic posters on corrupt and fraudulent practices:

1. Federal Government of Nigeria spends 2.6 trillion naira-- half of the State Annual Budget fueling cars under the dubious shade of petroleum subsidy. I explained that. Mr. Philip asked me truculently: How many cars do we have in Nigeria?

2. That Nigerians would revolt after 4 years; said by President Goodluck Jonathan, I equally explained and referred them to National Accord 29 Nov. 2011, Page I. Again, he interjected with sardonic bellicosity: 'is it 4 years then?'

There after Mr. Philip and his assistant, a young man started sleeping on their chairs. They collected our files, documents and the posters on corruption. I could remember him emphasizing that we must tell them our backers or sponsors. We told them that we had no sponsors but patriotic contribution from members.

We were taken to the counter and they handed us over to the local police, saying that they would come back the next day--Friday to continue with us. We were taken back to the cell. There we were packed with some other people.

Our female advocate Yetunde Fatoye was locked in the same room with us, about 10 people in that room. We slept in the same room with her till day! They had a bathroom which was too wide open for bathing privacy. It had no door.

Later in the night they arranged for wraps of soup and starch meal after collecting N200 for each. One boy who said he was the president of the cell demanded from us money for Izal and detergent. Patrick our scribe gave him N500.

Then in the morning around 11a m we were called out to the counter. The investigators from State CID this time around sent only one person. Mr. Philips did not come. The local policemen gave us back our shoes and other personal effects, still seizing our phones. We were discharged from there and driven to Wuse Zone 6 Magistrate Court at Cotonou Street.

Then our charges were prepared: unlawful assembly, public nuisance, incitement. Our lawyer Barrister Stan Dioka sent a counsel to plead for our bail. We were granted bail since the case, according to the Judge, "is ordinarily bailable". However, he placed stringent conditions on our bond: two grade level 12 public officers and above as sureties. How then was the case ordinarily bailable?

We were driven to Kuje prison for admission. At prison entrance Yetunde was collapsing due to excessive gastro-enteritis. She was driven back to Suleja Prison since, as the warders said, Kuje was not admitting female prisoners. Relatives of our advocates in conjunction with our lawyer Barrister Ezekiel Ugochukwu started working on the bail conditions for our release one at a time.

Our case was put off for October 7, 2013. I stayed three weeks in kuje prison and was released on Wednesday 25th Sept. 2013. Achason Friday was eventually released on Tuesday October 8, 2013. On the 14th of January 2014, the frivolous case was struck out for want of prosecution.

CHAPTER 4

WHY A REVOLUTION IN NIGERIA?

"The most compelling reasons for revolution throughout the ages were injustice, crushing poverty, marginalization, rampant corruption, lawlessness, joblessness and general dissatisfaction with the ruling elite. That these conditions exist is well known to the people in authority but the successive efforts have failed to yield the radical change from the present approach to a revolution one"--*Aminu Tambuwal, Speaker of the Nigerian House of Representatives, July 2, 2013*

On the 16th of July 2012, I ascended to the roof-top of the 9-strorey Head of Service Block Abuja unconventionally to expose to Nigerians the corruption, deceit and rot in that department. I was wheedled to descend by the management of the Head of Service. After flooring them in their grill, they handed me over to the SSS.

The SSS, a responsible and disciplined body, interviewed me briefly and not finding any fault in me, released me on escort. Since then the Anti-Corruption Revolution has spread to The Presidency, National Assembly, Federal Character Commission, Wuse Market Junction (many times) and other states in the Federal Republic of Nigeria. Yet on the 28th of May 2013, we were exhaustively screened by the ADIS Office of the SSS. Again, not finding us wanting, they said they 'don't want to waste our time.'

In spite of the fact that we had been cleared by the SSS, the police arrested some of us on 5 September 2013 and sent us to jail on frivolous charges. When I went to the office of the Commissioner of Police, Federal Capital Territory Abuja on 7 November 2013 to plead for the withdrawal of our case on the ground that we are protesting against corruption without violence, non anti government and serving our country in line with the constitution, I was stunned by the police men. The Investigating Police Officer (IPO), a spindly, black, debonair man said: I should sign an undertaking that I will not protest against corruption again anywhere in the Federal Republic of Nigeria.

I objected to their snare carrot, citing constitutional grounds to buttress our cause. Then they said if I would not sign that crap they would establish a fresh case against me. I told them they had no right to do that as it would amount to a civil suit which they don't handle. Then I consolidated my earlier statement that I would continuously speak out and fight against corruption in Nigeria.

I refused to kowtow to their deceit and ignominy. Their desultory shenanigans were too irritating to put up with. It equated to rankling with me; so, I signed and left. Is the Nigerian Police an advocate of the Corruption Establishment in Nigeria? Why do the police outrageously display visceral distaste for anti-corruption protests? Why are they bulwarks against corruption?

Do the policemen reap from today's resultant confusion? This is a conundrum for Nigerians because former Inspector General of police, Mr. Tafa Balogun, was sentenced to two years imprisonment for looting six billion Naira state funds. While being led to jail he was unremorseful and bragged: 'I will bounce back.'

Early in the morning of 30 January 2013, as I was driving to launch our anti-corruption Revolution, a truck coming from behind, lost brake and crushed my Mitsubishi 2000 Gallant irreparably. The crash, which occurred exactly athwart Mobile Filling Station Madalla, sent my vehicle flying into the bush at a speed I had never driven before, destination unknown. I eventually hit an electric pole, and then managed to creep out.

Turning back, the intermediate bus in the chain clash had been turned to its side. Officers of the Federal Road Safety Corps and the gathered crowd joined hands to push it back on its four wheels. They forced open the doors and brought out two dead mangled and bloody bodies. The traffic officers raced away with them in their pick-up van under ambulatory conditions. I was traumatized, woozy and fainting with that grisly image. No body attended to me.

Swiftly my assignment caught my attention. Then craning to the back seat, I drew out my satchel which contained the anti corruption message--The Wuse Market Declaration of Anti-Corruption Revolution in Nigeria. A Good Samaritan ferried me to Wuse. With the wounds on my legs I still ascended the 50-metre Airtel GSM sign post mast at Wuse Market Junction to declare Anticorruption Revolution.

The question is: Why are we engineering an Anti-Corruption Revolution in Nigeria? Are we just crying wolf or is the current cannibalistic corruption leading Nigeria into the deep-sea abyss? The unconscionable profundity of corruption and rot of the Nigerian State has been concisely compiled in the main compendium-THE EXPEDIENT NIGERIAN REVOLUTION HAS

EMERGED; Log in. Since the present text is a guide hand book, I entreat that patriotic reference should be made to that piece to explore this. However, the time line events (journals) section of the website of the Revolutionary Council of the Nigerian People-- www.revolutionarycouncil.org.ng.--equally subsumes a complete file of endemic corruption in Nigeria.

During the insufferable apartheid era, blacks, the owners of the land of South Africa were oppressed by brutish Boer segregationists. Their liberties and rights were disgracefully restricted. They were slaves in their mother country. There was hopelessness over blacks overcoming the ignominious rule. After visiting South Africa with his Eminent Persons Group to explore schemes to end racial segregation in February-May 1986, former Nigerian Military President, Olusegun Obasanjo, came back to tell Nigerians that only African black magic - 'Juju' could wipe out apartheid. He was so thrown off balance that he dwelt into pessimism.

While in prison, Nelson Mandela and other patriots set up non-violent machineries via dialogue to dislodge racial prejudice and secure independence for blacks. These negotiations were accelerated by Oliver Tambo and other supporters of independence then in the country and exile. Today the nation of South Africa, once in depression, is dwelling in overwhelming economic expansion and wealth.

Dr. Martin Luther King Jr. - black civil rights leader, discontented with the subjugation of Negroes in America, launched a crusade of non-violent civil disobedience and protests in 1954 to demand an end to racial isolation laws and practices, and restore freedom and equality to blacks and other browbeaten races. His struggle was carried out in the form of defiance campaigns, sit-ins, jail-ins, kneel-ins, bus boycotts, demonstrations, etc.

Through these tacks he could take apart most segregation laws pertaining to transportation, estate acquisition rights, civil rights and education. For resisting injustice and speaking the truth he was in and out of jail, despite his having been crowned with a Nobel Peace Price. Nevertheless, the barbaric Ku Klux Klan (KKK) and other white fanatics who wanted Negroes to remain perpetual slaves were fed up with him. They killed him in cold blood after his speech at Memphis in 1968.

In the present-day Negroes in the US, who were in the past under racial repression, enjoy equal rights and opportunities with whites, thanks to this struggle. Today too, a black man, Barack Obama is the President of the United States of America in realization of Dr. Martin Luther King's Great Dream at Chicago on August 28, 1963.

India was one time under murkiness of British imperialism - another regime of colonization. A valiant, firm and well thought-of man - Mahatma Gandhi initiated a non-violent crusade of Satiagraha (The Force of Truth and Love with firmness) and Ahimsa (non-hurting, non-violence) to unshackle India from the fetters of British Colonialism. Political machinations prompted the murder of Gandhi.

Mahatma Gandhi nonetheless died with a traumatized heart because, his liberated India regrettably sundered into Hindu India and Islamic Pakistan. No

254

matter what, he had delivered his people from hopelessness and misery. Assignment consummated!

Correspondingly, we are saying that despite the current turmoil, the nation of Nigeria shall again be built on self reliance, economic growth, prosperity, wealth, joy and happiness for all - the craving of all responsible humanity. The tack of achieving these patriotic goals is all-inclusive and calls for nationalistic sacrifice. Patriots who are unhappy with present circumstances of wretchedness and uncertainty in the Nigerian State must join hands to salvage their country from further descent to abyss. This is the sermon of the noble Sweeping Nigerian Revolution.

BUTTRESSES

It is very important to reaffirm to the Nigerian People that the only panacea to the present doom-laden government machination of corruption is 'public out cry and mass dissent', employing Passive Resistance line of attack. In other words, it is the non-violent Revolution of the Nigerian people that will eradicate deceit, squander mania and treasury looting in the polity and chart our noble state to the path of responsibility, discipline and ethics of the Federal Republic of Nigeria (section 23 of the 1999 Constitution as amended). This will incontrovertibly usher in urgently needed self-reliance, economic growth, prosperity, advancement, wealth, joy and happiness for all Nigerians.

This Revolutionary exhortation to National Duty has been patriotically advocated by some highly regarded personalities around the world. President Goodluck Jonathan hinted of the present Nigerian Revolution in Lokoja, Kogi State on November 28, 2011. There, at a political rally, he warned state governors and other political officers that:

"The Masses will revolt against them if after four years they (masses) still find themselves in hopelessness and wretchedness." [126]

Now ought we to wait until another four years when all the funds in the state treasury would have been looted? The depth of treasury pillage in 2011 was 2.6 trillion naira-- half of the State Annual Budget frittered away employing hazy fuel subsidy scheme. Politicians and the elite shamelessly have no scruples about engaging in official corruption and deceit. We must rise now!

While reflecting on insecurity in Nigeria at a seminar organized by the Public Complaints Commission in November 2012, former Head of State, General Yakubu Gowon, said:

"Unfortunately, corruption in Nigeria today has become monstrous and a national embarrassment. All hands must be on deck to arrest and eliminate this monster."[127]

This is an obvious patriotic entreaty on all Nigerians to engage in public dissent and mass outcry to salvage our dear nation from further descent to abyss. At a January 2013, Northern Peace Summit convoked in Arewa House, Kaduna State, former Nigerian Permanent Representative to the United Nations, Alhaji Maitama Sule, voiced that:

"Nigeria needs a Revolution." [128]

This is in accordance with our position that the problem with Nigeria is not Boko Haram. It is not tribe or geographical location but corruption, cupidity, selfishness and official recklessness.

Former President of Ghana, FL. LT. Jerry Rawlings had exhorted African leaders to engage in ferocious and constructive battles against ravenous corruption that is devastating the continent or risk calamitous upheaval from the people. Rawlings, while delivering his key note address in March 2013 at the 2nd Zik Lecture Series of the Faculty of Social Sciences, Nnamdi Azikwe University Awka titled 'Eradicating corruption in Africa,' said:

"Corruption arises from a state of deviation from the moral and spiritual norm. It is a deliberate refusal to operate, based on set rules, regulations and laws and

with a wicked, if not evil desire to circumvent the punitive actions that come with such deliberate action."

He restated his call for the people of African countries to engage in massive dissent and public outcry against corruption. At the same time, he cautioned leaders not to suppress and gag public protests, against corrupt government policies. Calling the electorate to be alert to their sovereignty and constitutional responsibilities he said:

"It is the willingness to 'tolerate the intolerable' that gives the motivation or momentum for persons or institutions with influence to perpetrate acts of corruption within our society. Corruption at the level of government directly affects the rule of law and debases the moral right of political leadership to serve as respected regulator of the affairs of the State."

Rebuking the suppression of corruption dissent by political leaders he posited:

"Leaders must understand that when you take away the power of the people to express moral outrage, you have effectively disempowered your capacity to fight corruption through the people. Let us have faith in our

people and respect them. We have statesmen and women of integrity on our continent. "[129]

Pope Emeritus, Benedict xvi, while on a pontifical mission to Benin Republic in November 2011, had this to say about African leaders:

"This time: there are too many scandals and injustices, too much corruption and greed, too many errors and lies, too much violence which leads to misery and death. Every people wish to understand the political and economic choices which are made in its name. " [130]

The G8 World Leaders due to meet in June 2013 in Northern Ireland, was to discuss extensively: squander mania, corruption and official recklessness in the Nigerian polity. World leaders and international agencies are highly concerned about perception of stupendous wealth amid wretchedness, squalor, poverty, hopelessness and insecurity in Nigeria. For example, US Microsoft behemoth billionaire, Bill Gates, is worried that:

"Nigeria really needs to think that relative to its level of wealth, it is really for behind."[131]

At his return from recess in September 2012, former Senate President David Mark, before the floor of the Senate, condemned the deceitful and foolhardy activities of those handling the nation's economy." According to him:

"Those who manage the economy cannot afford to chase shadows while the economy is in doldrums."[132]

On the 30th of June 2013 while addressing the votary at a National Conference on the Role of Muslim Scholars in Fostering Unity, Peace, And Security in Nigeria, organized by the Jama'atul Nasril Islam (JNI), the Sultan of Sokoto, Alhaji Muhammadu Sa'ad Abubakar 111, lamented that egregious leadership was ruining Nigeria. In his message to the participants, the President-General of JNI said:

"Many things are going wrong and nothing seems to be working". In other words, the country is in decadence and rot.

He bluntly stated that:

"Bad leadership is the cause of insecurity in Nigeria. If those in power are doing what is expected of them, we would not be having these problems. So many things are going wrong in this country. So many things are not working because the leaders refuse to allow them to work."[133]

The Speaker of the Nigerian House of Representatives, Aminu Tambuwal had tentatively repented and joined the Revolutionary Council of the Nigerian People. On the 2nd of July 2013 while speaking on the topic: 'The Role of the Legislature on Economic, Infrastructural, and Ethical Revolution in Nigeria' at the 2013 Distinguished Management Lecture organized by Nigerian Institute of Management(Chartered), Tambuwal called for a non-violent, Intellectual Revolution to rid Nigeria of the present corruption and decay. [134]

In his thesis to Nigerians released 15 January 2012, the radical Catholic Bishop of Sokoto Diocese, Rev. Dr. Hassan Kukah said:

"The inability of the state to punish criminals as criminals has created the illusion that there is a conflict hatred which leads to violence between Christians and Moslems. Nigeria is changing because Nigerians are taking back their country from the grip of marauders. Christians and Moslems together in solidarity are protesting against bad governance and corruption beyond the falsehood of religion. It is this poverty that produces jealousy and." [135]

On the 20th of September 2012, a member of the Nigerian Senate from Abia State, Senator Uche Chukwumerije, before the floor of the upper house, threatened to move a motion to impeach President GoodLuck Jonathan. Chukwumerije's grouse was that the President had refused to implement a November 2011 resolution of the Senate on Bureau of Public Enterprises

(BPE). The higher legislative body had revealed that the BPE violated the law since it did not obtain National Council on Privatization endorsement on some of its shady deals.

In his presentation before the floor of the Senate which was debating on a Bill for an Act to amend the Public Enterprises ACT CAP P38 LFN (2004), Chukwumerije said:

"The Ahmed Lawan report is the highest moral ground of the Seventh Senate so far. It was that report that convinced everybody that the hope of this Country lies with the Senate. The pattern in this Country all along had been one siphoning of the country's funds through all sorts of legal subtleties to private pockets and companies. And for the first time there was a bold report that exposed the rot and we called for a reversal of the pattern ...., unfortunately, it is business as usual."

In his impeachment warning he scorched:

"They are looting public funds with impunity and nobody is saying anything...when it comes to the stage of threatening impeachment I, Uche Chukwumerije, will move the motion." [136]

While chatting with journalists on his 73rd birthday, August 2014, former Military Head of State, General Ibrahim Badamasi Babangida, criticized the current militarization of the Nigerian polity. He avowed that public outcry and mass protests from the people would stop such undemocratic policies. According to him:

"I was already an officer in the Nigerian Army in the '60s, and there was no military presence in those days except the Nigerian Police and I think it is high time we restored the past glory of the force. But the time would come though. I am sure the military guys will not be involved in these civil duties. It cannot continue like this; you guys would shout your heads out; the public would shout and the administration would listen."[137]

In an exclusive interview with the National Trail newspaper in January 2014, former governor of old Kaduna State and leader of the Peoples Redemption Party, Alhaji Balarabe Musa, at Abuja stated that a coup or mass revolution was inevitable in Nigeria if endemic corruption and bad governance are not quickly addressed. According to the veteran social activist:

"If circumstances continue to be negative, there will either be a military coup, which we had before, or a social revolution which we have not experienced already, but we can't exclude it because other countries did not exclude it. It asserts itself. It is a historical reality."

Balarabe Musa therefore advised that:

"The solution is for us to stand firmly and make maximum sacrifices for the liberation of Nigeria and to restore the dignity of the human person in Nigeria. Let us bring true national unity and let us have a programme for even development across the whole country. We cannot attain

this if we have these two evils in Nigeria: corruption and criminal waste of resources. The second is that we cannot have free and fair elections leading to a legitimate government in Nigeria."

In a government defensive counter attack, Senior Special Assistant to President Good- luck Jonathan on National Assembly Matters, Hon. Chijioke Edoga, said:

"The kind of revolution we should be asking for is the one already going on in the country; if we look at the power sector, police reforms, telecommunications, agriculture and many other sectors, not the one that would plunge the country into chaos. If coups were a solution, we would not be having the problems we are having now because we have had many of them before." [138]

CHAPTER 5

REVOLUTIONARY NIGERIANISM IDEOLOGY

Along the evolution of the world men have practiced political and social models like capitalism, communism, socialism and 'welfarism'. Such anachronistic postulations served the regional interests of the operators at different times. However, these theories are no longer germane to the present-day Nigerian socio-political environment.

What we need in Nigeria today is a thought that will supplant the egregious order of endemic corruption and deceit in both polity and society. In other words, how do we obliterate this cancerous and catastrophic corruption and recast our country to the noble path of discipline, responsibility and ethics (section 23 of the Nigerian constitution as amended)? This is an expedient step to attain self reliance, economic growth, prosperity, wealth, joy and happiness for every Nigerian independent of tribe, religion or geographical bearing.

This principle invokes the realities in the landscape of the Federal Republic of Nigeria. I have thoughtfully given this ideology the name REVOLUTIONARY NIGERIANISM. Revolutionary Nigerianism employs the non-violent principles of public outcry and mass dissent by the people to demand an end to corruption and deception in Nigeria, and a rebirth of conscience, patriotism and responsibility.

There are two basic ideas enshrined in Revolutionary Nigerianism: The Demand and The Tack. The Demand is what the revolution seeks to introduce in Nigeria for the benefit of the people. In other words, when we confront the authorities in a non-violent demonstration, what do we demand that they do for the Nigerian people? The other part is The Tack-- the methodology or way of achieving these demands. These two principles underpin the thought (section 38) of Revolutionary Nigerianism. In our next discourse, we shall present to Nigerians the Charter of REVOLUTIONARY NIGERIANISM.

THE CHARTER OF THE REVOLUTIONARY COUNCIL OF THE NIGERIAN PEOPLE

WHEREAS endemic and monstrous corruption in the Nigerian polity and society has attained an unprecedented level such that high government officials and their private collaborators are looting N2.6 Trillion Naira-- half of the State Annual Budget-- fueling cars, under the dubious shade of petroleum Subsidy, contrary to section 16(2c) of the 1999 constitution as amended,

AND WHEREAS this deceit and treasury plunder has subjected the people of the Federal Republic of Nigeria to abject poverty, wretchedness, hopelessness misery, squalor and unconscionable insecurity,

AND WHEREAS respectable petitions on corruption and fraudulent practices in government Ministries, Departments and Agencies which challenge the integrity, dignity and sovereignty of the Federal Republic of Nigeria have been submitted to the following government departments: Inspector-General of Police, Secretary to the Federal Government, the Nigerian Senate, the House of Representatives, EFCC, ICPC, Human Rights Commission and Public Complaints Commission.

AND WHEREAS these government departments have received these petitions and have refused to clarify, prosecute and rectify where applicable, a clear indication that they want the treasury looting, corruption and squander mania to continue in the Nigerian state,

AND WHEREAS the Nigerian National Assembly has been a cesspit of corruption and deceit, turning deaf ears to responsible petitions from Nigerians contrary to sections 14(2a-c) and 24b of the Constitution of the Federal Republic of Nigeria as amended,

AND WHEREAS deadly insurgency groups have overrun north eastern Nigeria, causing carnage, destroying properties and livelihood, abducted over 200 school girls from Chibok and women--their fate at present unknown--rendering millions of Nigerian citizens homeless in and across the country,

AND WHEREAS these insurgency groups, consequent on their triumph over the Nigerian Army in the north east, have declared an alternative sovereignty of Islamic Caliphate State,

AND WHEREAS it is evident that this monstrous corruption and insurgency, if allowed to continue, will lead to collapse of the Nigerian state which will imperil future generations,

AND WHEREAS political and revolutionary opposition forces have been coupled to unseat the previous profligate and corrupt government of Goodluck Jonathan and a new people-bent administration under President Muhammadu Buhari installed and popularly welcome,

AND WHEREAS the government of the Federal Republic of Nigeria is continuity, with transfer of assets and liabilities from the past government to the new regime,

AND IN A BID to obliterate current endemic corruption and recast our country Nigeria to the path of responsibility, discipline and the national ethics (section 23), bearing in mind the collective interest of the Nigerian people,

THEREFORE, we the advocates of Corruption-free Government in Nigeria--The Revolutionary Council of the Nigerian People hereby today January 1, 2015, adopt for Nigeria, in accordance with sections 14 (2a-c), 24b, 38, 39, 40 and other relevant sections of the Constitution of the Federal Republic of Nigeria1999 as amended, the salvaging ideology of REVOLUTIONARY NIGERIANISM as follows:

THE CHARTER OF THE REVOLUTIONARY
COUNCIL

1. OUR VISION; OUR MISSION
   OUR VISION

Monstrous and endemic corruption, if allowed to continue, will lead to collapse of the Federal Republic of Nigeria which will imperil future generations. As this cannibalistic corruption has today attained an outrageous 2.6 trillion naira-- half of the Annual Budget of the nation stolen fueling cars under the

dubious shade of Petroleum Subsidy, Nigerians are today left with two critical options: the present obsession of corruption and deceit which evidently is leading us to devastation, destruction and doom, and the noble and patriotic pathway of Anti-corruption and ethics which correspondingly ushers in self reliance, economic growth, prosperity, wealth, joy and happiness for every Nigerian independent of religion, tribe or geographical bearing.

OUR MISSION

As a constitutional duty (section 24 (b), 38, 39and 40), we shall continuously mobilize the People of Nigeria to wage ferocious battles against fabric and ruinous corruption in the Nigerian polity and society though non-violent means of Public Out Cry and Mass Dissent. This Revolution of the Nigerian People will progress inexorably until corruption, squander mania and official recklessness are obliterated from the polity and the government is recast to the path of discipline, responsibility and ethics of the Federal Republic of Nigeria (section 23).

CORRUPTION-FREE GOVERNMENT IN NIGERIA (CFGIN)
THE REVOLUTIONARY COUNCIL OF THE NIGERIAN PEOPLE

DEMANDS OF THE NIGERIAN PEOPLE
A.   CORRUPT PRACTICES

That the Presidency and the National Assembly should investigate and rectify the following demands of the Nigerian People with appropriate punitive measures to indicted persons:

1. Why ₦2.6 Trillion–half of the Annual Budget of the Federal Republic of Nigeria is, under the dubious shade of petroleum subsidy, stolen, fueling cars. What is the impact of this deceit and treasury plunder on the masses? (Farouk Lawal House Committee on Petroleum: national accord; April 20, 2012, P.15; contravening section 16 (2c) of 1999 constitution.

2. Why the Senate of the Federal Republic of Nigeria demanded Two-billion-naira bribe from the Pension Reform Task Force to give it a pass mark (Mr. Abdulrasheed Maina, Chairman PRTF; DAILY SUN; April 13, 2012, p.1

3. Why the House of Representatives demanded N 44 million, 4,000 dollars (From SEC) and 3 million dollars bribe (Farouk Lawal and Odetola)? Where is the $600,000 bribe given to Hon. Farouk Lawal by Femi Otedola, owner of Zenon Oil?

4. Why the Presidency embezzled N701.5 billion Natural Resources Fund from 2000 -2012. (Senate PA Committee investigation; DAILY SUN, July 6, 2012, P.5)

5. Why 300-billion-naira Aviation Intervention Fund has been embezzled by industry operatives.

(National Assembly Joint Committee on
Aviation; DAILY SUN, June 22, 2012, P.8)

6. Why two billion naira has been embezzled in the
Environment Ministry without planting
Ecological trees in 36 states of the Federation in
2010. (House of Reps oversight on July 12, 2012;
PEOPLES DAILY, July 13, 2012, P.3)

7. Why the Ministry of Works was allocated a
whopping N3.97 billion in 2012 budget for non-
existent Survey projects and which they looted.
The same figure had been represented in the 2013
Budget defence (Senate Committee on States and
Local Govt. Admin Led by Sen. Kabiru Gaya;
DAILY SUN, Nov. 27, 2012, P.7)

8. Why the Petroleum Products Pricing and
Regulatory Agency, PPPRA, is paying annual
allowances and salaries of just 249 workers with
5.72 billion naira, an average of ₦23 million per
employee. (National Assembly Joint Committee
on Petroleum, downstream led by Sen. Magnus
Abbey. DAILY SUN Nov. 28, 2012 p.3)

9. Why 4 billion naira is looted monthly at the
Pension Department of Head of Service which
also runs a pay roll of 73, 000 ghost pensioners.
(Report by Mr. Abdulrasheed Maina, Chairman
PRTF, DAILY SUN, Nov. 5, 2012 P.6, The
ROAD March 8, 2012 P.1, 4)

10. Why a Banquet Hall was to be built at the State
House at a whopping cost of N2.2 billion naira and
Vice President's official residence gulped N16 Billion
when 80% of Nigerians live on less than ONE

DOLLAR--N200 a day--a livelihood of misery,
poverty wretchedness squalor and insecurity.
(FCT Minister 2013 Budget Defence Before the
National Assembly)

11. Why Federal Government assets – Transcorp
Sheraton, Nicon Luxury, Ajaokuta Steel, Volkswagen
of Nigeria (VON), Daily Times of Nigeria (DTN) and
others were sold at a paltry N300 billion and these
proceeds unaccounted for in contravention of Section
80 (4) of 1999 Constitution. The ROAD Dec. 1, 2012,
P.4)

12. How did the 400 million dollars grant from World
Bank for provision of portable water spent since
90% of Nigerians do not have access to good
drinking water? AIT News, 8.pm, 23 Jan. 2012)

13. Why ₦2.1 billion newly printed ₦ 1000 currency
notes were stolen at the Nigerian Security Printing
and Minting Company in December, 2012 (House
of Reps investigation. THE SUN, Jan.18, 2013, p.7)

14. Where is the 4.5 billion naira released by
President Good luck Jonathan as FG counterpart funding
for American Hospital Limited and American University
of Medical Sciences Project? Who have stolen that money
and abandoned the project? The ROAD April 17, 2012,
p.1

15. Why job placements in ministries, departments and
agencies (MDAs) have been hijacked by racketeers who
charge up to 2 million naira per person to give
employment to applicants (DAILY SUN, Jan.17, 2013,
p.1; March 5, 2013, p.1,5)

16. Why African First Ladies' Mission Mansion is to be built in Abuja with a whopping off-budget ₦ 4 billion. From which government subhead is this huge amount sourced? (THIS DAY, MARCH 18, 2013, p.18)

17. Why the Government of the Federal Republic of Nigeria is running a vacuous, decadent, banal, fraudulent and money-based education system that is producing empty heads, and these empty heads being the future leaders of the country.

18. Why Federal Government workers are depositing public funds in their personal bank accounts and homes as seen in Pension Dept of Head of Service (The ROAD, March 8, 2012, P.1, 4)
19. Why Stella Odua-Minister for Aviation recklessly bought two cars with 225 million naira public funds. (NATIONAL MIRROR October 21, 2013 p.1, A2-18)

20. Has the Nigerian National Petroleum Corporation (NNPC) refunded the sum of N236 Billion to the Consolidated Revenue Fund of the Federal Government as ordered by The Nigerian House of Representatives on May 13, 2013? (PEOPLES DAILY May 14, 2013, p.3) Has the NNPC refunded the sum of 1.48 billion dollars as ordered by Price Water House Coopers after their forensic report? (THE NATION April 28, 2015 p. 1, 2, 7)

21. Why the Budget Office embezzled Federal Government Contingency Fund totaling N4.9 billion, employing trivial, nebulous and phantom projects. DAILY SUN; June 19, 2013, p.1

22. Why the Immigration Department of the Ministry of Interior engaged in the recruitment scam of March 15, 2014 in which more than 20 citizens lost their lives and over 1000 wounded and hospitalized? (DAILY TRUST March 17, 2014, p. 1)

23. Why the Federal Government of Nigeria engaged in laundering of the sum of 9.3 and 5.7 million dollars cash successively to South Africa using two Nigerian citizens and an Israeli as carriers, causing us a national embarrassment before the International Community? (DAILY SUN Sept. 19, 2014 p.16)

24. Why major cases (Halliburton, Malabu, Siemens and former Central Bank Governor, Charles Soludo-- printing of shoddy polymer currency notes) have not been investigated and prosecuted.?

25. Why none of the petroleum subsidy thieves have been prosecuted and jailed? (DAILY SUN July 27, 2012, p.5)

26. Why the Federal Government has not investigated the allegation by the former CBN Governor, Sanusi Lamido Sanusi, that twenty (20) billion dollars Federal Government fund is missing? (THE NATION May 1, 2015, p.1, 4)

27. Why the Finance Ministry is running 45,000 ghost workers while hundreds of thousands of Nigerians roam about the streets, jobless; other suffering xenophobic attacks, incarceration and the death sentence in their bid to escape suffocation at home and earn a living overseas? (Vanguard March 2, 2015 p.8)

28. Why 50 firms doing contract jobs with the Ministry of Works operate without tax certificates thereby dodge mandatory financial contribution to the Tertiary Education Trust Fund (TETFUND)? (Report by the ICPC before the Senate on 27 February 2015, Vanguard March 2, 2015 p.8)

29. Why the Secretary to the Federal Government (SFG, David Babachir Lawal, looted the sum of 2.5 billion naira earmarked for Internally Displaced Persons in the north east, using his private company as conduit?

B.   REALIGNING   GOVERNMENT TOWARDS   RESPONSIBILITY   AND DISCIPLINE

1.That the Federal Government of Nigeria should convoke an Anticorruption National Conference (ANC) where Nigerians will discuss and agree on how to obliterate corruption in polity and society.

2. That the present National Assembly is a bogus and cumbersome enterprise. It is expensive, time-wasting and replete with excessive bureaucracy, duplicity and corruption. Hence the National Assembly should be resolved into a **mono cameral legislature** like Senegal.

3.That the principal function of the members of the legislature should henceforth be to make laws to obliterate corruption which has been the bane of any meaningful development and progress in Nigeria since 55 years.

4. That the structure of the Nigerian Civil Service should be reversed to the pre-1988 state in which it was impossible for government workers to transfer public funds into private bank accounts or siphon government money into their houses.

6. That the Federal Government of Nigeria should set up a committee made up of credible Nigerians, civil society groups, human rights organizations, Labour and international observers to investigate and implement these demands of the Nigerian people listed above.

6. **That in line with our covenant with the Department of State Security (DSS), on May 28, 2013, the Million–Man march-and-occupy protests** in Abuja and other towns in Nigeria will continue until fabric corruption is obliterated from the polity and society and government re-channeled to the part of responsibility, discipline and ethics of the Federal Republic of Nigeria (section 23 of 1999 Constitution) to usher in urgently-needed self reliance, prosperity, advancement, economic growth, wealth, joy and

happiness for every Nigerian independent of religion, tribe of geographical location.

7. The masses want from the Government that:

- 1 wrap of "akpu" to be sold at N5.00
- 1 mudu of "dawa" to cost N20.00
- 1 mudu of cassava garri at N50
- 1 mudu of rice costing N70.00
- 1 bottle of palm oil sold at N30.00
- 50kg mixed fertilizer at N200.00; 1 litre of petrol at N50
- 1 bag of Portland cement at N200.00; 1 litre of kerosine at N20
- To come to their homes and switch on light
- To have good drinking water around their homes
- Quality education where students will read and pass their examinations instead of buying certificates with sex and money

. To have cheap and affordable health care especially in the rural areas and not the mockery of using mosquito nets. I think

Nigerians this way, are not asking too much.

8. That the constitutional basis of THE CHARTER OF THE REVOLUTIONARY COUNCIL OF THE NIGERIAN PEOPLE is derived from the following and other relevant sections of the Constitution of the Federal Republic of Nigeria1999 as amended:

1. Section14 (2a): Sovereignty belongs to the people of Nigeria.

2. Section14 (2b): Security and welfare of the people shall be the primary purpose of government.

3. Section14 (2c): Participation of the people in their government.

4. Section 24b: Help to enhance the power, prestige, good name; and defence of country.

5. Section 38: Freedom of thought and conscience.

6. Section 39: Freedom of opinion and expression

7. Section 40: Freedom of association and peaceful assembly

In the service of Country, Society and Humanity, no sacrifice or pain is too big or great. May the peace of the Almighty God be beneficently multiplied unto all adherents to equity, justice and fairness, those who speak the truth and serve humanity! **Time is running out**.

Long live the People of the Federal Republic of Nigeria.

Long live the Federal Republic of Nigeria.

One Nigeria, No corruption

Vox Populi, Vox Dei, section 14(2a)

ALUTA CONTINUA, VICTORIA ACERTA

OKENWA

ENYERIBE.... B. Pharm.

Head: CORRUPTION-FREE GOVERNMENT IN NIGERIA

THE REVOLUTIONARY COUNCIL OF THE NIGERIAN PEOPLE

JUNE 1, 2015— www.revolutionarycouncil.org.ng

EXPOUNDING THE REVOLUTION

When we speak of a Revolution in an unpredictable country like Nigeria, nerves jangle at the prospect of a coercive deposing of the government by means of guns and bombs. That will, as anticipated, precipitate attendant bloodletting. It was the type of change undertaken by Flt. Lt. Jerry Rawlings of Ghana and military mutineers in Nigeria in 1966.

However, the new Sweeping Revolution of The Nigerian People is not an adventure with deadly weapons. It is a non-sanguinary patriotic project. This Great Change employs bombs and missiles, highly explosive devices (IEDs) that are biting and searing but corrective and penitentiary. These revolution bombs and missiles are the anti-corruption documents launched from the roof-top of Head of Service block on 16 July 2012 and are being disseminated to Nigerians everyday.

Our new Revolution is not like the putsches of the 20th century. It goes without blood-shed, a non-savage project. It is a revolution of the intellect, the conscience (section 38) and other instruments in the constitution of the Federal Republic of Nigeria as amended.

Politicians and the elite in Nigeria, cloistered in corruption and deceit, are today looting state treasury with inexcusable presumptuousness. They claim that they

281

have intellect. In this way, these dubious aristocratic demigods dwell under the delusion of grandeur. Therefore, we have to go with them into a battle of the brain and conscience-- an intellectual juxtaposition; knowing fully well that our country Nigeria today is in dire straits.

They are already destined to lose this war and the masses will manifestly triumph. Their daily preoccupation is to ruin the country! These treasury looters; the Adept Drivers of the Gravy Trains of Nigeria, the Heavy Hitters of the Nigerian Corruption Industry, the Engineers of the Corruption Superstructure, are already guilty before the spirit of the Nigerian State, humanity, before karma, the hereafter and before The Almighty.

This is because, replete with absolute poverty of the superego, they are prodigals who rob and rape the Federal Republic of Nigeria, leaving the state comatose and decadent and the people in abject poverty, wretchedness, hopelessness, misery and inadmissible insecurity. They do not have defence and will run to nary a place. The Nigerian masses will easily overshadow them. At the end, the odds are in favour of the Nigerian masses-- a sure fire victory.

Interestingly, certain hypocrites in the National Assembly will brazenly hypothesize that they are elected under the Nigerian Constitution; that is Abraham as their forebear. That defence is very weak and holds no water -- at best humbug! Are you elected under section 47-51 of the 1999 Constitution to engage in outrageous acts of deception, flippancy, debauchery, ineptitude, vacuity and emptiness? You are elected to serve the people in line with section 14(2b) which states that 'the security and welfare of the people shall be the primary purpose of government.' This elemental purpose of their election, they are violating everyday with impunity!

The same constitution under which these imperious demigods hide to commit atrocities of corruption, deceit and barbarity on the Nigerian People will be used to disgrace them. Then they will descend from the sublime to the ridiculous, in fact to ignominy. Their devilish and underhand machinations of treasury looting and squander mania will unquestionably precipitate this.

At a funeral service in honour of late Dr. Nelson Mandela in Aso Rock Villa Chapel on 8 December 2013, Nigerian President -- Dr. Goodluck Jonathan affirmed that Nigerian political leaders 'will not be great men, but tiny men'. Out bursting distaste with the politicians, the President said:

"If you listen to those of us who are politicians in Nigeria from all political parties - from PDP to now APC but

*beginning as AD to ACP and others - the way we talk.
Some of us talk as if Nigeria is their bedroom that they
have control over. Read the newspapers; listen to the
radio and television or go to the social media and see
how politicians talk. Some of us even think we are little
gods. We intimidate, we threaten, we show hate in our
communication. These are definitely not the virtues of
great men. They are shockingly the voices of tiny men."*

In painful conclusion, he avowed that:

*"It is probably easier for a camel to pass through the eye
of a needle than for a politician to be truly great."*[139]

This revelation is factual because Nigerian politicians are
devoid of responsibility, discipline and ethics, section 23.
These noble cultures they throw to the ash heap. They are
abounding with debauchery, mediocrity, ineptitude,
deceit, banality, vacuity and emptiness. There are five
conditions a man must fulfill for him to be truly great on
earth:

He must imbibe humility, ready to bow before even
children.

He must adhere to responsibility, discipline and
ethics.

He will relentlessly engage in assiduous service to
country, society and humanity without requesting for
personal gain.

He must invoke his talents and ingenuities to
engage in inventions, innovations to yield productivity for
the betterment of country, society and humanity.

He must be on the side justice, equity and fairness
at engagements.

These rare earth values and benchmarks are of the order of Dr. Nelson Mandela.

The year 2017 marks a decisive moment in the political history of Nigeria. It is the year of transformation from the outlandish and bestial path of deceit and pillage to the way of responsibility, discipline and ethics of the Federal Republic of Nigeria (section 23). It is no longer going to be business as usual. We are not fools. We are not mugs. The Revolution and the boorish state treasury looting arrangement form dialectic in the state of affairs in the Federal Republic of Nigeria, the resolution of which must be to adopt the path of responsibility and sanity.

This time around the Nigerian people have to show the world that after all, we are not 'black monkeys' as the white man identifies. The Federal Republic of Nigeria must, this time, be turned upside down for the betterment of all, independent of religion, tribe or geographical orientation. **We are tired of living like fools in twenty first century Nigeria!**

CHAPTER 6

CONSTITUTIONALITY OF THE REVOLUTION

At this point one may ask the curious but significant question: What constitutional rights do I have to engage in a non-violent mass outcry and public dissent Revolution in my country, the Federal Republic of Nigeria? The answers to this question lie in the spirit of nationalism and love for country, society and humanity. **If allowed to carry on, rapacious corruption will lead to collapse of Nigeria which will consequently devastate future generations! This we can't afford in the 3rd Millennium.**

The rights of the citizens to embark on a Revolution are clearly stated in Chapter 2 of the 1999 constitution: the duties of the citizen to the state and the duties of the nation to the citizen. I exhort the people of Nigeria to fervently pore over this chapter. Section 14(2a) stipulates that the sovereignty-- the overall power of the state to govern itself - belongs to the people. It is from this sovereignty that we, the people of the Nigeria give representatives a small power through elections. These 'Adamic extracts', instead of them to administrate in the way of responsibility, discipline and ethics of the country, adopt the vicious path of deceit and official recklessness. Hence, they subject the people of Nigeria to penury, wretchedness and insecurity.

Section 14(2b) also states that the security and welfare of the people shall be the primary purpose of government. In Nigeria today, where is security? What with the incessant bombings and killings coupled with kidnapping, armed robbery, paediatric trafficking and ever-present homicide cases! Where is welfare in a country that spends half of the Annual Budget, 2.6 trillion naira fueling cars under the devious claim of Petroleum Subsidy?

Where is welfare in a country that the Civil Service-- the moral fiber of any government-- is in decadence and rot? When you retire from government work you will not be paid your entitlements! You go and collapse at the pension centre, waiting to be captured! Without doubt, this is a disastrous arrangement. Is there welfare in a country where the education system is a pecuniary-based establishment which is producing empty heads? Marks, certificates and degrees are bought by students with sex and money!

Section 14(2c) have it that the participation of the people in the government shall be assured in accordance with the provisions of the constitution. This corroborates

Pope Benedict xvi who stated in November 2011, in Republic of Benin that 'the people should be made to know the decisions being made about their lives in government.' It is sheer insanity to squander 2.6 trillion naira public funds fueling cars contrary to section16 (2c) without clarification and accountability!

The denouement of this is that over 80% of Nigerians are sweltering on less than one dollar a day-- a habitation of hopelessness. How do you expect the citizens to swallow this hook, line and sinker? How can you maroon them without oars or sails?

Section 24b also stipulates that it is the duty of every Nigerian citizen 'to help to enhance the power, prestige and good name of Nigeria, to defend Nigeria and render such National Services as may be required'. On semantics, the holophrastic there is 'defend' which is the grist of line 4 of the National Pledge--To Defend Her Unity. Nigerians are hereby, in accordance with the Constitution, entreated to defend their country against treasury looting, profligacy and official recklessness.

The major public-oriented pathology of Nigeria in the present day is the naivity of the people towards what is happening and their inability to come forward and tell their befuddled defaulting authorities how they want to be governed. Hence the underhanded leaders have continued with debauchery, mediocrity, banality and emptiness unlimited. If we don't do this, the country will collapse as it is happening now and everybody will be affected. God forbids! We can't afford to allow our nation crumble.

Section 38 of the constitution guarantees freedom of thought, conscience and religion. My conscience and thought according to the inspirations and messages I have received is this: monstrous corruption will destroy the Federal Republic of Nigeria. Thus, there is the expedient need to fight it headlong for the country to survive and grow. We must cut to the chase now!

It is the constitutional requirements of sections 39 and 40 that the people of Nigeria shall have **unhampered freedom** to put across their opinions on detestable government policies. While cautioning Nigerians against 'unguarded and divisive statements', the past Inspector General of Police, Mr. Mohammed Abubakar said that the Nigerian Police Force

"... Is not ignorant of the fundamental rights of citizens such as the rights to freedom of speech..."[140]

They should have the liberty to assemble together to discuss the problems of their country and proffer solutions. They have to coalesce to answer the question: **How do we liberate our country from further descent along the abyss?**

From the foregoing, we can see that the people of Nigeria have bountiful instruments and protection in the constitution to wage vigorous battles against corruption and deceit in the nation. Thus the 1999 constitution as amended advocates a Passive Resistance Revolution. The question is: How is this war to be fought and won?

What is the modus operandi? What is the modus Vivendi? What are the risks involved? Don't be distraught; that takes us to the 'next level' according to radio jingoists.

CHAPTER 7

A CALL TO NATIONAL DUTY

Nigerians are hereby called upon to be fully watchful to their rights and constitutional responsibilities to our dear nation. Do not anticipate that members of the National Assembly and their dubious counterparts in the executive will provide you the urgently-needed salvation. No, they will not! They are having their pockets filled with loot every day-- a base indulgence of debauchery.

I was led to various high government departments and I witnessed what is happening there: the deceit, ineptitude, decadence, squander mania, profligacy and official recklessness, in fact psychosis. I saw no iota of display of love and responsibility to country, society and humanity. It is really outrageous! I was unreservedly disillusioned after my escapades in various Federal Government departments.

They don't think about you because when petitions on corrupt and fraudulent practices are sent to them, they treat the documents with disdain and hide them from the Nigerian people. What does that designate? That treasury looting must continue! Hence, we shall be subjected to deeper poverty, wretchedness, uncertainty and insecurity. God forbids!

The self-satisfaction and gullibility of the Nigerian People towards corruption was decried by Governor Rotimi Amaechi of Rivers State via Vanguard news online of December 15, 2013. In the bombshell titled: 'We steal because Nigerians don't stone us-- Amaechi', the Governor seared that political office holders revel on monumental corruption because Nigerians do not hold them answerable. According to the Rivers Governor:

"If you see a thief and you allow him to be stealing, what have you done? You have stoned no body; that is why we are stealing. Who have you stoned? They came out and started dancing oil 'subsidy, oil subsidy.'

'They told you that they stole N2.3 trillion, what did you do? Instead you are protesting bring more oil subsidy; the oil subsidy that is not reaching the poor. A few individuals are going away with the money and you have done nothing. You are mourning Madiba who lived up to 95, and he was very angry with Nigeria when he died."

At the funeral session in honour of late Dr. Nelson Mandela in Lagos, Rotimi in a fit of acerbity continued:

" You have heard that 50 billion dollars is missing and you have done nothing about it. In some countries people will go on the streets until they return that money. It is 8 trillion naira, it can change Nigeria.

"Me, I want to steal only one billion dollars, let them bring it. You read Obasanjo's letter and you are asking why is he writing the letter, is he a South-South man? In fact, when he was there what did he do? You, what have you done? If you don't take your destiny in your hands, we will go on and other leaders will come and continue stealing." [141]

I think this man has patriotically exposed to Nigerians what they must do to save their country from imminent collapse. Then how do we do it? Do we wait for dubious politicians and leaders on the way and haul stones at them? No, that is barbaric!

There is another tack of stoning, more piercing yet responsible and productive. These stones are the rollicking anti-corruption documents and speeches. They rebuke corruption, deceit and official recklessness in both polity and society. They are powerful tools of liberation. Booing is more disgraceful and scorching than mere stones.

The Revolutionary Process is simple: **public outcry and mass dissent** against treasury looting, scamming and official recklessness in the Nigerian State. **When ever we call, come out of your houses. Join the million-man march-and-occupy protests championed by the Revolutionary Council of the Nigerian people**

wherever they may be held in the country. This is a clarion call to defend our country (section 24b).

We have to occupy the National Assembly, other major streets in Abuja and elsewhere in Nigeria. There we shall be eating and drinking. We shall be sleeping there on our blankets (remember to bring them at alarm). The atmosphere will be echoing our solidarity songs of love for country. What a fantastic get together of patriotic, noble and responsible Nigerians!

Take a leaf: on the 29th of April 2014 Chibok women from north-eastern Nigeria staged a mini revolution in Nigeria. Clad in disparate revolutionary apparel, they stormed the National Assembly to demand the immediate release of their daughters kidnapped by insurgents. Legislative leaders came out of their hole-and-corner offices to receive and bear with them.

The members of the National Assembly (Senate and House of Reps) as well as high government officials will likewise be moved to come and ask us our demands. We shall tell them that we are tired of the government which is practicing treasury looting, debauchery, ineptitude, banality, deceit, vacuity and emptiness. We want a great change from the way of deception and squander mania to the path of responsibility, discipline and ethics of the Federal Republic of Nigeria (section 23). We shall then present our demands:

It will be left for them to set up a body comprising private individuals of integrity, civil society groups, human rights organizations, labour, respectable government officials and international observers. The work of this committee will be principally to investigate these corrupt and fraudulent practices and deliberate on how to run the government devoid of corruption and dubiousness. It will establish solid regulations on how to obliterate treasury looting and plunder and re-channel the polity to the path of economic growth, prosperity, self-reliance, wealth, joy and happiness for all.

It will furthermore be the duty of this committee to set up a Modus Vivendi between the Nigerian government and crucible of The People, the subject matter of which must be how to obliterate cancerous corruption from polity and society in order to move the country forward.

However, if these treasury looters in government remain recalcitrant and would not listen to us, we shall continue our march-and-occupy and force them to resign in the interest of the nation. **The underlying philosophy of democracy is diametrically athwart the underpinning philosophy of corruption. Corruption**

and good governance are a mismatch! Government is not by force!

If you are not ready listen to the yearnings of the people under section 14(2a-2c) of the constitution, that means your continued occupation of government office is a disservice to the Nigerian people-- a waste and therefore useless! Undoubtedly, the future of the Nigerian State is strewn with uncertainties while this deceit and robbery lasts.

Consequently, the outcry will continue until they resign. Ellie Wiesel declared that:

"There may be times when we are powerless to prevent injustice, but there must never be a time when we fail to protest." [142]

Then the Nigerian people will plan how to establish a government of responsibility, discipline and ethics of the Federal Republic of Nigeria. This is a task that must be accomplished to salvage our country from further descent to muck.

While this Revolution is taking its constitutional course, I have to warn fellow Nigerians that they should not allow themselves to be confused and derailed by religious sentiments, ethnic differences and geographical bearings. We have considerately made this Revolution to be independent of these critical factors. Among the wiles and antics of treasury looters and dubious base elements is the predilection to drive Nigerians into ethnic or religious conflicts. This is exactly what is happening in Nigeria today. Rev. Dr. Hassan KUKAH and Sheik Ibrahim EL Zazzakky have at different flora corroborated this position.

As the clashes rage on, devious politicians and elites seize upon the resultant confusion to loot State treasury. This had been manifested in the 2013 Budget where 500 billion naira was voted for security and another 500 billion naira for defence. What percentage of National Budget is one trillion naira and where was this money going to? Without equivocation, to the pockets of groveling sycophants, lip service men, praise singers, chameleons and thieves! Now what is the war chest for the incessant corruption-borne State of Emergency? [143] In line with the chameleonic alignment of the Nigerian state, and presumptuous disregard to constitutional requirements, we are not told.

Let us keep religion and tribalism apart and fight our common enemy- corruption. United we stand! Do not succumb to distractions of ethnicity and religion. Beware of the chicanery of treasury looters, sorcerers and thieves! Before going to war, try to be acquainted with your enemy and be solidly concurred in esprit de corps to wage ferocious battles against treasury plunderers, the prodigals of Nigeria.

Although painstakingly and unremittingly planned, this Revolution of the Nigerian People could be encumbered or prolonged by security agencies-- The Police, SSS and The Army. According to William Shakespeare: As fortune goes, so misfortune does follow! History has shown that social systems (like corruption) have a great eleventh-hour respiratory power; and the advocates of the status-quo are always ready with their oxygen tents to keep the old abominable order alive. I had earlier on warned them that **this is a civil matter**. We are non-violent.

Violence will open a Pandora's Box. We are not using guns, bombs or other dangerous weapons. So, let security agents stay apart and watch us the masses and the treasury looters use our brains to solve the problems of this country once and for all. Our dear country Nigeria is being haunted daily by a spectre of uprising. There are apparently grave threats to national security. Ubiquitous undercurrents of resentment to political corruption and deceit loom everyday.

As I stated to Nigerians in the Wuse Market Declaration, any attempt by security agents to give undue advantage and protection to treasury looters by

gagging and suppressing public dissent will be highly resisted. Security agents should critically understand the calamitous consequences of shooting at the citizens they are sent to protect. It is not going to be business as usual. It is either we change or we perish. The future of the Nigerian state is at stake!

CHAPTER 8
Nigerian Youths, Salvage Your Country

The youths of Nigeria spearheaded the nationalistic struggle of the 20th country that eventually led to independence in 1960. The Nigeria National Democratic Party (NNDP) headed by Herbert Macaulay dominated Black Nationalist politics in Lagos between 1923 and 1938 using its newspaper, the Lagos Daily News as medium of propaganda. The more nationalistic group the Nigerian Youth Movement (NYM) formed in 1938 equally disseminated its activities with the Lagos Daily service newspaper.

It was through those movements that Nigerian youths expressed their grievances at obnoxious colonial policies and also contested elections in the colonial legislative council to press for reforms in government. As a result of intense pressure from those Nigerian youths, the British colonial government introduced social, economic and political reforms in colonized Nigeria. Hence the representative British administration enacted the Colonial Development and Welfare Act of 1939 in which the government resolved to pursue vigorous development in education, health, communication and other sectors. Later, Nigerians were appointed into the colonial executive council for the first time and nationalists started forming majority in the legislative council.

The youths of Nigeria protested vehemently the killing in 1949 of about 20 black coal miners at Enugu by the colonial authorities. The protests were organized by the Zikist movement, a subsidiary of National Convention of Nigerian Citizens (NCNC) formed by Dr. Nnamdi Azikiwe. In April 1953, Anthony Enahoro, a youthful Action Group (AG) member of the colonial House of Representatives introduced a motion asking for Nigerian independence come 1956.[144] Towards independence Nigerian youths participated in the formation of parties like the Africa Group, Northern Peoples Congress (NPC), NCNC and others.

The late, Dele Giwa used his position as a journalist to fight against military dictatorship and demand a workable democratic government. Youths of the Niger Delta are today enjoying free education, technical skills, enterprise empowerment and improved social and environmental infrastructure which are the rewards of their years of militant struggle.

The Nigerian youths of today seem to be unaware of the doom threatening their country. Some are more occupied with fun in the entertainment industry dancing '**kukere**', while at the same time opening their behinds for the world to see. Others seek power and influence by joining misleading cult sects.

Cyber cafes and game betting centres are full of boys and girls who want to get rich quick, some through internet scam. Youth crimes such as drug trafficking, kidnapping and armed robbery have become precipitous in the country. Demands for Codeine linctuses and other intoxicants across the country are abusively increasing because youths take them to feel 'high' and engage in crimes.

It is rare to see youths engage in reading nowadays. Yet, in that lies the treasure of power! Students in secondary school's resort to passing examinations by mercenary bargain or out rightly buy their WASC or NECO certificates. Those in the universities and polytechnics pay one way or the other to pass examinations or even buy degrees--women with sex, men with money.

I agree with Charley Boy that undoubtedly the future of this country lies in the hands of few exceptional youths. [145] Where are they? Don't they see the rot in the country?

The African National congress (ANC) youth leader, Julius Malema has been advocating for nationalization of mines and banks and economic freedom for unemployed youths in South Africa.[146] It is high time the youths of this country irrespective of ethnic or religious background, understood actually the evil cankering their country. They should know that their government is abounding with corruption, dubiousness, profligacy, squander mania and recklessness. As long as they are led by a corrupt camarilla, they have no future in Nigeria. No government founded on corruption like Nigeria can work.

Articulating the rot in the Nigerian society and the panacea, Amara Femor Sesay, a youthful Sierra Leonian who had lived in the country for years revealed thus:

"I dream of a Nigeria that will no longer be Nigeria (in the sense that the word Nigeria is synonymous with crime and corruption). I dream of a Nigeria that will ever be Nigeria (in the sense of its blessings and beauty)." [147]

The youths of Nigeria should rise and emulate the nationalistic heroes of the 20th century to demand an end to corruption for our country to survive. They must form pressure groups with the coordinate aim of fighting corruption in all strata of Nigerian life. Anticorruption should be the watchword in schools, colleges, industries, market places, government institutions and every day conversations. Youths leave the future of their country in the hands of dubious and fraudulent kleptomaniacs at their own peril.

While speaking at the West African Regional Conference on Youth Empowerment in Dakar, Senegal, former Nigerian President Olusegun Obsanjo warned of an impending youth-oriented revolution consequent on massive unemployment and joblessness in Nigeria. Emphasizing the dangers imminent from this social maladministration at that November 12 occasion, Obasanjo said:

"I am afraid, and you know I am a General. When a General says that he is ahead, that means the danger ahead is real and potent."

He lamented the 'absence serious, concrete, short term and long-term solutions' to youth unemployment in Nigeria. According to him,

"Youth unemployment is breeding catastrophic societal crimes like kidnapping, internet scam, armed robbery, drug and currency running."[148]

In a chat with TS WEEKEND, international reggae maestro and Rastafarian prophet, Majek Fashek, reaffirmed his prediction of an impending Mass Revolution in Nigeria. He prophesied that:

"...Jah still warned me to continue to tell my people that bloody revolution would hit Nigeria soon and that the blood of evil men will be sacrificed to the gods of war. How it will happen, I don't know.

"Even the time it will happen, I don't know, but area boys, the poor masses will lead the revolution and the fight will not be a war of ethnicity. When it starts, in fact, JJ Rawlings' revolution in Ghana will look like a child's play when Nigeria's own comes! Nigerians will soon rise to fight" [149]

While putting on a solidarity rally on September 2, 2015 in support of the anti-corruption battle of the new regime, President of the National Association of Nigerian Students (NANS), Comrade Tijani Usman Shehu, told President Muhammadu Buhari that Nigerian students were united against corruption, cybercrime, prostitution, human trafficking, drug abuse and other vices. The student leader presented a document to Buhari's Special Senior Adviser on Media and Publicity, Femi Adesina, who promised to submit it to the President for evaluation and action. Tijani Usman said:

"Nigerian students demand that our future must be secured and we strongly believe in the President's zero tolerance for corruption".

In his address to the students read by the media aide, President Muhammadu Buhari asserted:

"Everything you have asked for are the things that will make for a good country, and what we are after is a good country, a country where our youths can have a future and a hope. We are totally committed to building a country where our youths can realize their full potential. You can be assured that your welfare and wellbeing are topmost n our minds and very soon you will see the things we have promised to come to fruition.

"During the campaign change was our slogan, but today it is no longer a mere slogan; it is now a reality and we will see it in every facet of our lives. The youths will feel it, the adults will feel it and old people will feel it, and we will get the country of our dreams." [150]

YOUTHS OF NIGERIA NOW ARISE (Poem)

.

Once more I push to say

That is expedient today

Youths of Nigeria now arise

And pay the value price

From corruption, your country free

Squander mania and profligacy spree

Only route to polity revival

For country headway and survival

You don't do this present better

You will live to remorse later

The looter indulges with apathy
As his father's estate property
Look, Populace groan in poverty

Lone voice in rotten wilderness
Fighting Nigerian regime recklessness
Attendant hypocrisy, dubiousness

Pushing masses to extreme hopelessness
Day by day accelerating wretchedness
Secure our future, uproot this madness
Then we will have lasting greatness
 Dismiss me, adieu!

CHAPTER 9

To You Swindlers of the Nigerian State

Woe unto you State Treasury Looters! You belong to the sect of 'prebendalists' and squander maniacs that existed at Nigerian Independence and has over the years metamorphosed into what you are today, a light-fingered army leading Nigeria to destruction. After independence you fortified your selfishness, cupidity and treasury looting. You created an uncontrollable crisis that eventually brought down the government in 1966. You instigated the military putsches of 1966 that subsequently plunged the country into a civil war.

Since the war ended you have continued hereditary transfer of the traits of deceit, falsehood, dubiousness and fund stealing to date. You have egregiously planted yourselves at every ministry, department or agency. This is to ensure that the government of Nigeria is relentlessly derailed for your selfish ends.

At present, you are not only interested in stealing public funds but also destroying the county. This is unmistakable in your current state of pillaging public money. It has reached an unparalleled level of N2.6 trillion-- half of the National Budget. You claim in your prevarication that you spent this mammoth amount fueling Nigeria cars in 2011. It has not occurred to you that as you scheme to 'spend' half of the National Budget on petrol, you are devastating the country.

You have allowed greed and selfishness to becloud your reasoning and conscience. Love for country you throw to the dogs. That is why you rape your country, leaving her desolate, wretched and hopeless.

You arrange with your co-thieves to store government funds in graves you dig in your houses or private bank accounts. Government work now ends in your houses. The nation's purse is now your pockets.

Simple reckoning will tell you that your country is going down into the deep-sea abyss. You are the captain of this disastrous voyage. What do you foresee on this journey?

It is because of your dubious intrigues that nothing works in any sector in this country today: no electric power, degenerate education, agriculture in rubbles, porous and decayed health care, death traps on the high ways and citizens now sleeping with 'one eye open'. These are the results of your diffusion of government plans through treasury looting and embezzlement.

You are not ashamed of the rot to which you have led your country. You glory in big cars, big caps and dresses and magnificent houses. Regrettably you don't know that these things are a mockery because you have no output in Nigeria.

Break and ask your co-fraudster jail bird, James Ibori, incarcerated by the London South Wark Crown Court, the use of this ill-gotten wealth. Look at his waterloo. The same thing is going to happen to you one way or the other as you continue with these vices. It is just a question of time.

Are you justified in stealing billions of naira of public funds some of which you squander on jamborees overseas? Do you feel happy packing government money into your pockets while the Nigerian masses groan under the weight poverty and hunger? Do you take liberty in turning fellow citizens into beggars?

You go overseas to enjoy your loot, but what you do is apparent mockery considering the crimes you commit at home and how you have left your country desolate and wretched. You send your children abroad because Nigerian environment is not conducive to them. Unfortunately, you don't know that these kids sojourn as slaves in another man's land. In that bid, their productivities are retarded.

Even at home here, your life is a sham; you are living with pollutant generators that are a nuisance to the public. All your loots have not provided you immunity against epidemics. You still suffer 'plasmodiasis' and conjunctivitis (Apollo). The last Ebola epidemic made you extremely disconcerted. The present insecurity which is a consequence of your devilish machinations is haunting you too.

When you fly British Airways from London you have to hover in Abuja airspace for 1 ½ hours because there is no light at the tarmac, since you have also looted the funds for power. You eat parboiled (low nutrient) rice from Asia because you have extinguished rice production in Nigeria. Inhalation of dust on the roads equally rewards you with respiratory tracts diseases (RTD).

Naturally, the spirit of these poor people you defraud, traumatize and dehumanize everyday will continue to torture you. As you walk, you keep on looking behind to see if they are coming'. However, when they come; you will not know.

It is better to let you appreciate what is going to befall you in this your ruinous cannibalistic capitalism. As you continue devouring these poor citizens, starving them, it will reach a point when they will have nothing to eat. Then they will turn around and eat you up, that is 'reverse cannibalism'. Your Mephistophelian machinations of treasury plunder will precipitate this.

Therefore, it is expedient that you repent and exorcize yourselves of deceit and hypocrisy in the Nigerian society. For you to escape the impending doom, it is time for you to make amendments. The Panacea is to make Nigeria a place where you can stay comfortably with these ordinary people.

The common man doesn't need flamboyant life style like you. The masses just need village food (*akpu and dawa*), water to drink, light in their homes and treatment for poor man's sicknesses. You can never be content with life in a country where you have made over 80% of the people to live on less than one dollar (N360) a day--a habitation of misery, wretchedness and hopelessness!

 In order that the system may not devour you, there must be deviation from your current selfish and greedy acts to the way of decency, responsibility and discipline. These are the noble cultures of the founding fathers of our great nation that is now decadent. You have defiled these values for selfish ends. Stop looting State treasury. Stop embezzling and misappropriating public funds.

Become productive to your country instead of wantonly raping her. Adopt discipline of service to your country without requesting for personal gain. This is how Western countries where you go to deposit your loots developed- by selfless service.

The message that General Muhammadu Buhari delivered on 1st January 1984 is still on the marble for your perusal. He said that the present generation and in fact future generations have no place which we shall call our own except Nigeria. Therefore, we shall live in it together and salvage it together. No country has ever been developed by foreigners.

Create a level playing field for you and 80% of the Nigerian population living in misery. That is the stand point of your security. Developments in North Africa and elsewhere around the world are clear harbingers to you. The masses cannot continue to watch you pack their money into your pockets, private houses and bank accounts in the name of government.

This is time for you to regress to the principle of CORRUPTION-FREE GOVERNMENT IN NIGERIA (CFGIN). That is the road to growth, prosperity, advancement, self reliance, joy and happiness for all. The other road you have been taking for 54 years is the path of destruction and doom which I have said, will eventually consume you.

Hence your mockeries, sorcerers, profligates, squander maniacs, chameleons, hypocrites and deceivers in the Nigerian polity, 'the die is cast'. Choose between good and doom. The people have spoken; Vox populi, Vox Dei!

AND TO YOU PENTECOSTAL PASTORS AND CHURCH LEADERS IN NIGERIA,

It is inopportune that you cause 50% of the fraud taking place in the Nigerian polity and society. You go about promising your followers success, breakthrough, wealth, big cars and houses. Zealots, acting on your dubious predictions, have continued to engage in crimes.

They are the people who plot to embezzle public funds and loot the state treasury. If they conclude such inhuman machinations undetected, that means they have been "successful". They have made a break through. They will bring you part of the loots as offering or tithe. [151]You will accept and 'bless them'.

Verily, verily, I say unto you; the iniquity of their crimes will visit you with double potency! You have the word of God which is repentance from sins as a condition to have reconciliation with Him. Yet you leave this basic theology to preach wealth and riches. You despite theosophy, revel in ignominious Theo-cupidity. You induce people to steal public funds.

You relish big cars, big houses, Western Country Visas and private jets in difference to spreading The News. How many houses, cars or boats did Jesus Christ own? Did you see anywhere he did any promos of success, break through and riches?

You pastor, you derail, you derail and you pervert the word of God for personal aggrandizement. Your sole aim of establishing a church is to be wealthy. Your daily pre-occupation is presumptuous hankering for wealth and money. The more offerings you get the happier you are. You are no longer interested in proselytism and winning souls but money.

Therefore, repent oh ye epicurean pastors and follow the sacred line of your mission. Understand the discreteness of true Christianity with respect to lust for affluence. Stop deceiving the children of God. Pastors must help Nigeria come back to life by changing your recipe of sermon from material wealth acquisition to anti-corruption.

Preach eloquently against embezzlement of funds, abuse of public office, treasury looting and other forms of scamming in government. Remember that the way of corruption which you insidiously induce is calamity, devastation and doom as we see in present day Nigeria. On the other hand, the way of true, corruption-free government is prosperity, economic growth, progress, peace and happiness. Therefore, lead your followers the way of truth and justice.

You church leaders; you side with the rich and disregard the poor. Hence you boost up wretchedness of the people. May the Almighty God who you project to serve bless you as you help to revolutionize this country for His glory and peace of human kind! Meanwhile this is a guide for your subscription: **CORRUPTION-FREE GOVERNMENT IN NIGERIA** (CFGIN).

LOOKING AT YOUR CRYSTAL BALL

(poem)

> Looking at your crystal ball fellow man
>
> Looking at your crystal ball
>
> Tell me, what do you see Niger man?

Looking at your crystal ball

I say I see darkness everywhere
Hunger, squalor here and there
I see wretchedness, hopelessness, joblessness
Precipitates of deviousness and recklessness

And now I see education in shambles
Sacred legacy--agriculture in rubbles
Health care for man now decadent
Aviation; a death-trap apparent

You destroy citadels of excellence!
Fracture incubators of eminence
Outrageously encumber productivity
Any hope then for national prosperity?

See them along the cosmic plane
With 2.6 trillion naira to the drain
That novelty mutant emergent
Doom-laden Mephistophelian agent
They loot state treasury and property
Weighing neither scruples nor sympathy

Where is our refuge?

Any escape from this deluge?
Not even in our matchbox shanties
Barricades against barbaric non-entities

As the zebra dance head posited
And Ghana's Rawlings entreated
You the people, the majority
Are to blame for this monstrosity

Do you welcome indescribable oppression?
And applaud cupidity, obscene possession?
When you have latitude to fight corruption
Employing instruments of your Constitution

Unshackle Nigeria from marauders
These adept gravy train commanders
Then have your peace and prosperity
Want of all responsible humanity

Sage, have national sovereign government
Not this dubious contraption establishment
An arrangement of cheat, triteness and banality
Charade of facetiousness and mediocrity
Cesspool of deceit and debauchery
Bandwagon of chameleons and treachery

AND TO YOU THE INTERNATIONAL
COMMUNITY:

Know it today that the problem with Nigeria is strictly corruption. Nigeria is a country that runs the complete range of corrupt practices: treasury looting, bribery, squander mania, official recklessness, profligacy, debauchery and deceit. These are extremely risk factors in institutional capacity moulding. We are dead beat of your falsehearted loans, grants and aids which inexorably find themselves in the private pockets of Mephistophelian politicians and the privileged--those who inhabit the twilight zones on the fringes of the Nigerian society.

We want this ruinous corruption in Nigeria to be tabled at the United Nations. That is the only way the International Community led by the objective United States President, Donald Trump, can help Nigeria exit from the present decadence and plunge into the abyss, not dubious grants and aids. If you want to help Nigeria escape from the present mess, initiate constructive measures that will facilitate eradication of corruption, which without doubt, must include appropriate sanctions.

TIME IS RUNNING OUT

I call on Nigerian patriots to arise so that we join forces and fight this war. This is the only option left for the people of the Federal Republic of Nigeria in the face of governmental deviousness and profligacy. From ancient times till date there has been the struggle for The Universe between God and Satan, between good and evil, between the id and the superego; and Nigerian politicians and leaders have reprehensible poverty of the superego. The government has failed the people. Leaders likewise have disappointed Nigerians.

There comes a time in life when time itself is ready for change and men are no longer willing to be plunged along the abyss of corruption, duplicity and unconscionable insurgency. In consequence, there comes a time in life when the cup of endurance flows over and men are no longer willing to be driven along the disgrace of wretchedness, poverty, squalor and unconscionable insecurity. What we need in Nigeria today is a group of men and women who will stand up for right and oppose what is wrong-- the corruption and debauchery. Along the way of life, someone must have reason enough and morality enough to cut off the chain of corruption and evil afflicting Nigeria.

With the present rape and robbery of the Nigerian state by politicians and the elite, Millennium Development Goals and Vision 202020 flaunted by the government officials in their avaricious quest to deplete the state treasury is obviously a wild goose chase, a mirage. It will be blithering sorcery for a country devoid of responsibility and discipline to have forethought (vision) and engage in development. This is a governmental machination where the leaders shamelessly inflict inadmissible barbarity on the masses employing long-winded sanctimoniousness and guile.

Then where is our hope?

Where is our refuge?

Where are we safe?

Not even in our match-box houses where we barricade ourselves against the rape, deceit, trauma and dubiousness of the Nigerian state! Our faith, unmistakably, is now in our own hands. It is either we allow corruption and deceit to flourish in Nigeria and be doomed or we stand up and fight. **Enough of verbosity and story-telling, time for action!**

In the course of our awareness in this Sweeping Nigerian Revolution, we discovered that Nigerians still tremendously fear and suspect each other based on tribe and religion. It should not be so. The Nigerian People should freely approach one another without fear and share ideas. Thus, we can overcome our differences and plan a strong, peaceful and prosperous nation. The new Nigeria ought to be based on patriotically productive ideology rather than religion, educational status or ethnicity.

We are struggling for freedom and justice, not for power. However, there is a social affiliation between power and love. Power without love is irresponsible and abusive. Love without power is over-romantic and anemic. Power cannot go resourcefully without love. Some people segregate power from love; which is reckless and negligent. Power with love is responsible and productive to country, society and humanity.

It is crucial we understand that freedom fighting by political party opposition has been so hackneyed that it is now a feeble force to liberate the people of Nigeria from the present decadence and rot. Events in the Nigerian polity buttress this. In 2011 just immediately after the elections half of State Annual Budget was looted under the veneer of petroleum subsidy--looted evidently by people who contributed to the 2011 elections. How much would be stolen in 2015>?

Today the Nigerian Army is porous and corrupt. In alignment with the Nick and other security agencies they have abandoned their duties and allegiance to the state to be stooping before individuals in authority – a bummer indeed. Hence, I wish to state that the empirical tack of salvation of the Nigerian state, as it is today, is by a well-articulated and punctiliously executed revolutionary opposition which is not frontally competing for power but puissantly campaigning to liberate the country from current abyssal descent. I stand to be confuted. Unfolding proceedings in Nigeria will vindicate this stance.

Although this Revolution seems cranky and newfangled, it is the only way forward for corruption-ridden Nigeria. Astute embracing and implementation of The Charter of this Great Change will, unarguably, obliterate corruption, deceit and current calamitous insecurity, and thrust Nigeria towards a diamond-borne future. This is the elusive thirst of The Nigerian People.

In the service of country, no sacrifice or pain is too huge or grand. So, did Neil Armstrong at the dusty crust of the moon on 20th July 1969 and Nelson Mandela at South African prisons for 27 years. Once more, may the Almighty God bless and rescue Nigeria from the shackles of sorcerers, charlatans, cannibals, 'prebendalists', groveling sycophants, squander maniacs and robbers of the state!

May His Peace be benevolently multiplied unto all votaries to equity, justice and fairness, those who speak the truth and serve country, society and humanity! Time is running out. **The wretched people of Nigeria cannot**

continue to watch you pack their money into your pockets in the name of government. I restate; time is running out!

Long live the Federal Republic of Nigeria

One Nigeria, No Corruption

Vox populi, Vox Dei (section14 (2a)

Aluta Continua, Victoria Acerta!

OKENWA ENYERIBE -   B. Pharm.

Head, CORRUPTION-FREE GOVERNMENT IN NIGERIA

The Revolutionary Council of the Nigerian People

BIBLIOGRAPHY

1. **We'll find abducted schoolgirls - Jonathan:** THE SUN Nig., May 5, 2014, p. 7

2. **Missing girls: Mark opts for total war against Boko Haram:** ibid May 6, 2014 p.5

3. Theguardian.com, Saturday 10 May 2014

4. *FRANCE 24 with AP, AFP: May 10, 2014)*

5. **Leadership Nig. Online**: May 10, 2014

6. **Hillary Clinton: Under Jonathan, Nigeria Squandered Oil Wealth, Breeds Corruption;** Sahara Reporters Posted May 9, 2014

7. **BOKO HARAM'S PEACE DEAL: Militant group offers abducted school girls in exchange for detained members. New video shows girls reciting Quran in captivity. DSS: Shekau is dead. FG: we're studying video:** THE SUN Nig., May 13, 2014, p.1)

8. **Soldiers shoot GOC**: PEOPLES DAILY Nig., May 15 2014, p.1; **Efforts to rescue schoolgirls complicated - US; Soldiers Mutiny: Army removes GOC:** THE SUN May 16, 2014, p.1, 5, and 16)

9. **Corruption stalls Nigeria's war against B'Haram – US**: ibid May 22, 2014, p.2

10. **Direct your protests to terrorists – Jonathan**: The PUNCH Nig., May 23, 2014, p.8

11. **Chibok Girls: Rival group attacks protesters:** DAILY TRUST May 29, 2014, p. 6, 11

12. **Boko Haram releases new video of abducted school girls in desperate pleas.**

    Some of the girls are ill, says negotiator: DAILY SUN June 2, 2014, p.16

13. **CHIBOK GIRLS: We didn't ban rallies in Abuja - IG**: Vanguard Nig., June 4, 2014 p.1, 5

14. **Boko Haram: Obasanjo blames FG for stalling talks. Says 'I have access to the insurgents'**: PEOPLES DAILY June 13, 2014, p.1, 2

15. **Police can't stop rallies over abducted girls, Court rules**: PEOPLES DAILY June 13, 2014 p.3

16. **German Parliament visits #Bring Back Our Girls at Abuja:** www.revolutionarycouncilng.org/journals June 20, 2014

17. **Chibok abduction kingpin arrested, Businessman, woman in custody as troops bust Boko Haram intelligence network, says DHQ**: THE SUN July 1, 2014 p.1)

18. **Malala Yousafzai visits Nigeria to #BringBackOurGirls**: theguardian today UK 14 July 2914; ABC News Online; The Associated Press and Reuters, **I'll help free Chibok Girls, says Malala** PEOPLES DAILY: July 14, 2014, p.3)

19. **I owe Nigerians victory over Boko Haram – Jonathan, Chibok Girls: fresh facts emerge on aborted meeting with Jonathan:** THE SUN July 17, 2014 p. 6, 8

20. **Jonathan meets Chibok Girls, 100 days after; Jonathan meets Chibok parents**: Vanguard; Daily Trust July 23, 2014 p.1

21. Ezekwesili **Narrates Airport Harassment by SSS:** BellaNaija.com 23.07.2014

22. Jonathan's **N100m largesse splits Chibok Community:** PEOPLES DAILY July 30, 2014 p.1), **Chibok Elders: Presidency shared money to parents**: DAILY TRUST July 31, 2014 p.1

23. www.revolutionarycouncil. org. ng. /journals

24. ibid www.revolutionarycouncilng.org August13, 2014

25. **Chibok abduction: #BBOG vows to continue protest until girls are rescued** – PEOPLES DAILY September 2, 2014 p.3

26. **Washington Post blasts Jonathan for campaign slogan:** The Washington Post Sept 9, 2014

27. **#BringBackJonathan2015: The Wages of Impunity by Wole Soyinka**: Sahara reporters September 13, 2014

28. **Red Cross involved in secret Boko Haram prisoner swap to bring back kidnapped girls -** Colin Freeman: The Telegraph18 Sept. 2014

29. **Escapee Chibok Girl with DMI**: DAILY TRUST Nig. Sept. 29, 2014, p.9

30. **School girls flee Boko Haram after three-week walk through jungle**: The New York Post October 13, 2014, **Four More Girls escape Boko Haram**: The New Telegraph Nig, October 14, 2014 p.1

31. **Chibok girls: March on Villa ends in tears, anger**: THE NATION October 15, 2014 p.1, **With Agency Reports from Reuters and AFP**, 14/10/2014

32. **Alicia Keys demonstrates in NY for Nigerian girls**: ABC News, AFP, 14/10/2014

33. **Chibok girls: We've reached deal with Boko Haram — CDS**: THE NATION: News, Politics, Home October 18, 2014 p.1, **Nigeria, Boko Haram Reach Cease-Fire, Agree to Free Schoolgirls**: VOA **Listen News / Africa** 📌Pin it   October 18, 2014, **Soldiers kill 25 B/Haram insurgents, ceasefire collapses**: www.mydailynewswatchng.com/ News/ 20/10/2014

34. **Respect Ceasefire Deal, Obama Warns FG, Boko Haram**: LEADERSHIP Oct. 21, 2014

35. **CIT35** Bring Back Our Girls Wins Case at High Court: www.revolutionarycouncilng.org/journals/ Octoer 30, 2014

36. **Chibok Girls: BBOG Group Organizes Hands-on-head March**: LEADERSHIP October 4, 2014 p.4

37. Chibok Girls Married Off: News24.com/2014/11/01; theguardian.com, Saturday 1 November 2014 16.27 GMT

38. **Chadian Embassy Reschedules BBOG Group's Visit:** Leadership November 27, 2014 p.2

39. **Chibok red day: Agitators shut down Abuja at one year anniversary, protests aboard; DAILY SUN Nig.** April 15, 2015, p.1; **One Year Without Abducted Girls, We are in Pain**—Ezekwesili: Leadership April 14, 2015, pp 6-8; CITXXX **Leadership Nig., April 14, 2015, p. 8**

40. **Oby Ezekwesili attends Time 100 Gala, wants Obama to rescue Chibok girls:** BellaNaija.com 22.04.2015; www.vanguard.com /2015/04/oby-ezekwesili-attends-time-100-gala-wants-obama-to-rescue-chibok-girls

41. **HORROR IN SAMBISA, Our Ordeals in Sambisa Forest:** DAILY SUN May 4, 2015 pp 1-6

42. **Chibok Girls Deserve Justice—EU Commissioner:** Leadership June 20, 2015, p. 2 http/uncover.com/June 19, 2015

43. **Bring Back Our Girls: Buhari laments state of Nigeria's military**: Vanguard News July 09, 2015; http://www.vanguardngr.com/2015/07/bring-back-our-girls-buhari-laments-state-of-nigerias-military/#sthash.rShbrfUE.dpuf; **Buhari faults Jonathan's handling of Chibok girls' saga:** THE NATION News July 09, 2015; Chibok girls campaigners meet Buhari, demand action: **Daily Trust** Lead stories Thursday, 09 July 2015 04:01; **Buhari laments reliance on neighbours to fight terrorism, President still compiling shopping list to G7 leaders**: DAILY SUN Nig. July 9. 2015 p.5

44. www.metronaija.com/.../boko-haram-offers-to-swap-detainees-for.html o8 07 2015; *Chibok Girls: Boko Haram proposes swap deal: THE SUN July 9, 2015 p.5*

45. **Buhari exposes oil thieves. We'll reclaim every inch of Nigerian territory under Boko Haram control--Buhari:** DAILY SUN July 23, 2015 p.1, 5, 23

46. War & Conflict, Africa, Nigeria, Cameroon, Boko Haram http://www.aljazeera.com/30 Jul. 2015

47. **Chibok Girls: US Congress Urges BBOG Group to Continue Advocacy, Chibok Girls are Heroes --US:** LEADERSHIP August 5, 2015, p.2

48. **Day 500 Commemoration: BBOG Group Begins with Islamic Prayers; Non-release of Chibok Girls Harmful To Nigeria – Anglican Primate:** Leadership Nig. Aug 21, 25, 27, 2015.

49. **Chibok Girls: NHRC To Establish Missing Persons Register:** Leadership September 3, 2015 p.

50. **BBOG Group Commemorates 18 Months since Chibok Girls Abduction:** Leadership October 15, 2015 p. 2

51. www.revolutionarycouncil.org.ng /journals/15/10/2015

52. **Universal Children's Day: BBOG Group Calls for Implementation of Child Rights Act:** Leadership Weekend November 21, 2015, p.2

53. **Elimination of Violence against Women: BBOG Urges FG TO Prioritize Education:** Leadership November 27, 2015 p.2

54. **NEMA Records 410 births, 187 Marriages Recorded At IDP Camps** UNTOLD.COM/NEWS 02122015; This Day live/NEWS/02-12-2015; Vanguard.com/News

55. **600 Days of Chibok Girls Abduction, Saddening—BBOG Group:** Chika Mefor and Ejike Ejike, Leadership Dec. 6, 2015 p.2

56. **Chibok Girls: Buhari Storms Out Of Meeting with Parents:** Naij.com/14/01/2015
PMB Orders Fresh Probe Over Chibok Girls Abduction: Leadership Friday January 15, 2016 p.5; www.revolutionarycouncil.org.ng/journals

57. **CIT 57 Denmark Pledges to Take BBOG Rescue Campaign to the World:** Leadership February 24, 2016, p. 2

58. **www.revolutionarycouncil.org.ng**

59. www.revolutionarycouncil.org.ng

60. **Don't Consider Chibok Girls Secondary, Pastor Bkare Urges FG:** Leadership April 13, 2016 p.2; 2nd Anniversary:

61. **Chibok Girls Alive in New Video:** Leadership April 14, 2016 p.6

62. **Police deny BBOG access to the Villa:** Vanguard April 15, 2016 p.1; **Chibok Girls; 2 Years On, Police Stop BBOG from March to Villa:** Leadership Friday April 15, 2016 p.2, 5

63. **CIT 62 Six Chibok school girl's dead--rescued victim, Amina found nursing 4-month old baby as 'Boko Haram Commander' husband is arrested**: DAILY SUN May 19, 2016 p.1, 2 **Buhari hosts Amina, says she must return to school; troops rescue another school girl in Borno: DAILY SUN May 20, 2016 p.7**

64. **Presidency to BBOG: don't give up:** THE NATION July 12, 2016 p.43

65. **Chibok school girls weep in new video:** DAILY SUN August 15, 2016 p.1, 6

I Miss My Boko Haram Husband—Rescued Chibok girl, Amina Nkeki speaks:
www.naijacnnpoint.com/nigeriannews/i-miss-my-boko-

haram-husband--rescued-chibok-girl-amina-nkeki-speaks-with-cnn/16/08/2016

66. **Chibok Girls: BBOG Urges PMB to Constitute Rescue Operation Monitoring Team:** Leadership Tuesday August 23, 2016 p.2

67. **Bring back our girls or resign, Chibok families tell Buhari:** Premium Times August 26, 2016

68. Sunnewsonline.com/chibok-buhari-gives-fresh-conditions-for-swap/29/08/2016

69. **Chibok: Drama as BBOG, pro-Buhari group clash;** Again, police stop campaigners from entering Aso Villa: THE SUN 7th September 2016 p.1; Nigeria Newspapers online 6 September 2016

70. This Administration Has Made Three Attempts to Rescue Chibok Girls – Lai Mohammed: NAN16.09.2016

71. **CIT71 Chibok: Buhari invites UN as negotiator:** The Sun News--23 September 2016 P.6 •**Says we are ready for swap**

72. Boko Haram releases 21 Chibok girls to Nigerian government: CNN NEWS **13/10/2016;** BringBackOurGirls group confirms names of 21 released Chibok girls Premium Times Nige

73. **Chibok girls: we stayed without food for 40 days:** THE NATION 17 October, 2016 p.1

74. Breaking: Troops rescue another Chibok girl, Maryam--pmnews November 5, 2016

75. **Another Chibok girl found with baby; Boko Haram: Women sell sex to survive in Lake Chad Basin—Red Cross** DAILY SUN 6 January, 2017 p.2, 6

76. www.revolutionarycouncil.org.ng/journals

77. www.revolutionarycouncil.org.ng/20 April, 2017

78a. **Hot Fm News 6 am /02082017;** **www.revolutionarycouncil.org.ng/journals/01082017**

78b. **BBOG AGAIN STORMS ASO ROCK FOR MISSING 113 CHIBOK GIRLS**: Agency reports from African Independent Television, ITV and Agence France Press, 17/11/2017

79. **Those who sponsor Boko Haram –Murtala Nyako:** PEOPLES DAILY Nig., March 25, 2014, p. 48)

80. **Boko Haram - growing security headache:** ibid Nov. 11, 2011, p.2

81. **Jonathan goes tough on Boko Haram:** PEOPLES DAILY Nov.16, 2011, p.1; March 20, 2012, p.3

82. **Military Cdr. to FG: Dialogue with Boko Haram:** ibid Jan. 24, 2012, p.1

83. **ANPP Urges Jonathan to dialogue with Boko Haram:** The ROAD Nig., Nov. 9, 2011, p.16

84. **Edwin Clarke to Jonathan; Negotiate with Boko Haram;** FG open to dialogue, says Mark: PEOPLES DAILY August 2, 2012, p.1

85. **The Constitution of the Federal Republic of Nigeria, 1999** as amended Section 38-40, Official Gazette; The Federal Government Printer Lagos 7th March 2011

86. **AIT News:** 8pm Sept. 21, 2011

87. **Leadership Failure Caused Boko Haram, says Lamido**: PEOPLES DAILY Feb. 29, 2012, p.3

88. **Boko Haram; Suspected Killers of Hostages Arrested:** DAILY SUN 15 March 2012, p.8

89. **I would have joined Boko Haram –Ex military Gov.:** Vanguard Nig., Nov.8, 2012, p.16

90. **Dialogue can't curb Insurgency-Zazzakky:** The ROAD Jan.11, 2013, p.1

91. **Buhari predicts Bloody 2015, says FG is biggest Boko Haram:** The ROAD May 15, 2012, p.1, 4

92. **Gen. Muhammadu Buhari: Nyanya bomb blast and the fight against terrorism in Nigeria**: DAILY TRUST April 22, 2014 p.56

93. **Boko Haram: We are all guilty-Borno Gov.:** DAILY SUN Dec.7, 2012, p.6

94. **Rev. Dr. Oliver Dume, Bishop of Maiduguri Diocese**, Homily at St. Theresa's Catholic Church Madalla on Sunday 4th February ,2013

95. **Hassan KUKAH:** Be still and know that i am God: Virtual Insignia, Sokoto Diocese, Jan.2012, pp6-8

96. **Boko Haram can't break up Nigeria – Soyinka**: NIGERIAN PILOT July 3, 2014, p.6

97. **Boko Haram: Sheik Dahiru Bauchi blames govt officials for lingering crisis:** PEOPLES DAILY July 26-27, 2014 p. 6

98. **Only Nigerian Army can rescue Chibok Girls – Gen Babangida:** Saturday Mirror August 16, 2014, p.14

99. **Australian Negotiator Insists Modu Sheriff, Ihejirika Sponsor Boko Haram, Exonerates Buhari, El-Rufai:** http://saharareporters.com/ SAHARAREPORTERS, NEW YORK Aug 31, 2014

100. **Prosecute Boko Haram sponsors now, APC tells FG**: THE SUN Nig., Sept 3, 2014 p.1)

101. **2015: Nobody can stop Jonathan – Dokubo Asari:** NIGERIAN PILOT Sept.1, 2014 p. 16, 41)

102. **Gowon offers to mediate in Boko Haram Crisis:** PEOPLES DAILY October 10, 2014 p.

103. **Nigeria cannot defeat Boko Haram alone – UN:** DAILY TRUST 29 January 2015 p.6) The Guardian January 31, 2015 p.1; AU Proposes 7,500 Troops against Boko Haram www.revolutionarycouncil.org.ng.

104. **No peace for you, Bin Laden's son tells US:** THE SUN July 11, 2016 p.18

105. **B'Haram: We'll bomb Aso Rock. Shekau, sect leader vows in new video. We've defeated terrorists, Buratai insists:** Daily Sun August 9, 2016 p.1, 6
We will slay Muslims and raze down mosques-- Niger Delta Revolutionary Crusaders: Vanguard 5th August 2016 p.1

106. **We will stop bombings if-Boko Haram as Jonathan begins talks with group:** PEOPLES DAILY March 16, 2012, p.2

107. **Boko Haram ready for Cease Fire…. A welcome development if it'll bring peace-FG:** DAILY SUN Nov. 2, 2012, p.5

108. **Nasir EL RUFAI: Budget 2012(4): The rewards of insurgency:** PEOPLES DAILY Feb. 10, 2012, p.48

109. **The Road Leading to Disaster:** *Reflections of Comrade Fidel Castro*, **21 March 2012;** PEOPLES DAILY Nig. 29 March, 2012, p. 31

110. **Middle East Peace Vanishing--Carter:** DAILY SUN Oct.24, 2012, p.14

111. **Boko Haram: Dasuki, Dangiwa, Giro, our men:**

The ROAD March 19, 2012, p.1, 4: **FG, Boko Haram Parley Suffers Setback**: DAILY SUN March 19, 2012, p.3

112. **David Mark, govs, clerics, others condemn Kano bombings:** DAILY SUN March 20, 2013, p.7

113. **U.S. to Nigeria; Develop North, beat Boko Haram:** PEOPLES DAILY March 6, 2012, p.2

114. **Presidency explains release of Boko Haram suspects:** Daily Trust May 23, 2013, p.1

115. **Jonathan Grants Amnesty to Boko Haram Sect**: LEADERSHIP April 4, 2013, p.1; **FG Renews Amnesty for Boko Haram:** PEOPLES DAILY May 30, 2014, p.1

116. **Boko Haram, a finger of God:** DAILY SUN March 7, 2012, p.42

117. **How poverty-stricken teenagers resort to scavenging for a living:** PEOPLES DAILY July 26-7, 2014 p.2

118. http://punchng.com/dont-bomb-niger-delta-umar-warns-buhari/; **Col Umar: Don't go to war in the Niger Delta**—DAILY SUN August 31, 2016 p.1

119 **Niger Delta crisis: FG negotiating Nigeria's sovereignty—Soyinka:** DAILY SUN September 26, 2016 P.1, 6

120. **DSS, Gowon clash over agitators:** HE SUN NEWS 3rd August 2017

121. **Obasanjo on Boko Haram:** DAILY SUN Sept. 19, 2011, p.5

122. **Boko Haram: Police foil attempt to bomb NNPC HQ:** The Punch July 4, 2011, p.1; **60 killed in Kano bus park bombing:** Vanguard March 19, 2013, p.1

123. **Boko Haram abducts 100 female students; Women Protest Abuja (Nyanya) Bomb Blast; FG: 72 now dead, 164 injured:** DAILY SUN: April 16, 2014, p.1, 5

124. **President Good Luck Jonathan to State Governors:** national accord Nov. 29, 2011, p.1

125. **All hands must be on deck to eliminate monstrous corruption in Nigeria-Gen. Yakubu Gowon**; DAILY SUN Nov. 21, 2012 p.6

126. **Nigeria Needs Revolution –Maitama Sule:** The ROAD Jan.11, 2013, p.1

127. **Nigeria must fight corruption to avoid Arab spring-Jerry Rawlings**: SATURDAY SUN March 9, 2013 P.7

128. **Pope Emeritus, Benedict xvi, in Benin Republic renews hope**: The ROAD, Nov. 25, 2011 p.7.

129. **Obama, Cameron, G8 World Leaders to discuss Nigeria's controversial oil wealth wastage**; National Accord Feb. 4, 2013 p. 31

130. **Jonathan soft-pedals on N5000 Notes as Mark lamb lasts Okonjo-Iweala, Sanusi, others**; PEOPLES DAILY Sept. 20, 2012 p.1, 2

131. **Nigerian leaders have failed--Sultan**: PEOPLES DAILY July 1, 2013 p.1

132. **Nigeria Needs Revolution -Tambuwal**: THE SUN July 3, 2013 p.1

133. **Hassan KUKAH:** Cit 33

134. **Impeachment: Senators shout down Chukwumerije**: DAILY SUN Sept. 21, 2012 p.5

135 **Only Nigerian Army can rescue Chibok Girls – Gen Babangida:** Saturday Mirror August 16, 2014 p.13

136. **Coup, Mass Revolt Inevitable Unless... Balarabe Musa:** national TRAIL Jan. 27-Feb. 2, 2014 p.1, 4)

137. **Nigerian politicians lack Mandela's qualities-Jonathan:** THE SUN December 9, 2013 p.7

138. **Terrorism: IG spits fire, warns against provocative comments:** PEOPLES DAILY April 2, 2014 p.3

139. **'We steal because Nigerians don't stone us'-Amaechi:** http/www.vanguardngr.com/2013/12

140. **Elie Weisel:** The Kingdom of Memory Reminiscences (New York Random House Digital, 2011); **Achebe Chinua**: THERE WAS A COUNTRY A PERSONAL HISTORY OF BIAFRA; Penguin Books London 2012 p.249

141. **Jonathan to Extend State of Emergency; Security situation remains dicey...**National Trail 7-13 April 2014 p.1

142. **Eluwa et al; A History of Nigeria:** Africana Nig., 2011 p. 245

143. **Charlyboy: An intellectual Madman:** The ROAD

Nov.18, 2011, p. 38

144. **Malema - A South African Dilemma:** National Accord Nov.2, 2011, p.22

145. **A Sierra Leonean writes Nigerians:** The ROAD April 25, 2012 p.40

146. **Revolution Coming, Obasanjo says:** DAILY TRUST Nov.12, 2012 p.1

147. **Majek Fashek Exclusive - I CONFESS:** TS WEEKEND; DAILY SUN Oct. 26, 2012 pp 28-29

148. **Anti-graft War Will Secure Tour Future, PMB Tells Students:** Leadership September 3, 2015 p.5

149. **EFCC accuses Atuche of using depositors' funds to pay N45m tithe:** PEOPLES DAILY Nig., Sept. 28, 2012 p.4

Further Reading

1. **MARTIN MEREDITH:** THE STATE OF AFRICA, A HISTORY OF FIFTY YEARS OF INDEPENDENCE: FREE PRESS, LONDON, 2006

2. **The Autobiography of MARTIN LUTHER KING, JR**. edited by CLAYBORNE CARSON, IPM ABACUS London, 2008

3. **Rolihlahla Nelson Mandela:** LONG WALK TO FREEDOM; Little, Brown and , New York, 1995

4. **Achebe Chinua:** THERE WAS A COUNTRY A PERSONAL HISTORY OF BIAFRA; Penguin Books London, 2012

5. KIRK-Green AHM: Crisis and Conflict in Nigeria; A Documentary Sourcebook, 1966-1970, Oxford University Press, 1971

6. **GHANDI:** AN AUTHOBIOGRAHY; THE STORY OF MY EXPERIENCE WITH TRUTH; Beacon Press, Boston, 1993.

7. Toyin Falola et al: The Rise and Fall of Nigeria's Second Republic, Zed, 1984

8. ARISTOTLE: Book One, Politics 11

9. **Olusegun Adeniyi**: POWER, POLITICS AND DEATH - A front-row account of Nigeria under President Yar'Adua; Prestige-Kachifa, Yaba Lagos 2011

10. **Okenwa Enyeribe: WIN THE WAR ...Inside Biafra**; Dabiton International Press Abuja Nig., 2012

11. **Okenwa Enyeribe: AN ANTHOLOGY OF THE NIGERIAN STATE; ISBN--10**:1973244209; **ISBN--13**: 9781973244202

INDEX

Neil Armstrong, 180
Nelson Mandela, 140, 156, 180
New York Post, on released Chibok girls, 38
New Zealand, campaigners for Chibok girls, 48
Niger Delta:
    Avengers, militant group, 130
    Republic, struggle for, 130
    Revolutionary Crusaders declaration, 126, 187
    Volunteer Force, 123
Nigeria:
    Air Force (*NAF*), analysis and technical war room, 99
    National Democratic Party, 166
Nigerian:
    Army, 18, 100, 126, 141, 143, 180
    Constitution, 97, 146, 156
    Independence, 166, 171
    Police, banning BBOG protests, 21
    Youth Movement, 166
    Youths, scavenging on garbage, 129
    Youths, sold as slaves in Libya, 129
Niyi Osundare, corruption in Nigeria, 10

Nkosazana Dlamini-Zuma, on rise of Boko Haram insurgency, 125

Nnamdi Azikwe, University Awka, 142
NNPC, kidnapped oil explorers, 109, 113
Northern Ireland, meeting of G8 on Nigeria, 143
Nura Khalid, Apo Mosque, 59, 75, 104
Oliver Dume, Maiduguri Catholic Diocese, 118
Olusegun Obasanjo, contact with Boko Haram, 24
Operation *Lafiya Dole*, Borno State, 94

Made in the USA
Middletown, DE
15 July 2021

44257849R00213